ICAEW

The Institute of Chartered Accountants in England and Wales

AUDIT AND ASSURANCE

For exams in 2019

Study Manual

www.icaew.com

Audit and Assurance
The Institute of Chartered Accountants in England and Wales

ISBN: 978-1-50972-020-0
Previous ISBN: 978-1-78363-710-2

First edition 2007
Twelfth edition 2018

The content of this publication is intended to prepare students for the ICAEW examinations, and should not be used as professional advice.

British Library Cataloguing-in-Publication Data
A catalogue record for this is available from the British Library

Originally printed in the United Kingdom on paper obtained from traceable, sustainable sources.

The publishers are grateful to the IASB for permission to reproduce extracts from the International Financial Reporting Standards including all International Accounting Standards, SIC and IFRIC Interpretations (the Standards). The Standards together with their accompanying documents are issued by:

The International Accounting Standards Board (IASB)

30 Cannon Street, London, EC4M 6XH, United Kingdom.

Email: info@ifrs.org Web: www.ifrs.org

Welcome to ICAEW

As the future of our profession, I'd like to personally welcome you to ICAEW.

In a constantly changing and volatile environment, the role of the accountancy profession has never been more important to create a world of strong economies, together. ICAEW Chartered Accountants make decisions that will define the future of global business by sharing our knowledge, skills and insight.

By choosing our world-leading chartered accountancy qualification, the ACA, you are not only investing in your own future but also gaining the skills and values to meet the challenges of technological change and contribute to future business success.

Joining over 150,000 chartered accountants and over 27,000 fellow students worldwide, you are now part of something special. This unique network of talented and diverse professionals has the knowledge, skills and commitment to help build local and global economies that are sustainable, accountable and fair.

You are all supported by ICAEW as you progress through your studies and career: we will be with you every step of the way to ensure you are ready to face the fast-paced changes of the global economy. Visit page viii to review the key resources available as you study.

It's with our training, guidance and support that our members, and you, will realise career ambitions, develop insights that matter and maintain a competitive edge.

I wish you the best of luck with your studies and look forward to welcoming you to the profession.

Michael Izza
Chief Executive
ICAEW

Contents

The Auditing and Assurance module develops your understanding of the critical aspects of managing an assurance engagement (including audit engagements); acceptance, planning, managing, concluding and reporting.

Questions within the Study Manual should be treated as preparation questions, providing you with a firm foundation before you attempt the exam-standard questions. The exam-standard questions are found in the Question Bank.

Permitted texts

At the Professional and Advanced Levels there are specific texts that you are permitted to take into your exams with you. All information for these texts, the editions that are recommended for your examinations and where to order them from, is available on icaew.com/permittedtexts.

Professional Level exams	Permitted text
Audit and Assurance	✓
Financial Accounting and Reporting	✓
Tax Compliance	✓
Business Strategy and Technology	x
Financial Management	x
Business Planning	No restrictions

Advanced Level exams	
Corporate Reporting	No restrictions
Strategic Business Management	No restrictions
Case Study	No restrictions

The exams which have no restrictions include the following:

- Business Planning: Banking;
- Business Planning: Insurance;
- Business Planning: Taxation;
- Corporate Reporting;
- Strategic Business Management; and
- Case Study.

This means you can take any hard copy materials into these exams that you wish, subject to practical space restrictions.

Although the examiners use the specific editions listed to set the exam (as listed on our website), you **may** use a different edition of the text at your own risk.

This information, as well as what to expect and what is and is not permitted in each exam is available in the Instructions to Candidates. You will be sent the instructions with your exam admission details. They can also be viewed on our website at icaew.com/exams.

Key resources

We provide a wide range of resources and services to help you in your studies. Here is some of what we have to offer.

Take a look at the online resources available to you on icaew.com/examresources:

Syllabus, skills development and technical knowledge grids

This gives you the full breakdown of learning outcomes for each module, see how your skills and technical knowledge will grow throughout the qualification.

Study guide

This guides you through your learning process, putting each chapter and topic of the Study Manual into context and showing what learning outcomes are attached to them.

Exam webinars

The pre-recorded webinars focus on how to approach each exam, plus exam and study tips.

Past exams and mark plans

Each exam is available soon after it has been sat, with mark plans available once results have been released. Remember that if you're accessing an exam from 2018, it may not reflect exams for 2019. To access exam-standard questions that reflect the current syllabus, go to the Question Bank.

Errata sheets

These are available on our website if we are made aware of a mistake within a Study Manual or Question Bank once it has been published.

Exam software

You need to become familiar with the exam software before you take your exam. Access a variety of resources, including exam guide, practice software, webinars and sample exams at icaew.com/cbe

Student support team

Our dedicated student support team is here to help and advise you throughout your training, don't hesitate to get in touch. Email studentsupport@icaew.com or call +44 (0)1908 248 250 to speak to an adviser.

Vital and *Economia*

Vital is our quarterly ACA student magazine. Each issue of Vital is packed with interesting articles to help you with work, study and life. Read the latest copy at icaew.com/vital.

What's more, you'll receive our monthly member magazine, Economia. Read more at icaew.com/economia.

Online student community

The online student community is the place where you can post your questions and share your study tips. Join the conversation at icaew.com/studentcommunity.

Tuition

The ICAEW Partner in Learning scheme recognises tuition providers who comply with our core principles of quality course delivery. If you are not receiving structured tuition and are interested in doing so, take a look at our recognised Partner in Learning tuition providers in your area at icaew.com/dashboard.

CABA

Access free, confidential support to help you take care of your wellbeing, at work and at home. CABA's services are available to you, and your family, face-to-face, over the phone and online. Find out more at caba.org.uk

ICAEW Business and Finance Professional (BFP)

This exciting new designation has been developed as a form of recognition for professionals who have gained the essential knowledge, skills and experience necessary for a successful career in business and finance. Once you have completed the ICAEW CFAB qualification or the Certificate Level of the ACA, you are eligible to apply towards gaining BFP status. Start your application at icaew.com/becomeabfp.

Skills within the ACA

Professional skills are essential to accountancy and your development of them is embedded throughout the ACA qualification.

The following shows the professional skills that you will develop in this particular module. To see the full skills development grids, please go to icaew.com/examresources.

Assimilating and Using Information

Understand the situation and the requirements

- Identify the needs of customers and clients
- Explain different stakeholder perspectives and interests
- Identify risks within a scenario
- Identify elements of uncertainty within a scenario
- Identify ethical issues including public interest and sustainability issues within a scenario

Identify and use relevant information

- Interpret information provided in various formats
- Evaluate the relevance of information provided
- Filter information provided to identify critical facts

Identify and prioritise key issues and stay on task

- Identify business and financial issues from a scenario
- Work effectively within time constraints
- Operate to a brief in a given scenario

How skills are assessed: students may be required to demonstrate:

- the regulatory, professional and ethical issues relevant to accepting, carrying out and managing assurance engagements; and

- how quality assurance processes mitigate risks.

Structuring problems and solutions

Structure data

- Identify any information gaps

- Frame questions to clarify information

- Use a range of data types and sources to inform analysis and decision making

- Structure and analyse financial and non-financial data to enhance understanding of business issues and their underlying causes

- Present analysis in accordance with instructions and criteria

Develop solutions

- Identify and apply relevant technical knowledge and skills to analyse a specific problem
- Use structured information to identify evidence-based solutions
- Identify creative and pragmatic solutions in a business environment
- Identify opportunities to add value
- Identify ethical dimensions of possible solutions
- Select appropriate courses of action using an ethical framework

How skills are assessed: requirements will include planning assurance engagements in accordance with the terms of engagement and appropriate standards, taking account of:

- managing audit and other assurance engagements;

- reliance on controls;

- reliance on the work of internal audit or other experts;

- reliance on the work of another auditor;

- extent of tests of control and of substantive procedures, including analytical procedures

- use of analytical procedures including data analytic routines to identify the risk of misstatement; and

- number, timing, staffing and location of assurance visits.

Applying judgement

Apply professional scepticism and critical thinking

- Recognise bias and varying quality in data and evidence
- Identify assumptions or faults in arguments
- Identify gaps in evidence
- Identify inconsistencies and contradictory information
- Assess interaction of information from different sources
- Exercise ethical judgement

Relate issues to the environment

- Appreciate when more expert help is required
- Identify related issues in scenarios
- Assess different stakeholder perspectives when evaluating options
- Retain an overview of the business issue or scenario
- Appraise the effects of alternative future scenarios
- Appraise ethical, public interest and regulatory issues

How skills are assessed: students may be required to:

- identify significant business or audit risks from a given scenario, explain their impact on the financial statements, and recommend audit procedures to mitigate the risk of a material error. Requirements will test the ability of students to filter those issues which are more relevant than others in a given scenario.

- distinguish the quality of data or evidence to be tested in two potential ways. (i) Students will need to distinguish between data generated from within an organisation and that generated by a third party, the latter being less susceptible to management bias; and (ii) students will need to appreciate the effect on the quality of evidence that bias caused by specific factors can have eg, where profits are used to determine a bonus payment to be made to the company's management.

- identify the impact of specific economic and political factors on a set of financial statements eg, in the context of dealing with customers or suppliers based outside the UK that (i) political instability may cause problems which prevent the customer or supplier from trading, ultimately leading to going concern issues for the audited entity; and (ii) economic factors may cause exchange rate fluctuations leading to the risk of misstated balances in the financial statements.

- evaluate the effect of uncertain future events when describing the procedures to be performed in carrying out an examination of a company's financial forecasts.

- assess the materiality of a particular matter (eg, an unadjusted error) in the context of a set of financial statements or other financial information. This assessment should then inform the student's judgement as to whether or not to modify the opinion given in a statutory auditor's report or modify the conclusion in a non-audit assurance report.

- judge the potential independence risks involved in accepting or continuing an audit or other assurance engagement, and the procedures to mitigate those risks; and consideration of the required steps upon the discovery of fraud/money laundering.

- display the ability to present a structured argument to a client eg, in situations where management is questioning the extent of audit work performed.

Concluding, recommending and communicating

Conclusions

- Apply technical knowledge to support reasoning and conclusions

- Apply professional experience and evidence to support reasoning

- Use valid and different technical skills to formulate opinions, advice, plans, solutions, options and reservations.

Recommendations

- Present recommendations in accordance with instructions and defined criteria

- Make recommendations in situations where risks and uncertainty exist

- Formulate opinions, advice, recommendations, plans, solutions, options and reservations based on valid evidence

- Make evidence-based recommendations which can be justified by reference to supporting data and other information

- Develop recommendations which combine different technical skills in a practical situation

Communication

- Present a basic or routine memorandum or briefing note in writing in a clear and concise style

- Present analysis and recommendations in accordance with instructions

- Communicate clearly to a specialist or non-specialist audience in a manner suitable for the recipient

- Prepare the advice, report, or notes required in a clear and concise style

How skills are assessed: students may be required to:

- advise on the regulatory, professional and ethical issues in carrying out an assurance engagement;

- conclude and report on assurance engagements, including determining whether to modify a report with or without a modified opinion/conclusion; and

- identify deficiencies in financial information systems, their potential consequences and recommendations for improvement.

CHAPTER 1

Reintroduction to audit and assurance

Introduction

Examination context

TOPIC LIST

Summary and Self-test

Technical reference

Answers to Interactive questions

Answers to Self-test

Introduction

Learning outcomes

- Revise the concept of assurance from your Assurance paper ☐
- Revise the concept of audit from your Assurance paper ☐
- Understand the specific benefits of an audit ☐

Syllabus links

This chapter revises key concepts from your Assurance paper.

Examination context

This chapter is revision of what you have previously been examined on in your Assurance paper.

You will need an understanding of what assurance services are – audit in particular – that will be brought forward from your lower level paper to answer any questions at this level.

1 Assurance defined

Section overview

- An assurance engagement is one in which a practitioner expresses a conclusion designed to enhance the degree of confidence of the intended users, other than the responsible party, about the outcome of the evaluation or measurement of a subject matter against criteria

- Key elements are: three party involvement, subject matter, suitable criteria, sufficient appropriate evidence, written report

- Different levels of assurance may be given in assurance assignments: reasonable and limited

- An audit is an example of an assurance engagement giving reasonable assurance

Definition

Assurance engagement: An engagement in which a practitioner aims to obtain sufficient appropriate audit evidence in order to express a conclusion designed to enhance the degree of confidence of the intended users other than the responsible party about the subject matter information (that is, the outcome of the measurement or evaluation of an underlying subject matter against criteria).

Assurance engagements include primarily audits but also other services such as reports on internal control and review of a business plan.

In recent years businesses world-wide have been publishing sustainability and corporate responsibility reports, in an attempt to demonstrate accountability for the impact of their activities on society and the environment. Such reports may be the subject of assurance engagements that provide limited assurance to management on reported elements such as key performance indicators, adherence to voluntary codes etc.

1.1 The elements

Any assurance engagement needs:

- a responsible party
- a practitioner
- a user of the report
- a subject matter
- criteria
- sufficient appropriate evidence to support the conclusion
- a written report containing a conclusion

The engagement will be governed by its terms of engagement (found in an engagement letter).

The engagement will need to be:

- planned
- performed
- concluded upon
- reported on

1.2 Levels of assurance

The International Federation of Accountants (IFAC) recognises two types of assurance engagement:

- Reasonable assurance engagements, which result in a positive expression of opinion and where the level of assurance given is deemed to be high

- Limited assurance engagements, which result in negative assurance and where the level of assurance given is deemed to be moderate

Engagements could be either type, and this would need to be specified in the terms of engagement.

So for a report on the effectiveness of management's system of internal control, it might be agreed that the report should read as follows:

- "In our opinion management has operated an effective system of internal control"- a positive form of opinion deriving from a reasonable assurance engagement; or

- "Nothing has come to our attention that indicates material internal control weakness" - a negative form of assurance deriving from a limited assurance engagement.

No report on an assurance engagement can ever provide absolute assurance, because of the nature of the evidence available.

Assurance type	Assurance level	Opinion/conclusion	Example
Reasonable	High	Positive	Audit of financial information
Limited	Moderate	Negative	Review of financial information

1.3 Benefits of assurance

A key feature of assurance services is that they are provided by independent professionals who therefore give an objective, unbiased opinion. They give the following benefits to users:

- Enhances the credibility of the information being reported on

- Reduces the risk of management bias, error or even fraud in the information being reported on

- Draws the attention of the user to any deficiencies in the information being reported on

Assurance services also give added credibility to the wider share market:

- They ensure that high quality, reliable information circulates in the market
- They give investors added faith in the market
- They improve the reputation of organisations trading in the market

Worked example: Assurance engagement

Predator plc, a large listed company, is considering taking over Target Limited, a small, family owned company.

Predator has asked Talbot and Co, chartered accountants, to carry out due diligence in relation to this prospective purchase. They want them to review the financial statements of the last three years and ensure that they were prepared under generally accepted accounting practice in the UK. They also want them to review the budgets for the coming twelve months and ensure that they are reasonably and internally consistent.

You can see the elements of the assurance service as these:

- Practitioner: Talbot and Co
- Responsible party: Target Ltd management
- Users: Predator plc management
- Subject matter: Financial statements/budgets
- Criteria: UK GAAP/reasonable and internally consistent

Talbot and Co will plan and carry out work to obtain sufficient appropriate evidence to support their assurance opinion, which will be given in a written report.

The benefits of this service to Predator plc are that:

- they are given assurance that the financial statements are in line with UK GAAP and therefore are understandable and comparable with other companies they might be considering for takeover.

- they are given assurance that the budgets are reasonable and internally consistent and therefore can be trusted as an indicator of the company's future operating ability.

- they can therefore make an informed decision about whether to buy Target and for how much.

Interactive question 1: Benefits of assurance

During the night of 7 June 20X3 strong gales caused the brick chimney of the factory to crash through the roof of Hancock Ltd's assembly area. Production was severely disrupted for a period of two months.

In addition to claiming from its insurers for the cost of repairing the premises and for the equipment and inventories destroyed in the accident, the company is also including a considerable claim under the loss of profits provision of its policy. The directors have prepared detailed calculations of the loss of profit and have requested the company's auditors to review this claim and provide an assurance report which they will submit with it to the insurers.

Requirement

What advantages would the directors expect to gain from having this report?

See **Answer** at the end of this chapter.

2 Audit defined

Section overview

- An audit is a key example of an assurance service in the UK, where many companies are required to have audits by law

- An audit is an exercise designed to enable an auditor to express an opinion whether the financial statements are prepared, in all material respects, in accordance with an applicable financial reporting framework

- An auditor usually expresses a conclusion as to whether the financial statements "give a true and fair view"

- The 'audit threshold' is the legal qualification for a company to have an audit

- The benefits of audit are much the same as the benefit of assurance services generally. Users of financial statements subject to an audit are given assurance that the financial statements meet legal requirements as well as accounting ones

Definition

Audit of financial statements: According to ISA (UK) 200 *Overall Objectives of the Independent Auditor and the Conduct of an Audit in Accordance with International Standards on Auditing (UK)*, the overall objectives of the auditor in conducting an **audit of financial statements** are as follows:

- To obtain reasonable assurance about whether the financial statements as a whole are free from material misstatement, whether due to fraud or error, thereby enabling the auditor to express an opinion on whether the financial statements are prepared, in all material respects, in accordance with an applicable financial reporting framework; and

- To report on the financial statements, and communicate as required by the ISAs (UK), in accordance with the auditor's findings.

Worked example: How audit is an assurance engagement

The key criteria of an assurance engagement can be seen in an audit as follows:

(1) Three party involvement

- The shareholders (users)
- The board of directors (the responsible party)
- The audit firm (the practitioner)

(2) Subject matter

- The financial statements

(3) Relevant criteria

- Law and accounting standards

(4) Evidence

The auditor is required by international standards on auditing (ISAs) to obtain sufficient and appropriate evidence to support the audit opinion.

(5) Written report in a suitable form

As required by ISA (UK) 700 *Forming an Opinion and Reporting on Financial Statements*, the auditor's report is a written report issued in a prescribed form.

2.1 The audit threshold

For many years all companies registered in the UK were required to be audited. In the early 1990s certain very small companies were granted exemption from audit and this exemption was later extended to all small companies fulfilling certain criteria as defined by the Companies Act 2006.

Small companies are exempt from mandatory audit if they can satisfy two out of three of the following criteria:

- The company has no more than 50 employees
- The company's turnover does not exceed £10.2 million
- The company's gross assets total does not exceed £5.1 million

Since January 2016, most subsidiary companies have been exempt from audit if certain conditions are met; one of the main conditions being that the parent company must guarantee the liabilities of the subsidiary.

Companies that take advantage of the audit exemption must include a statement to that effect in the financial statements.

Even if a company comes under the audit threshold, an audit must be carried out if:

- the articles of association require one
- shareholders who own at least 10% of the shares ask for one
- the company is a non-dormant public company
- the company is involved in the insurance or banking markets

2.2 The benefits of being audited

The case for audit for those companies where it is not required by statute usually revolves around the protection of those who, apart from management, nevertheless have a financial interest in the company, for example:

- Banks and other providers of finance
- Minority shareholders

The rationale for doing away with the need for audit for small companies was made by the UK Department of Trade and Industry (as it then was). A White Paper from the DTI made the very valid point that if the purpose of the audit was to protect shareholders who are not involved with managing the business, and the vast majority of smaller companies were owner managed, what purpose did the audit serve for those companies?

Many would argue (and the auditors of smaller companies have found this to be true) that, in many cases, the audit is valued by management because of the following:

- They value having their business scrutinised by another set of professional eyes

- It provides additional assurance to third parties such as taxation authorities concerning the reliability of the financial statements

- A growing business will one day require an audit

- Audit may have subsidiary benefits, such as the auditors recommending improvements in company systems.

There are, however, some disadvantages relating to having an audit from the entity's point of view. These drawbacks include the following:

- Cost
- Staff time required in providing information, etc
- Disruption to client's business
- Time spent on the initial appointment process
- Dealing with confidentiality
- Expectations gap, particularly surrounding fraud detection
- Inherent limitations of audit

3 Audit and other assurance compared

Section overview

- The earlier sections of this chapter looked at the similarities between audit and other examples of assurance

- All assurance assignments follow the same basic outline with the key difference being the level of assurance given in the final opinion

- This has practical implications at various stages of the assignment

The specific differences relating to agreement of terms and acceptance of appointment are covered in Chapters 6 and 14. The differences in the detailed content of reports are covered in Chapters 13 and 14.

3.1 Nature of work undertaken

In the Assurance paper you studied in detail the sources of audit evidence and the types of procedure that are generally performed on an audit. For other types of assurance assignment, where lower levels of assurance are being provided, the amount and type of evidence required will be less.

The following table compares the main audit procedures as outlined in ISA (UK) 500 with those that would be carried out in an engagement to review financial statements following the guidance of International Standard on Review Engagements (ISRE) 2400, and with those that would be carried out in examining prospective financial information under International Standard on Assurance Engagements (ISAE) 3400:

ISA (UK) 500	ISRE 2400	ISAE 3400
• Inspection of documentation • Inspection of assets • Observation • External confirmation • Recalculation • Reperformance • Analytical procedures • Inquiry	• Inquiry, eg, into the accounting principles in place, the accounting systems in use, and concerning material assertions • Analytical procedures, eg, comparison with prior periods, comparison with anticipated results, and analysis of expected patterns in elements of the financial statements	• Assessment of assumptions • Recomputation • Written representations

From the above it should be clear that the scope of work differs considerably between ISRE 2400 and ISAE 3400. Under ISRE 2400 the work will be based on historical information that can be tested and, in some instances, verified after the fact. A review under ISAE 3400, on the other hand, will be looking at prospective information. This means that the work will revolve around scrutinising management assumptions and will rely on written representations rather than obtaining evidence by direct testing.

For reviews of interim and historical financial information performed by the entity's own independent auditor, specific guidance is given in ISRE 2410.

3.2 Quality of evidence

It is clear that far less evidence is obtained during a review assignment, and the evidence is generally less reliable as some of the most reliable sources, such as third party confirmations and evidence generated by the assurance provider, are not required.

In some cases, the nature and quality of the evidence that can be obtained is further affected by the nature of the subject matter of the assignment. If the firm is appointed to carry out a review of forecast figures to be presented to potential lenders then again analytical procedures and inquiry will be employed but the reliability of the evidence will be even lower due to the uncertainties involved. The figures being reviewed relate to transactions and events, some or all of which have not yet occurred at the time the opinion is given. The information is based on subjective estimates.

3.3 Reporting

In both of these cases the assurance provider can give only a low level of assurance and in the case of prospective information, such as the forecast figures, may include additional warnings to readers of the assurance opinion about the nature of the information and the assurance that can be given.

Chapter 14 looks at the content of such reports in more detail.

Interactive question 2: Review and audit compared

The directors of Connelly Ltd are concerned about the reliability and usefulness of the monthly financial management information that they receive.

As a result, the company's auditors have been engaged to review the system and the information it generates, and to report their conclusions.

Requirement

Contrast this assignment with the statutory audit of the company's financial statements with regard to the scope of the assignment and to the report issued.

See **Answer** at the end of this chapter.

Interactive question 3: Benefits of an audit

Acrylics Ltd was established in June 20X0 to produce acrylic products which are used as display units in the retail industry. The shares are owned equally by two executive and two non-executive directors.

The company's revenue increased steadily over the first two years of trading. The results for the first year of trading indicated an operating profit margin of 15%, and the management accounts for the second year of trading indicate that this has increased to 18%. The directors are currently negotiating a contract worth £600,000 to supply a major retailer which has over 100 outlets throughout the UK. The company will require an increased overdraft facility to fulfil the order.

The finance director of Acrylics Ltd has prepared a business plan for submission to the company's bankers in support of a request for a larger overdraft facility. The plan includes details of the company's products, management, markets, method of operation and financial information. The financial information includes profit and cash flow forecasts for the six months ending 31 December 20X2, together with details of the assumptions on which the forecasts are based and the accounting policies used in compiling the profit forecast. The company's bankers require this financial information to be reviewed and reported on by independent accountants.

Although the company's revenue was below the threshold for a statutory audit for its first year of trading, the company was required by its bankers to have an audit of its financial statements for the year ended 30 June 20X1. Your firm conducted this audit in accordance with auditing standards and issued an unqualified report.

Requirements

(a) Describe the benefits, in addition to continuance of its overdraft facility, to the company and its directors and shareholders from having an audit of its annual financial statements.

(b) Explain how and why the level of assurance provided by a report on profit and cash flow forecasts differs from the level of assurance provided by an auditor's report on annual financial statements.

See **Answer** at the end of this chapter.

Interactive question 4: Examination of cash flow forecasts

Your firm has been engaged to examine the cash flow forecasts prepared by the management of a company whose principal activity is the installation of electrical systems for customers in the retail, construction and industrial sectors in the UK.

All contracts are fixed-price. Customers pay 95% of the contract on completion of the work and withhold 5% of the contract price for up to six months from the date of completion in case remedial work is required. The materials and components used are bought from UK suppliers who require payment within 30 days of the invoice date.

As a result of a significant fall in demand for its services the company has closed two of its regional depots and put both premises up for sale. It has also made 25% of its employees redundant.

Requirements

(a) Identify the specific matters you would consider when examining the assumptions underlying the receipts and payments included in the company's cash flow forecasts.

(b) Explain the level of assurance that will be provided in your assurance report as a result of your examination.

See **Answer** at the end of this chapter.

Summary and Self-test

Summary

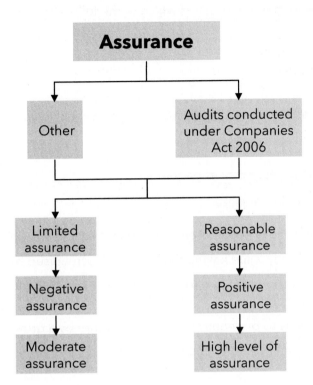

Self-test

Answer the following questions.

1   Define an assurance engagement.

2   Any assurance engagement requires which of the following elements?

    A   A user
    B   A responsible party
    C   A subject matter
    D   Criteria

3   In a reasonable assurance engagement, a negative conclusion is drawn.

☐ True   ☐ False

4   An audit is a limited assurance engagement.

☐ True   ☐ False

5   Which of the following is not a potential benefit of having an audit?

    A   Management may value having their business scrutinised by a set of professional eyes

    B   Assurance may be given to parties other than management who have a financial interest in the company

    C   An audit is likely to be required in the near future by a growing company

    D   Fraud will be uncovered by the auditors

Exam-style question

7   **Treetops Ltd**

Your firm acts as external auditor for Treetops Ltd, a company whose principal business activity is the manufacture and export of hammocks. Due to recent changes in the statutory audit exemption thresholds, Treetops Ltd is no longer required by law to have an audit of its financial statements for the year ended 28 February 20X5.

The directors of Treetops Ltd have asked you to set out the main advantages of the company continuing to have a statutory audit and also to provide them with examples of some of the other types of assurance work which your firm may be able to carry out for them.

The company's managing director has also requested a meeting with you. He has recently discovered that his purchase ledger clerk has diverted £10,000 of company funds into his own bank account. The managing director wants to know why this was not discovered during the course of your audit for the year ended 29 February 20X4. The company's retained profit for that year was £350,000.

Requirements

(a) Briefly describe the advantages to the directors and shareholders of Treetops Ltd of continuing to have a full audit under the Companies Act 2006 when exempt from the statutory audit.

    (4 marks)

(b) Provide examples of four other types of assurance engagement where the scope of the work is agreed between the assurance firm and the company. For each engagement identified, briefly set out the nature of the assurance given in the accompanying report and, where applicable, identify potential users of the report other than the company's management.

    (8 marks)

Now, go back to the Learning objectives in the Introduction. If you are satisfied you have achieved these outcomes, please tick them off.

Technical reference

1	Assurance defined	FRC Glossary of Terms – Ethics and Auditing (Updated January 2018)
2	Audit defined	ISA (UK) 200.11
3	Audit and other assurance compared	n/a

Answers to Interactive questions

Answer to Interactive question 1

Advantages of report regarding loss of profits

- Independent opinion from external source
- Enhanced credibility of compilation of claim
- Confirmation that data subjected to review and examination
- Comfort to insurers that risk of inflated claim reduced
- Could accelerate processing of claim

Answer to Interactive question 2

Scope	
This assignment	Statutory audit
Agree between parties	In accordance with Companies Act 2006
Restricted to instructions	In accordance with audit regulations
	In accordance with ISAs (UK)

Report	
This assignment	Statutory audit
Addressed to board	Addressed to members
Format wholly discretionary	On true and fair view
Private report	Format prescribed
	Report in public domain

Answer to Interactive question 3

(a) Benefits, additional to continuance of overdraft facility, of having an audit:

   (i)   Shareholders who are not involved in the day-to-day management of the company (non-executives) will have assurance that their interests are protected (ie, company assets are not abused).

   (ii)   Financial information is likely to be more reliable, resulting in more informed decisions.

   (iii)   An audit improves a company's governance – management benefits from:

      – Assurance that they are complying with their statutory responsibilities (including the prevention and detection of fraud, as the audit may act as a deterrent);

      – By-products of the audit, such as the identification of weaknesses and recommendations for improvement; and

      – Reducing risks and improving performance.

   (iv)   An audit imposes financial discipline which is useful for growing companies.

   (v)   It may be easier to obtain credit, as suppliers and credit rating agencies regard the additional assurance provided by an audit important.

(b) How and why the level of assurance provided by a report on profit and cash flow forecasts differs from the level of assurance provided by an auditor's report on annual financial statements.

   (i) An audit conducted in accordance with auditing standards provides a high level of assurance which is reasonable but not absolute.

   (ii) The delay between the reporting date and the date of the auditor's report means that even items such as provisions/estimates can often be substantiated.

   (iii) A review of forecasts is only likely to provide a moderate level of assurance.

   (iv) This is because financial statements are based on historical information, and forecasts are based on assumptions which are subject to uncertainty.

Answer to Interactive question 4

(a) The following matters should be considered when examining the reasonableness of the assumptions underlying the receipts and payments:

Receipts:

Trading receipts reflect:

- The reduction in demand in the construction sector
- Potential loss of business following the closure of the two depots
- 95% of the contract price is received on completion and 5% received six months later
- The fact that amounts due may not ultimately be paid

Receipt from sale of premises:

- Realistic proceeds from the sale of the two depots that reflect local property values

Payments:

- Payments for components and raw materials reflect the 30 day credit terms
- PAYE, NIC and other taxes are paid on the due dates
- Redundancy payments are in accordance with legal/contractual obligations
- Ongoing wages reflect reduced workforce following the redundancies
- Any extra costs (eg, transportation costs) involved in servicing contracts from distant depots and a fall in overheads after the sale of the two depots are reflected
- Professional costs (eg, legal and selling agent) involved with the sale of depots are included

(b) An examination of cash flow forecasts is likely to provide only a moderate level of assurance. This is because forecasts are based on assumptions which are subject to uncertainty.

Answers to Self-test

1   An assurance engagement is one in which a practitioner expresses a conclusion designed to enhance the degree of confidence of the intended users other than the responsible party about the outcome of the evaluation or measurement of a subject matter against criteria.

2   All of the elements listed are required, as well as a practitioner and sufficient and appropriate evidence, leading to a written expression of opinion.

3   False. A positive opinion is given in a reasonable assurance engagement.

4   False. It is a reasonable assurance engagement.

5   D – Although an audit may act as a deterrent to fraud, it does not certify that one has not occurred. We shall look at the responsibilities of auditors in relation to fraud in the next chapter.

Exam-style question

7   **Treetops Ltd**

(a) **Benefits of audit**

(i)   The credibility of financial information would be enhanced

(ii) Enhances the value of accounts for business valuation purposes in the event of a sale

(iii) Authorities such as HM Revenue & Customs can have more faith in the figures

(iv) Avoids the future cost of extra work by the auditor when audit exemption limits are exceeded

(v)   Avoids a potential future qualification over the opening inventory figure

(vi) Makes it easier to raise finance

(vii) May act as a deterrent to fraud/management abusing assets/reduce risk of management bias

(viii) More reliable information results in more informed decisions

(ix) Provides management/shareholders with assurance that the financial statements are true and fair/prepared in accordance with accounting standards

(x)   By-products of the audit such as identification of weaknesses and recommendations should reduce risk and improve performance (management letter)

(xi) Imposes discipline on management and accounts staff if they know that the figures will be subject to third party scrutiny, and therefore encourages best practice

(xii) Gives management comfort that they are complying with their professional responsibilities/the accounts comply with the Companies Act

(b) **Four other types of assurance engagement**

Fraud investigation

The conclusion/assurance will be based on the extent of the work carried out.

The report will:

(i)   identify likely causes of fraud
(ii) attempt to quantify the level of fraud

Potential users would be:

(i)   legal experts in a court case
(ii) the Police
(iii) internal or external auditors

Working capital reports/reports on inventory and trade receivables recoverability

The report will state whether:

(i) trade receivables are likely to be received
(ii) inventory can be sold profitably in the near future

Potential users would be:

(i)   potential buyers
(ii) investors
(iii) banks
(iv) internal or external auditors.

Internal control reports

Such a report would:

(i) comment on the effectiveness of internal controls and highlight weaknesses
(ii) make suggestions for the improvement of controls.

Potential users would be:

(i)   regulatory bodies
(ii) shareholders
(iii) internal or external auditors

Reports on business plans/cash flow forecasts

The assurance given would be negative/limited/moderate, ie, "Nothing has come to our attention".

The report would state whether:

(i)   the business plan/forecasts have been prepared in line with stated assumptions;

(ii) nothing has come to light to indicate that the assumptions are not a reasonable basis for the plan;

(iii) the accounting policies used are consistent with the annual accounts; or

(iv) the plan is consistent with the past performance of the company.

Potential users would be:

(i)   bankers
(ii) other lenders
(iii) external auditors

Note: Additional credit was given for mentioning the following alternative engagements (½ mark for each, up to a maximum of 2 in total for all types of engagement identified).

- Value for money studies
- Environmental audit
- Circulation reports
- Cost/benefit reports
- Due diligence
- Branch audit
- Review of specific business activities
- Internal audit
- Report on website security

CHAPTER 2

Responsibilities

Introduction

Examination context

TOPIC LIST

Summary and Self-test

Technical reference

Answers to Interactive questions

Answers to Self-test

Introduction

Learning outcomes

1 Legal and other professional regulations, ethics, accepting and managing engagements and current issues

Students will be able to understand and advise on the regulatory, professional and ethical issues relevant to those accepting, managing and carrying out assurance engagements. Students will be able to understand the processes involved in accepting and managing assurance engagements and how quality assurance processes mitigate the risks to those conducting the engagement.

- Identify and advise upon the legal, professional and ethical issues that may arise before accepting or during a specified assurance engagement ☐

- Judge when to raise legal and ethical matters arising from assurance work with senior colleagues for review and possible referral to external parties ☐

- Discuss the purposes and consequences of UK laws and other regulatory requirements surrounding assurance work ☐

- Explain, using appropriate examples, the main ways in which national legislation affects assurance ☐

- Describe the principal causes of audit failure and their effects and the gap between outcomes delivered by audit engagements and the expectations of users of audit reports ☐

2 Planning engagements

Students will be able to plan assurance engagements in accordance with the terms of the engagements and appropriate standards.

- Outline the aspects of employment and social security law which are relevant to statutory audit ☐

Syllabus links

The issue of responsibilities is usually clarified in an engagement letter, which was introduced in your Assurance paper.

Examination context

Various areas of auditor responsibility are covered regularly in the short form section of the examination paper, including fraud, responsibilities with regard to a review of projected information and compliance with laws and regulations.

1 Management responsibilities

Section overview

- Management is responsible for the following:
    - Managing the business so as to achieve company objectives
    - Assessing business risks to those objectives being achieved
    - Safeguarding the company's assets
    - Keeping proper accounting records
    - Preparing company financial statements and delivering them to the Registrar
    - Ensuring the company complies with applicable laws and regulations
- It is not the responsibility of the auditors of a company to do any of the above

The approach adopted in this section is to identify the responsibilities which are either defined by ISAs (UK) as being attributable to management, or set out in the UK Companies Act 2006 as being the responsibilities of the company's directors.

It follows, therefore, that these duties cannot belong to the auditor or assurance firm.

1.1 Managing the company

First and foremost it is the directors' job to **manage the business** so that its objectives are achieved. This may mean producing suitable returns for shareholders or the achievement of other targets.

It also means **assessing what business risks face the company** and **devising the necessary strategies to deal with them**.

Clearly it is not the auditor's responsibility to set these strategies. However, the auditor does need to understand the risks facing the business and to understand how it will impact on their approach to the audit or other assurance engagement. We will look at this in more detail in Chapters 9 and 10.

1.2 Directors' responsibilities under the Companies Act 2006

The directors' statutory duties primarily come from the responsibilities laid out in the Companies Act. It is important that the directors of a company fully understand these, as in some cases there are criminal consequences for failing to carry them out correctly. The general duties of directors under the Companies Act are to **act in the way most likely to promote the success of the company** for the benefit of its members as a whole.

Safeguarding assets

It is the directors who have the legal responsibility for safeguarding the assets of the company. It is therefore for them to take reasonable steps for the prevention and detection of fraud and other irregularities.

To carry out this responsibility they need to implement systems and controls to safeguard the company's assets and they then need to ensure that the systems and controls operate effectively. Such procedures may include the following:

- The safekeeping of documents of title to land and buildings and other assets
- The setting of authority limits, ie, the limitation of what any one individual can do without consulting someone else
- Implementing other procedures to prevent fraud and reduce the likelihood of error

We looked at internal control systems in your studies for Assurance.

Books and records of the company

It is also the directors who are legally responsible for keeping proper accounting records which disclose with reasonable accuracy at any time the financial position of the company.

This requires records of the following:

- The cash payments and receipts
- What the payments and receipts relate to
- The assets (including non-current assets and inventory)
- The liabilities

The nature of the books and records is not laid down by statute and can take many forms, including manual books, loose-leaf folders, computer records or even a shoebox full of invoices with an add listing attached.

Preparation and delivery of company financial statements

Company law also places on the directors the obligation to prepare financial statements for each financial period (usually a year). These statements must give a true and fair view of the affairs of the company at the end of the accounting period and of the profit or loss of the company for that period.

In preparing those financial statements, the directors are required to:

- select suitable accounting policies and then apply them consistently

- make judgements and estimates that are reasonable and prudent

- comply with applicable accounting standards

- prepare the financial statements on the going concern basis unless it is inappropriate to presume that the company will continue in business

Once the financial statements have been prepared, it is the directors' responsibility to ensure that they, together with the auditor's report, are laid before the members of the company in general meeting and delivered to Companies House within the specified time.

Interactive question 1: Directors' responsibilities

You are finalising the audit of a company. The audit highlights memorandum indicates that the company has failed to maintain proper books and records. This is because there is no non-current asset register and it was not possible to draw up a register, as some of the invoices were missing. The director is furious that the audit firm says this makes it impossible to give an unqualified audit opinion. He says that the audit firm prepared the accounts and therefore it is simply a matter of the auditors' incompetence.

Requirement

Explain the directors' responsibilities in relation to the books and records of the company.

See **Answer** at the end of this chapter.

1.3 Compliance with laws and regulations

It is the responsibility of management to ensure that the company complies with the laws and regulations which have an impact on its operations.

This includes laws and regulations concerning the following:

- Money laundering
- Health and safety
- Public liability
- Employer's liability
- PAYE and payroll matters

Background

Following the Enron scandal, the Sarbanes-Oxley Act was rapidly passed into US law in 2002. It introduced a number of measures to attempt to improve the quality of financial reporting, including the following:

- Having Chief Executive Officers (CEOs) and Chief Finance Officers (CFOs) attest to the veracity of the financial statements

- Much greater disclosure of the amendments made to the financial statements during the audit process

    Companies have had to review systems to ensure that CEOs and CFOs can make such attestations, as there are criminal penalties for making them falsely. This has also affected UK subsidiaries of US companies.

2 Assurance providers' responsibilities

Section overview

- The assurance provider is responsible for the following:

    - Carrying out the assurance service in accordance with professional and ethical standards

    - Carrying out the assurance service in accordance with the terms of engagement

- In the case of statutory audit, the auditor is, in addition, responsible for the following:

    - Forming an independent opinion on the truth and fairness of the annual accounts

    - Confirming that the annual accounts have been properly prepared in accordance with the Companies Act 2006

    - Confirming that the information contained within the directors' report is consistent with the annual accounts

- While the assurance provider does not bear the management responsibilities outlined above, many of them will impact strongly on the audit and, in particular, the risk assessment that the assurance provider carries out

2.1 General

The responsibility of the external provider of assurance services is determined by the following:

- The requirements of any legislation or regulation under which the engagement is conducted; and/or

- The terms of engagement for the assignment, which will specify the services to be provided (you learnt about engagement letters in your studies for Assurance);

- Ethical and professional standards;

- Quality control standards.

2.2 Statutory audit

The legal requirements are contained in the Companies Act 2006 (CA 2006).

In the case of an audit of annual accounts under the CA 2006, it is the external auditor's responsibility to:

- form an independent opinion on the truth and fairness of the annual accounts
- confirm that the annual accounts have been properly prepared in accordance with the CA 2006
- state in their auditor's report whether in the opinion the information given in the directors' report is consistent with the annual accounts.

To achieve these objectives the auditor has to ensure that:

- the audit is planned properly (see Chapters 7, 8, 9 and 10)
- sufficient appropriate audit evidence is gathered (we covered this in detail in Assurance)
- the evidence is properly reviewed and valid conclusions drawn (see Chapter 13).

In accordance with the law and ethical standards the auditor must maintain independence from the client.

In particular, as stated above, appointment as the Companies Act auditor does not lead to responsibility for the following matters:

- The design and operation of the accounting systems.
- The maintenance of the accounting records.
- The preparation and accuracy of management information.
- The preparation of the financial statements.
- The identification of every error and deficiency in the accounts and the accounting records.
- The prevention of fraud in a company.
- The detection of immaterial fraud in the company.
- Ensuring that the company has complied with the laws and regulations that are relevant to its business (except insofar as it affects the financial statements).

All these remain the responsibility of the management of the company; they have the responsibility to manage and cannot delegate or pass this responsibility on to the external auditor.

All impact on the financial statements to a greater or lesser extent, and systems and controls, impact on the way the auditor conducts the audit. However, it is important to know where these responsibilities lie:

- Business risks
- Fraud and error
- Non-compliance with laws and regulations
- Accounting policies

We shall look at how far auditor responsibilities extend in these areas in the following sections of this chapter.

CA 2006 also grants auditors certain rights to enable them to fulfil their responsibilities. Examples of these rights are as follows:

- The right of access at all times to the company's books and accounts
- The right to obtain any information necessary for the audit from any officer or employee of the company
- The right to attend any general meeting of the company

A person who, knowingly or recklessly, provides the auditor with false or misleading information commits an offence under the Act.

2.3 Non-assurance services

A firm which is engaged by management to provide additional non-statutory and non-assurance services is only responsible for providing the services specifically negotiated with management. Such engagements do not result in the firm taking responsibility for any aspects of the company's operations or procedures.

For example, a firm may be engaged to perform services additional to the audit such as:

- Assisting the company with the maintenance of its accounting records
- Assisting the company with preparing management information
- Preparing the financial statements of the company
- Preparing the corporation tax return of the company

The key point is that management retains the overall responsibility for all of these matters; the firm is employed as a support to management, providing expert assistance.

The principles and rules concerning the provision of non-audit services by the **audit** firm to its audit clients are set out in the FRC's Ethical Standard and are dealt with in Chapter 4.

Background

The Sarbanes–Oxley Act, mentioned above in the context of management responsibilities, also has provisions which relate directly to auditors. In particular:

- There is stricter enforcement of the auditor independence rules as a result of the Act.

- A Public Company Accounting Oversight Board (PCAOB) has been set up to inspect audit files of US listed and other public interest clients.

PCAOB is entitled to inspect the audit files of major subsidiaries of US listed companies, so US domestic law can impact overseas where the subsidiary is not US based. Auditors of subsidiaries of US listed companies must register (for a fee!) with PCAOB and are liable to inspection.

3 Error

Section overview

- Auditors are responsible for obtaining audit evidence that provides reasonable assurance that the financial statements are free of material misstatements, some of which may be caused by error

- Management are responsible for designing and implementing a system of internal control which is capable of preventing, or detecting and correcting, errors in the financial records

- Auditors are required to assess the system of internal control as part of their audit in order to determine whether to rely on the system of controls or carry out extended tests of details

- Auditors are required to report to those charged with governance on material weaknesses in controls which could adversely affect the entity's ability to record, process, summarise and report financial data potentially causing material misstatements in the financial statements

- Auditors are responsible for giving an opinion whether the financial statements are free from material misstatement caused by error. This means that they should design procedures that are capable of detecting errors

- As we set out in your Assurance manual, the two types of test generally carried out as part of an audit are tests of control and tests of detail. The more reliance that can be placed on controls (assessed by testing controls), the fewer tests of details may be carried out

Definitions

Error: An unintentional misstatement in financial statements, including the omission of an amount or a disclosure.

Internal control: The process designed, implemented and maintained by those charged with governance, management and other personnel to provide reasonable assurance about the achievement of an entity's objectives with regard to reliability of financial reporting, effectiveness and efficiency of operations, and compliance with applicable laws and regulations. The term "controls" refers to any aspects of one or more of the components of internal control.

Auditor's assessment of internal controls

As we also outlined in your studies for assurance, the auditor is required to assess the system of internal controls as part of his risk assessment, and determine whether he believes it is capable of preventing or detecting and correcting errors.

If he determines that it is capable of this, it will affect the way that he carries out his audit, as ISA (UK) 315 *Identifying and Assessing the Risks of Material Misstatement Through Understanding of the Entity and its Environment* requires auditors to:

- obtain an understanding of controls relevant to the audit
- evaluate the design of those controls and
- determine whether they have been implemented

If testing of controls reveals that the system is not only capable of preventing or detecting and correcting errors, but it operates efficiently, the auditor will be able to conclude that the system is strong and the risk of the financial statements containing errors is reduced. This, in turn, will result in a lower level of tests of details being carried out.

ISA (UK) 330 *The Auditor's Responses to Assessed Risks* requires the auditor to test controls if:

- the auditor intends to rely on the operating effectiveness of those controls or
- substantive procedures alone cannot provide sufficient appropriate audit evidence.

Reporting on deficiencies in internal control

ISA (UK) 265 *Communicating Deficiencies in Internal Control to Those Charged with Governance and Management* sets out that auditors should determine whether audit work has identified any deficiencies in internal control. Where, in the auditor's judgement, those deficiencies are significant, they should be communicated in writing on a timely basis.

A significant deficiency in internal control is one that, in the auditor's professional judgement, is important enough to be brought to the attention of those charged with governance.

Summary

In summary:

- Auditors are responsible for detecting material errors in the financial statements, which they may do by carrying out tests of control or tests of details

- Management are responsible for internal control systems capable of preventing or detecting error

- Auditors are responsible for assessing whether that system is capable of preventing or detecting errors

- If the material weaknesses are found, auditors are responsible for:

    - Reporting these to management

    - Carrying out additional tests of details to uncover any potential errors as a result of the weakness

4 Fraud

Section overview

- The auditor is responsible for drawing a conclusion as to whether the financial statements are free from material misstatement (which can be caused by fraud)

- The auditor's responsibilities with regard to fraud are set out in ISA (UK) 240 *The Auditor's Responsibilities Relating to Fraud in an Audit of Financial Statements* and include the following:

  - Assessing risks of material misstatement

  - Discussing the susceptibility of the financial statements to material misstatement caused by fraud

- A key issue in relation to discovering material misstatements caused by fraud is professional scepticism

- When the auditors become aware of possible non-compliance, they should evaluate the possible effect on the financial statements and on other audit evidence obtained and need to make reports to management

4.1 Definition of fraud

Fraud is a word we normally use to cover a wide range of illegal acts.

For audit purposes, ISA (UK) 240 *The Auditor's Responsibilities Relating to Fraud in an Audit of Financial Statements*, identifies two types of risk of misstatement which can arise from fraud:

- Misstatements arising from fraudulent financial reporting; and
- Misstatements arising from misappropriation of assets.

In order to have a reasonable expectation of detecting fraud or error, auditors should follow the procedures in ISA (UK) 240.

4.2 Responsibilities regarding fraud

ISA (UK) 240 sets out management and auditor responsibilities regarding fraud.

Regarding management, the ISA (UK) states that the primary responsibility for the prevention and detection of fraud rests with both those charged with governance of the entity and with management. To fulfil this responsibility, various actions can be taken including the following:

- Demonstrating that management follow a culture of honesty and ethical behaviour and communicating that they expect all employees to adhere to this culture

- Establishing a sound system of internal control

- From the point of view of those charged with governance, ensuring that management implement policies and procedures to ensure, as far as possible, the orderly and efficient conduct of the company's business.

Regarding the auditor, the ISA (UK) states that the auditor must obtain reasonable assurance that the financial statements, taken as a whole, are free from material misstatement, whether caused by fraud or error. The auditor does not therefore offer complete assurance that the financial statements are free from fraud and/or error as audit testing is not designed to provide this assurance.

4.3 Risk assessment

Part of an auditor's work must include assessing the risk of a fraud existing. We will consider risk assessment procedures in more detail in Chapter 9. Appendix 1 to ISA (UK) 240 is a very useful document as it gives examples of fraud risk factors.

However, it should not be used as a list to be regurgitated in the examination, as risks are always specific to the client.

ISA (UK) 240 sets out that auditors are as follows:

- Entitled to accept representations as truthful and records as genuine, unless there is evidence to the contrary; but also

- Required to bring professional scepticism (as defined) to the work.

Auditors should also carry out a discussion of the susceptibility of the entity's financial statements to fraud. This will usually include a consideration of the following:

- Where the company's system is weak and how management could perpetrate fraud

- The circumstances that could indicate earnings management which could lead to fraudulent financial reporting

- The known internal and external factors that could be an incentive to fraud being carried out

- Management's involvement in overseeing employees with access to cash or other assets which could be misappropriated

- Any unusual or unexplained changes in behaviour/lifestyle of management or employees

- The need for professional scepticism

- The type of circumstances that could lead to suspicions of fraud

- How unpredictability will be incorporated into the way the audit is carried out

- What audit procedures might be responsive to fraud

- Any allegations of fraud that have been made

- The risk of management override of controls

4.4 Where fraud is suspected

If the auditors identify misstatements which might indicate that fraud has taken place, they should consider the implications of this for other aspects of the audit, particularly management representations which may not be trustworthy if fraud is indicated. This may lead to a limitation in the scope of the audit.

4.5 Written representations

Auditors are required to obtain particular written representations from management that management acknowledges its responsibility to design and implement internal controls to prevent and detect fraud and that management has disclosed any known or suspected frauds by management, employees with a significant role in internal control, or any other frauds which might have a material impact on the financial statements to the auditor.

In addition, management confirm in writing that it has disclosed the results of its own assessment of whether the financial statements may be materially affected by fraud.

4.6 Reporting frauds or suspected frauds

The ISA (UK) requires that the auditors should discuss suspected or actual fraud with management and those charged with governance and make the appropriate reports, as set out below:

Management	If they actually discover fraud
	If they suspect fraud
Those charged with governance	Unless all of those charged with governance are involved in managing the entity and the auditor has identified or suspects fraud involving management
Third parties eg, regulatory and enforcement authorities	The auditor shall determine whether there is a responsibility to report the occurrence or suspicion to a party outside the entity

If fraud or error causes the financial statements to not give a true and fair view or there is a fundamental uncertainty, it should be included in the auditor's report in the usual way, **thereby notifying the shareholders.**

Interactive question 2: Fraud

During the course of your audit of Slipstream Ltd the credit controller asks for a private interview with you. During this interview she makes it known that she suspects the chief accountant of misappropriating company funds received from debtors and altering the books.

Requirement

What steps would you take to enable you to assess whether the credit controller's suspicions are reasonable?

See **Answer** at the end of this chapter.

Interactive question 3: Reporting fraud

During the course of the audit you discover that the wages clerk has been defrauding the client through not deleting leavers from the payroll until two months after departure, and was pocketing the money herself.

Requirement

What should you do with regard to:

(a) Informing the client?
(b) The auditor's report?

See **Answer** at the end of this chapter.

4.7 Concluding on fraud

Fraud is a major cost for business and the statutory audit is not designed to identify every fraud in an audit, merely those with a material effect. However, many users of accounts expect that the audit process should uncover all instances of fraud in a company. This is a feature of the expectations gap (discussed below in section 8).

From time to time, the issue of whether auditors' duties should be extended in relation to fraud is discussed. It can be argued that the auditors have closer contact with an organisation than any other external advisers and therefore they are in a position to gain a detailed understanding of the organisation and its systems which should lead to an ability to discover all frauds at an organisation.

However, this argument ignores the inherent limitations of the audit process, which you are aware of from your earlier studies in Assurance, and also opens up the possibility that audit becomes seen simply as a fraud investigation and the wider objective of reporting on the financial statements is lost.

Another key issue is the cost to businesses that this would represent, as the level of testing in a fraud investigation would be far more detailed than the sample based testing required for the purpose of an audit, which most businesses would find prohibitive.

It must be concluded that attempts to make auditors more responsible for discovering fraud also miss the point that management ultimately is responsible for everything within the company, including the prevention and detection of fraud. Management should not be able to hide behind the auditors when fraud is eventually discovered or blame the auditors for not discovering the fraud earlier. Implementing and reporting on the principles of corporate governance is one way to enhance the performance of management in establishing effective systems, managing the risks to the security of the organisation's assets and promoting high standards of conduct by all those within the organisation.

Lastly it must be emphasised that this expectation gap with relation to fraud is generally associated with the statutory audit. If an assurance firm is engaged to carry out a different assurance engagement, or a non-statutory audit, then the terms of that engagement will be set out between the parties and all parties should be very clear what the role of the assurance providers in relation to discovering fraud, will be on that assignment. Bear in mind that the cost of providing a service to uncover frauds might be high and therefore this might be rare in practice. Of course, in order to close the gap in understanding of what the purpose of a statutory audit is in relation to fraud, the auditors' responsibilities are set out in the audit engagement letter. However, this letter is a private matter between the directors and the firm, and therefore this measure does not tackle the issue that the view is widely held in 'society at large' that auditors should detect frauds.

5 Compliance with laws and regulations

Section overview

- Management is responsible for ensuring that the company complies with laws and regulations

- Auditors are responsible for concluding that the financial statements are free from material misstatements caused by non-compliance with laws and regulations

- Auditors are required to have a general understanding of the legal and regulatory framework within which the company operates

5.1 Non-compliance with laws and regulations

Definition

Non-compliance: Acts of omission or commission intentional or unintentional, committed by the entity, or by those charged with governance, by management or by other individuals working for or under the direction of the entity, which are contrary to the prevailing laws or regulations. Non-compliance does not include personal misconduct unrelated to the business activities of the entity.

Auditors are interested in two categories of law and regulations:

- Those which have a direct effect on the financial statements, for example, the Companies Act
- Those which provide a legal framework within which the company operates

The auditor should obtain an understanding of the legal framework within which the company operates as part of his understanding of the entity and its environment (discussed in Chapter 8).

Areas of law which affect all businesses will be as follows:

- Employment law (for example, the auditor should note if work on the payroll appears to indicate that the company pays employees less than the minimum wage.)

- Social security law (for example, the auditor should ensure that the company appears to be paying over the correct amounts to HMRC in respect of PAYE, NI and payments such as maternity pay and paternity pay.)

- Health and safety law (for example, the auditor might notice if a company did not have clear safety notices on manufacturing premises and did not display clear fire exit and procedures notifications.)

5.2 Risk assessment

As part of their risk assessment procedures, auditors should assess the risk that the company is not complying with any relevant law or regulation. Risk assessment procedures will be considered in more detail in Chapter 9.

5.3 Evidence about compliance

The auditor is required by ISA (UK) 250A *Consideration of Laws and Regulations in an Audit of Financial Statements* to obtain sufficient appropriate evidence about compliance with those laws and regulations that have a direct effect on the determination of material amounts in the financial statements (ISA (UK) 250A: para. 14).

Auditors should:

- make inquiries of management
- inspect correspondence with relevant licensing or regulatory authorities.

(ISA (UK) 250A: para. 15)

The auditors should obtain written representations that management has disclosed all known instances of actual or suspected non-compliance with laws and regulations

5.4 Non-compliance suspected or identified

When the auditors become aware of information regarding non-compliance, they should first obtain an understanding of the non-compliance, together with information to evaluate its effect on the financial statements (ISA (UK) 250A: para. 19).

If, after doing this, the auditors suspect non-compliance, then they must discuss the matter with the appropriate level of management unless prohibited by law, for example Anti-Money Laundering Regulations (discussed below in 5.6) (ISA (UK) 250A: para. 20).

If the auditors cannot obtain sufficient appropriate evidence about the suspected non-compliance, this might represent a limitation on the scope of the audit, which will result in the auditors not being able to give an unmodified opinion (ISA (UK) 250A: para. 21). (We shall look at reporting in more detail in Chapter 13.)

5.5 Communication and reporting of non-compliance

ISA (UK) 250 requires the auditors to communicate discovered instances of non-compliance with laws and regulations to those charged with governance (the directors) without delay, and make appropriate reports, as set out below:

Those charged with governance	If the auditors suspect non-compliance with laws and regulations. If the auditor suspects that management or those charged with governance are involved in non-compliance, the auditor shall communicate the matter to the next higher level of authority at the entity, if it exists, such as an audit committee or supervisory board. Where no higher authority exists, or if the auditor believes that the communication may not be acted upon or is unsure as to the person to whom to report, the auditor shall consider the need to obtain legal advice (ISA (UK) 250A: para. 25).
Shareholders	**Only** if non-compliance causes the financial statements to not give a true and fair view or there is a fundamental uncertainty – in which case it should be included in the auditor's report in the usual way (see Chapter 13).
Third parties eg, regulatory and enforcement authorities	The auditor shall determine whether the auditor is required to report the identified or suspected non-compliance to parties outside the entity under law, regulation or ethical requirements.

5.6 Money Laundering Regulations

In December 2017, the FRC added an Appendix to ISA (UK) 250 which contains guidance for UK auditors on Anti-Money Laundering Legislation. The key point is that although "Anti-Money Laundering Legislation does not extend the scope of the audit", it does require the auditor to make reports where it is known or suspected (ISA (UK) 250: Appendix, para. 13). This is not just for matters that are material to the financial statements – all instances of suspected money laundering are relevant. This guidance is covered in more detail in section 7 of this chapter.

The auditor must take care not to commit the offence of 'tipping off', where the suspected/ identified non-compliance could fall within the scope of the Money Laundering Regulations. This means that they must consider the Money Laundering Regulations when they are deciding whether to communicate non-compliance with management or those charged with governance.

5.7 Bribery Act 2010

The Bribery Act 2010 introduced severe penalties for individuals and organisations that engage in bribery. The offences relating to individuals are:

- offering a bribe
- accepting a bribe
- bribing a foreign public official

Commercial organisations can be penalised for failing to prevent bribery by persons associated with that organisation, including employees, agents and subsidiaries.

Auditors will need to analyse the risk to a client of non-compliance and will need to ensure that adequate procedures are in place. Auditors may also have a duty to report suspicions of bribery to the National Crime Agency (NCA) under the Proceeds of Crime Act 2002 (POCA).

As commercial organisations in their own right, audit firms will themselves need to have bribery prevention policies in place. The government suggests that the bribery prevention policies should focus on six principles:

- Proportionate procedures designed to mitigate risks and prevent unethical conduct

- Top-level commitment that creates a culture in which bribery is unacceptable

- Risk assessment that is periodic, informed and documented

- Due diligence procedures that take a proportionate and risk based approach

- Communication (including training) to ensure that bribery prevention is embedded and understood throughout the organisation

- Monitoring and review, and making improvements to procedures where necessary

The Act regards a payment as bribery if it leads to "improper performance by another person, which amounts to a breach of an expectation that a person will act impartially and in good faith". A facilitation payment, for example, made to a foreign country in order to gain access to its internal markets, is a form of bribery and should be avoided. Genuine hospitality and donations to recognised charities, on the other hand, are acceptable in the normal course of business. The legal test of what is and is not a proper payment is "what a reasonable person in the UK would expect of a person performing the relevant function or activity".

5.8 Concluding on reporting non-compliance with laws and regulations

Businesses are faced with ever increasing amounts of legislation across all areas of their activities. It is reasonably asked, "can auditors be expected to become sufficiently expert on every single regulation that exists?"

Many regulations are concerned with matters that are not recorded in accounting systems, for example, issues relating to employment, health and safety and building planning consents. Auditors already face the problem of how to get sufficient and appropriate evidence in relation to their very limited responsibilities, as evidence in this area can be subjective and general. There must be a limit to how much further into the company's total records auditors should be expected to go.

It is possible that it would be better for companies to have a 'regulations audit' carried out by an industry insider who genuinely understands the types of regulations with which the business has to comply and how compliance should occur.

6 Related parties

Section overview

- Accounting standards require that all transactions with related parties are disclosed
- Auditors need to consider the risk of there being undisclosed related party transactions
- The auditors should ask the directors for a list of related parties and watch out for transactions with those parties during the course of testing
- Auditors need to carry out specific tests to seek to identify related parties
- The auditors need to ensure that appropriate disclosures have been made about related party transactions
- Written representations about related parties must be obtained from directors

6.1 The nature of related party transactions

Transactions with related parties may be carried out on terms which may not be the same as in an arm's length transaction with an independent third party. The approach adopted in financial reporting standards is to disclose the relevant amounts and relationships so that the readers of the financial statements can decide for themselves whether such transactions have led to a manipulation of the financial statements.

Related parties are those people or companies that might have, or be expected to have, an undue influence on the company being audited. So as examples (but the full list is much longer), the directors and key management of a company, together with their families, are regarded as related parties of that company, as are other companies controlled by them, other companies in the same group, and so on.

A director might well be in a position to tell an employee to arrange for the company:

- To sell to the director some goods at a cut down price; or
- To buy from another business owned by the director services at above-normal prices.

Because these transactions may not be at the normal market rate, company law and accounting standards require all transactions with related parties, even those conducted at the market rate, to be disclosed. The party that controls the company being audited must also be disclosed in the accounts, even if there are no transactions between them.

ISA (UK) 550 *Related Parties* details the audit work required in respect of related party transactions. The work can be split into the three main stages of the audit:

- Planning
- Detailed work
- Review

6.2 The planning stage

The auditor needs to consider the risk of there being undisclosed material related party transactions. This is an extremely difficult area, because the materiality rule for related party transactions is not just the normal one. The normal rule judges materiality by reference to the company being audited, whereas material related party transactions are judged both by that and by reference to the individual related party (which may be much smaller than the company being audited).

ISA (UK) 550 recognises that risks of material misstatement are higher where there are related party transactions because of the following:

- The complexity of related party relationships and structures

- Information systems that may be ineffective at identifying related party transactions

- Normal market terms may not apply, for example transactions may be conducted with no exchange of consideration

The auditor will also need to bear in mind that fraud may be more easily committed through related parties, and audit procedures will need to be designed accordingly.

6.3 The detailed testing stage

The auditors should ask the directors, who are, after all, responsible for the proper preparation of the financial statements (which will include full disclosure of related party transactions), for a list of related parties and consider if this is complete. The whole audit team should be aware of the list so that they can keep an eye out for those names when carrying out all of the other audit work needed. For example, an entry in the cash book may give an indication of a related party, so it needs to be picked up by the person auditing cash and bank.

ISA (UK) 550 sets out specific procedures that should be carried out:

- Detailed tests of transactions and balances (such as would ordinarily be carried out on audits)

- Reviewing minutes of meetings of shareholders and directors to observe if any related parties or transactions with them become apparent

- Reviewing records for large or unusual transactions or balances, particularly those recognised near the end of the reporting period

- Reviewing confirmation of loans receivable and payable and confirmations from banks (which might indicate guarantor relationships)

- Reviewing investment transactions, for example, when the company has invested in another company

Audit evidence in relation to related parties and transactions with them may be limited and restricted to representations from management. Due to this, the auditor should try carry out procedures such as:

- Discussing the purpose of the transactions with management/directors

- Confirming the terms and amount of the transaction with the related party

- Inspecting information in the possession of the related party

- Corroborating the explanation of the transactions with the related party

- Obtaining information from an unrelated third party if possible

- Confirming information with persons associated with the transaction, such as banks, solicitors, guarantors and agents

Where related party transactions are found the auditor checks that the appropriate disclosures are made in the accounts. Remember that all transactions with related parties need to be disclosed, even if they are at a normal market rate. However, any disclosures should include information that is needed for a proper understanding of the transaction and this would, of course, include whether the transaction was or was not at a market rate.

6.4 The review stage

Written representations should always be requested from directors, who are in the best position to know the identities of related parties. The auditor then reviews the accounts, together with the audit evidence available, in order to reach a conclusion on the appropriate audit opinion.

Interactive question 4: Related party transactions

The training partner in your office is aware that you have covered ISA (UK) 550 *Related Parties* in your Professional Stage studies. He has asked you to help him prepare for a training session he is about to give.

Requirements

Prepare notes for a training session for junior staff on how to identify related party transactions. Your notes should include:

(a) A list of possible features which would lead you to investigate a particular transaction to determine whether it is in fact a related party transaction.

(b) A summary of the general audit procedures you would perform to ensure that all material related party transactions have been identified.

See **Answer** at the end of this chapter.

7 Money laundering

Section overview

- Accountants have substantial responsibilities in respect of suspected or actual money laundering

- Money laundering is defined as a wide range of activities in relation to criminal property, including using, acquiring, concealing and removing from the UK

- Accountants are required to report a suspicion of money laundering to the National Crime Agency

- Failure to make a report is a criminal offence

- There is also an offence called "tipping off" – making the money launderer aware that a report has been made

7.1 Background

The auditor's responsibilities in respect of money laundering are substantial. It is not the purpose of these notes to go into all the implications of these responsibilities, but you do need to be aware of the duties laid on your firm and, from your very first day of work as an accountant, on you.

7.2 What is money laundering?

The purpose of money laundering is to:

- disguise the origins of funds derived from illicit sources, and
- enable illicit funds to be used by those who control them.

As you know from your law studies, as a result of the Proceeds of Crime Act 2002 the definition of money laundering has been expanded to include the following:

- Using
- Acquiring
- Retaining
- Controlling
- Concealing
- Disguising
- Converting
- Transferring
- Removing from the UK

Criminal property is also rather widely defined as the **benefits of criminal conduct**.

The definition extends well beyond the "obvious" examples involving a criminal, say, a drug dealer, passing the takings of his crimes through the books of a "front" business, such as a restaurant.

Other examples of criminal conduct and criminal property include the following:

- **Tax evasion**

    - This could relate to direct tax such as corporation tax or to indirect tax such as VAT.

- **Offences that involve saved costs**

    - These could result from environmental offences, or from failure to implement health and safety requirements.

- **Offences committed overseas that are criminal offences under UK law**

    - These could involve payments that are deemed to be bribes.

7.3   Your responsibilities

The duty to report

The Proceeds of Crime Act and the related Money Laundering Regulations both single out accountants (along with, among others, banks, lawyers, estate agents and casino operators) as having special responsibilities. If an accountant has **grounds for suspicion** that money laundering is taking place at a client, **that accountant must report it**. The exception to this rule is where the accountant is offering advice to a client on areas such as compliance with taxation legislation and the accountant claims Legal Professional Privilege (LPP) and may not therefore be required to make a report. Remember that LPP does not apply to audits.

The regulations override the duty of confidentiality (see the discussion of professional ethics in Chapter 4) towards the client and it is important to note the words '**grounds for suspicion**' – if an accountant waits for incontrovertible evidence, it might be too late.

Accountants do not automatically benefit from any professional privilege under the law. Lawyers do, to some extent, but accountants **generally** do not, unless they are providing legal services, and have always had to tread a fine line of discretion between their duty to their client and the public interest.

An accountant's duty to report money laundering includes reporting actual knowledge or reasonable grounds for suspicion of money laundering. Non-reporting is not an option but mere speculation should not be reported.

Auditors are concerned primarily with the risk of material misstatement of the financial statements, and the audit procedures adopted are designed accordingly. It may be, therefore, that an auditor does not become aware of immaterial matters and there is nothing in the auditing standards to compel the auditor to seek them out. However, if an auditor does come across any misstatement, material or otherwise, this must now be considered from a money laundering perspective.

For non-audit engagements, the terms of engagement will determine whether materiality needs to be considered or not. But here again, any misstatement, regardless of its materiality in whatever context, must be considered for its Proceeds of Crime Act implications.

It would seem that there are considerable amounts of money in the economy which derive from criminal activity – drugs, terrorism, organised crime – and these amounts must go somewhere.

There is therefore a clear ethical imperative (as well as a legal one) to report knowledge or reasonable suspicion of such activity.

If a client is doing well and you do not understand where the money has come from, after exhausting all reasonable lines of enquiry then you have grounds for suspicion and a duty to report without 'tipping off' either:

- the client; or
- anyone who could prejudice an enquiry into the matter.

Report to whom?

Accountants must report to the money laundering nominated officer in their assurance firm, which fulfils their responsibility. Note that ISA (UK) 250 refers to this officer as a money laundering reporting officer.

The money laundering nominated officer then has to decide on whether to report the matter to the National Crime Agency (NCA) and, if appropriate, to make the report.

The legislation protects professionals from any claims for breach of confidentiality even where suspicions are later proved to be ill-founded.

7.4 Offences and penalties

Failing to report and to comply with the regulations – including the need to provide suitable training – are offences under the legislation.

There is also an offence called '**tipping off**' designed to avoid the money launderer being able to escape before the forces of law and order catch up with him or her.

The penalties for non-compliance by accountants are potentially quite severe – for some offences a jail term of fourteen years is a possibility.

7.5 A paradox

The auditor's responsibility is to form an opinion as to whether or not the financial statements give a true and fair view. If included in the company's revenue are material amounts resulting from money laundering, it is probable that the financial statements do not, in fact, give a true and fair view. If the auditors qualify the report, however, they could be accused of tipping off.

7.6 Concluding on money laundering

Money laundering issues affect almost all aspects of an accountant's work and, particularly, due to the privileged position of the auditor, carrying out audit work.

A case has been made to the government by both the ICAEW and the Scottish Institute that, due to the professional standards under which their members operate (which we shall look at in the next two chapters) they should be allowed to use their discretion in making reports to NCA.

The government has said broadly: "This is the 'trust me I'm an accountant' argument and past experience of submissions of 'suspicious transactions reports' suggest that not many come from accountants. So we're doing something about it. If you wish to argue to the public that you should have specific rights not to report drugs and terrorist money, go ahead, but we don't think the public will be convinced."

Yet there is an argument that the profession has, over the years, done much to encourage compliance with the tax laws and the introduction of better business practices and that possibly the wide definition of money laundering in the Proceeds of Crime Act 2002 does not provide the best mechanism for resolving the problem.

There is concern that the reporting requirements of the POCA are set too low putting pressure on accountants to carry out 'extra' work.

7.7 Money laundering and the audit approach

The introduction of the Proceeds of Crime Act 2002 (POCA) and the Money Laundering Regulations (MLR) bring added complications to the auditor's work.

This legislation has regulatory and ethical implications which we have dealt with. Another key principle stressed by the authorities dealing with Money Laundering in the UK and worldwide is **KYC – know your client**.

- The firm will need to have checked the client's identity, when they first became a client and will need to keep the evidence on file for six years after they cease to be a client.

- Where does the money come from? Auditors should think about the real nature of the business' sales, but also about the source of the start-up capital and any other equity and loans raised.

- Remember the money launderer wants to overstate income and loves paying tax on the excess, which goes against the grain of the way most auditors think.

In December 2017, the FRC added an appendix to ISA (UK) 250A, which incorporated the old APB PN 12 into the ISA (UK). The appendix summarises the auditor's duties under UK law, as covered in this section.

Further guidance is available from the CCAB's *Anti-Money Laundering Guidance for the Accounting Sector*, which sets out some 'prompts' that clearly illustrate how money laundering suspicions could arise during the planning and risk assessment phase of an audit, or even during the detailed evidence gathering phase.

(1) What is its purpose in entering into any transaction forming the basis of the proposed engagement or its purpose in seeking services where not related to a specific transaction?

(2) What are the entity's main trading and registered office addresses?

(3) What are its business activities or purposes and sector?

(4) Who controls and manages it (ie, has executive power over the entity – this may be directors, shadow directors or others depending on the circumstances)?

(5) If the client is audited, were the accounts qualified and, if so why?

(6) Name and check that the person (s) purporting to represent the entity is/are who they say they are.

(7) Who owns it – ultimate beneficial owner (s) and steps in between (as a minimum for companies provide details of any ultimate beneficial owners of more than 25% – for trusts, supply details of trustees and settlors and details of either beneficiaries with more than 25% interest, or the classes of beneficiary, and or collective investment funds to other similar arrangements provide details of the general partner and/or investment manager together with details of any person with more than 25% interest)?

(8) What is its business model/intended business model (ie, the mechanism by which a business intends to generate revenue and profits and serve its customers – in terms of broad principles)?

(9) What are the key sources of:
- Income (eg, trading, investment etc,); and
- Capital (eg, public share offer, private investment etc)?

(10) The history and current (also forecast if readily available) scale of its entity's:
- Earnings (eg, turnover and profits/losses); and
- Net assets.

(11) The entity's geographical connections, so that you are in a position to ask such questions as "Why is it getting so much money from that place?" and "Why is it sending assets to that place?"

(12) Has the entity been subject to insolvency proceedings, or is it in course of being dissolved/struck-off, or has it been dissolved/struck-off?

8 Expectations gap

Section overview

- The expectations gap is the gap between the expectations of users of assurance reports and the firm's responsibilities in respect of those reports

- There are a variety of misunderstandings about the nature of assurance work

- The expectations gap has been narrowed by the following:
  - Improving the required auditor's report
  - Inserting paragraphs relating to directors'/auditors' responsibilities in the engagement letter
  - The role of audit committees, which liaise with auditors

8.1 What is the expectations gap?

This so-called 'gap' is between the expectations of users of assurance reports, particularly of auditor's reports under the Companies Act, and the firm's legal responsibilities. For example, users of the financial statements may well expect that an assurance engagement involves the checking of every single transaction, while the firm judges that checks on a test basis are sufficient.

This is further compounded by confusion over the meaning of the report that the auditor gives. The misunderstandings made by lay users of financial statements can be summarised as follows:

- Many believe that responsibility for preparing financial statements lies with the auditor, rather than with management.

- It is widely believed by the general public that the auditor's principal duty is to detect fraud, when in fact the duty is to make a report as to whether or not the financial statements are materially misstated, irrespective of whether such misstatement arises as a result of fraud.

- In most cases the users of the financial statements will also have little perception of the concept of materiality and believe that the auditors check all the transactions that the company undertakes.

- The public generally perceives that an auditor's report attached to the financial statements means that they are 'correct', rather than just meaning that there is reasonable assurance that they give a true and fair view.

8.2 Narrowing the expectations gap

Various steps have been taken to try to reduce the expectations gap.

Expanding the auditor's report

The content of the Companies Act auditor's report has been expanded to do the following:

- Set out responsibilities of auditors and directors
- Explain how an audit is conducted:
  - On a test basis, which implies sampling
  - By assessing significant estimates and judgements
  - So as to give reasonable assurance on the financial statements
  - So as to detect material misstatements – in relation to fraud, error or any other irregularity

In the case of listed companies the report has been expanded further to explain to the users of the financial statements that the auditors review statements made by the company about its corporate governance procedures, and consider other information included with the financial statements to ensure it is consistent. The revised ISA (UK) 700 requires the auditor to report on risks of material misstatements identified by the auditor, and on how the auditor has applied the concept of materiality. The auditor is also required to provide an overview of the scope of the audit, demonstrating how the risks identified have been addressed. This is discussed in more detail in Chapter 13.

Engagement letter

When the firm issues an engagement letter, the letter includes a paragraph reminding the directors of their responsibilities and setting out the firm's responsibilities. Additional detail on the engagement letter can be found in Chapter 6.

Directors' responsibilities

The reporting requirement was extended by the guidance on the preparation of auditor's reports, to include a statement of the directors' responsibilities. This serves to make the respective responsibilities of management and auditors clearer to the users of the financial statements.

Audit committees

Various statements on the principles of corporate governance developed for listed companies have recommended that companies should establish an audit committee of the board to liaise with and receive reports from both external and internal auditors. (Internal auditors are people who work for a company and help the directors to ensure that accounts are properly kept and business risks are minimised. 'External auditors' is the phrase used to describe those involved in the independent Companies Act audit.) The existence of an audit committee serves as a reminder of the division of responsibilities between auditors and management. The disclosures made in the company's annual report about its corporate governance practices should include comments about the operations of its audit committee.

8.3 So why do things still go wrong?

Sometimes companies fail. Sometimes people commit fraud. Sometimes people make genuine mistakes when financial statements are being prepared.

These events are never the fault of the auditor – although as we have seen, the expectations gap means that the users of financial statements do not necessarily understand this.

Sometimes – and these tend to be the most difficult cases – events like this occur, the auditors do not detect them, but no audit failure takes place.

How can this be?

The auditors may not be at fault if:

- the effect is immaterial;

- the accounts, in spite of the event taking place, still give a true and fair view; or

- the auditor's procedures were properly planned, executed and documented but the event could not be detected for some reason, perhaps a carefully executed fraud or a sudden, cataclysmic change leading to the company's collapse.

Nevertheless, corporate collapses do happen and the auditors are found to have been negligent in some way. Clearly, in these cases, something must have gone wrong in:

- planning the audit
- performing the audit
- drawing conclusions from the work done

These failures can usually be traced to one of four main causes:

- The failure to assess audit risk properly

- The failure to respond appropriately to audit risk

- The failure to recognise and respond to situations where the auditor's objectivity is threatened

- The failure to recognise and respond to situations beyond the auditor's area of competence

Summary and Self-test

Summary

Self-test

Answer the following questions.

1 Which one is management not responsible for?

☐ The safeguarding of company assets

☐ Keeping proper accounting records

☐ Preparing financial statements

☐ Auditing financial statements

2 Auditors have a duty to detect frauds which have a material impact on the financial statements.

☐ True

☐ False

3 The Sarbanes–Oxley Act requires CEOs to certify that the accounts are true.

☐ True

☐ False

4 Which two of the following are auditors not necessarily required to do?

A Assess the risk of fraud causing material misstatement in the financial statements

B Discuss the risk of fraud causing material misstatement in the financial statements

C Detect instances where fraud has caused a material misstatement in the financial statements

D Report material misstatements caused by fraud to the police

5 Auditors may be required to report instances of non-compliance with laws and regulations to which of the following?

☐ Shareholders

☐ Directors

☐ Regulatory authorities

6 Management are responsible for making appropriate disclosures concerning related parties in the financial statements.

☐ True

☐ False

7 An auditor fulfils his duty to report a suspicious transaction in relation to money laundering if he makes a report to the money laundering nominated officer in his firm.

☐ True

☐ False

8 Which of the following is not a measure designed to close the expectations gap?

A Auditors required to attend company board meetings

B More detailed engagement letter sent to audit clients

C Auditor's report format revised and extended

D Statement of directors' responsibilities included in the financial statements

Exam-style questions

9   During the course of the audit of Gamma Ltd (Gamma) an employee of the company informed you that a substantial cash deposit was paid into the company's bank account and a month later, the same amount was paid by direct transfer into a bank account in the name of Epsilon, a company based overseas. The employee also informed you that the managing director of Gamma had instructed him not to record the transaction in the accounting records as it had nothing to do with Gamma's business.

State, with reasons, what further action you should take in relation to this matter.   **(3 marks)**

10   Your firm is the auditor of Alpha Ltd (Alpha). The managing director of Alpha discovered that the assistant accountant had used company cheques and bank transfers fraudulently to pay his own personal expenses. The expenditure was reported as company expenses in the statement of profit or loss. Although the amounts involved are immaterial in the context of the financial statements, it transpired that this had been going on for several years. The managing director has expressed concern that your firm did not discover this fraud and has requested a meeting to discuss this matter.

Using Alpha's fraud as an example, compare and contrast the responsibilities of the auditors in respect of fraud with the expectation of the managing director of Alpha.

(3 marks)

11   If brought to their attention, auditors should consider the implications of any breaches by their clients of employment and social security legislation.

Outline the consequences of not considering the implications and provide examples of such breaches.   **(4 marks)**

12   You are the auditor of a company with numerous branches spread throughout the United Kingdom. Revenue for the year ended 31 December 20X1 was £25 million, profit before tax was £1,500,000 and net assets were £9,500,000. Your auditor's report was signed in March 20X2 without qualification. Your report to management after the audit pointed out that internal controls were weak at the branches due to the small number of staff.

You have been telephoned by the finance director, Ray Gosling, and told that the sales ledger clerk at the Goose Green branch had been caught 'teeming and lading'. His investigations so far show that during the year to 31 December 20X1 the sales ledger clerk had diverted £50,000 of receipts from customers to his own bank account. Ray has asked you to attend a meeting with him to discuss the matter. He is particularly concerned as to why the fraud was not discovered during the course of the audit and what the effect on the accounts might be.

At 31 December 20X1 the Goose Green branch had net assets of £400,000. For the year ended on that date the branch had revenue of £1,000,000 and made a small loss.

Your re-examination of your audit working papers shows that your staff had visited the Goose Green branch, that no grounds for suspicion arose during the audit and that appropriate audit procedures were carried out.

Requirements

(a)   Prepare notes to guide you in your discussions with the finance director.   **(6 marks)**

(b)   Following the meeting the finance director has asked you to carry out additional assurance work to establish the extent of the fraud. Outline the main areas to which you would direct your attention in order to establish the extent of the fraud and the loss to the company and state why you would consider those areas.   **(6 marks)**

(12 marks)

Now, go back to the Learning objectives in the Introduction. If you are satisfied you have achieved these outcomes, please tick them off.

Technical reference

1	Management responsibilities	Companies Act 2006 ss. 170-181 and s. 386
2	Assurance provider's responsibilities	Companies Act 2006 ss.495-498
3	Error	FRC Glossary of Terms
4	Fraud	ISA (UK) 240.3, 11, A1 (main references)
5	Compliance with laws and regulations	ISA (UK) 250A.11
6	Related parties	ISA (UK) 550.10
7	Money laundering	Proceeds of Crime Act 2002 s. 330
8	Expectations gap	n/a

Answers to Interactive questions

Answer to Interactive question 1

Directors are responsible for:

- Keeping proper accounting records
- Disclosing with reasonable accuracy at any time the financial position of the company
- Ensuring that the financial statements comply with the Companies Act 2006

Answer to Interactive question 2

- Review and obtain photocopies of documents which have aroused her suspicions

- Enquire into reasons for altered pages in books/documents etc

- Investigate any apparent override/circumvention of company procedure, eg, cancelling a sales invoice instead of raising a credit note

- Review previous management letters for any weaknesses facilitating misappropriations

- Consider credit controller's motives for putting chief accountant under suspicion, eg, working relationship/job threat

- Take note of chief accountant's standard of living; make enquiries about his lifestyle.

- Consider whether past dealings with chief accountant have ever cast doubt on his integrity

- Increase analytical procedures on revenue and receivables, eg, monthly revenue/receipts of major customers/extend circularisation if trade receivables collection period has increased

- Discuss with engagement partner, who may wish to discuss with client (eg, board of directors)

Answer to Interactive question 3

(a) Informing the client

    (i) Report to appropriate level of management

    (ii) If believe that management or employees with significant roles in internal control are involved or fraud results in material misstatement in financial statements report to those charged with governance (eg, audit committee)

    (iii) If integrity/honesty of management or those charged with governance is in doubt, seek legal advice

(b) Auditor's report

    (i) If error is corrected, no need to qualify

    (ii) If no correction is made, then report should be appropriately qualified

    (iii) If outcome of fraud is uncertain then a significant uncertainty paragraph should be included

    (iv) If outcome can be determined and amount is not adjusted in the financial statement except for/material misstatement

Answer to Interactive question 4

Notes for a training session for junior staff on how to identify related party transactions

Purpose of the training

To assist junior staff in the application of IAS 24 *Related Party Disclosures* and ISA (UK) 550 *Related Parties,* and specifically on how to identify related party transactions.

Related parties

IAS 24 defines related parties as individuals or entities (eg, companies) with more than a simple business relationship with the client. This would be because they are directors, owners or major investors of the client and can include family and close friends of the directors or owners.

At the start of each audit you will be provided with an up-to-date list of known related parties. It is important that if you come across any transactions involving these parties during the audit you should record them on the audit file.

The directors should provide us with a complete list of these related party transactions. However, we need to be certain that their list is complete, and by comparing the transactions you find with the list from the directors we can obtain evidence as to its reliability.

General audit procedures

Unless we determine that the risk of non-disclosure of related party transactions is high, we gain a significant amount of evidence needed from general audit procedures. These are listed in (b) below.

Additionally, they may intentionally or otherwise leave out certain transactions from the list they provide and you therefore need to be aware of indicators of potential undisclosed related party transactions. These are given in (a) below.

If you notice any such transactions, record them on the audit file. If there is a significant number of such transactions, immediately ask the manager for specific guidance on what action to take.

(a) List of possible features which would lead you to investigate a particular transaction to determine whether it is a related party transaction.

    (i) Transactions which have unusual terms of trade, eg, unusual prices, interest rates, guarantees and repayment terms.

    (ii) Transactions which appear to lack a logical business reason for their occurrence.

    (iii) Transactions which are overly complex.

    (iv) Transactions which involve previously unidentified related parties.

    (v) Transactions which are processed in an unusual manner.

(b) Summary of the general audit procedures you would perform to ensure that all material related party transactions have been identified.

    (i) Obtain a list of current known related parties, eg, directors, other companies with common directors, family members of directors, significant private company investments of directors, associate or joint venture companies, key personnel and significant investors (>20%).

    (ii) Ensure that the permanent file is updated for related parties.

    (iii) If it is the first year of the audit perform company search; otherwise review statutory records to confirm directorships, other directorships and significant investors.

    (iv) Discuss the list of related parties as disclosed by the directors as to its accuracy and completeness.

(v)   Enquire of directors as to whether there have been any material transactions with the related party, eg, loans, purchase or sale of assets, consultancy fees.

(vi)   List all transactions disclosed by the directors.

(vii) Review the accounting records before and after the year end for any large or round sum amounts; investigate and analyse with reasons.

(viii) Analyse all loans receivable or payable, and seek confirmation of identity of lender or borrower.

(ix)   Review board minutes and enquire as to whether the company has provided any guarantees.

(x)   Analyse the details of guarantees given and review the terms.

(xi)   Include confirmation of all related party transactions or lack of them within the letter of representation.

(xii) Check the accuracy of disclosure within the context of IAS 24.

Answers to Self-test

1 Auditing financial statements

2 True, as auditors are giving an opinion whether the financial statements are free from material misstatements, they should plan and perform procedures designed to discover material misstatements even if they result from a fraud.

3 True

4 C - Detect fraud causing a material misstatement - auditors are required to plan in a manner that tries to uncover material misstatement caused by fraud, but as fraud is by its nature concealed, they might not necessarily uncover it. D - Report fraud to the police. They are required to report to directors, but may be precluded from reporting outside the entity by their duty of professional confidence.

5 All of them, although again, in the case of reporting outside of the organisation, the auditor must take care not to breach his duty of professional confidence.

6 True

7 True

8 A - And in fact, this could be a breach of the auditor's professional duties if the auditor attended in a management capacity for example.

Exam-style questions

9 **Actions**

- Check bank statement to confirm employee's assertion
- Report to nominated officer/ money laundering officer in firm
- Avoid tipping off

Reasons

- Represents proceeds of crime under Proceeds of Crime Act 2002/money laundering
- Criminal offence if auditor does not report suspicions of money laundering

10 **Auditor's responsibilities**

- To identify material misstatements in the financial statements
- Plan, perform and evaluate work in order to have a reasonable expectation of detecting material misstatement in the financial statements
- No obligation to prevent fraud although it may act as a deterrent

MD's perception

- Auditor responsible for ALL fraud
- Lacks an understanding of materiality
- Directors often rely on auditors for monitoring they should undertake themselves

Alpha

- Fraud was not material to Alpha financial statements and consequently not auditor's responsibility

11 Failure to comply may result in penalties/fines requiring provision or disclosure

Serious breaches may have going concern implications (closure, inability to pay fines)

May be indicative of poor control environment

Examples

- Minimum wage and working time directives
- Health and safety at work regulations
- PAYE & NI compliance
- Pension scheme requirement

12 (a) **Notes for meeting re fraud**

Before meeting

(i) Check terms of engagement letter. Were there any special duties agreed with client (specifically, any extra work on branch audits)?

(ii) Schedule responses to this letter from the client.

(iii) Check that the letter contained the usual paragraph re purpose of audit procedures.

Why fraud not discovered

(i) Remind Ray that the prevention and detection of errors and fraud are primarily the responsibility of management.

(ii) The purpose of audit procedures is not to discover errors and fraud, but to enable the auditor to form his opinion on the financial statements: reasonable expectation of discovering error and fraud.

(iii) Weaknesses were pointed out in the last management letter, covering all branches of similar size, together with suggestions for improvement.

(iv) Discuss management's response – reasons why suggestions not implemented.

(v) Audit working papers give details of the work done at Goose Green, which was in accordance with ISAs (UK).

Effect on the accounts

(i) Amount material in context of branch – particularly as it may have turned a profit into a loss – but probably not in the general context of the company (3.3% of profit before tax). 20X1 accounts do not need adjustment unless fraud found to be more extensive.

(ii) Potential effect of control weaknesses not considered material enough to warrant a qualification in 20X1 accounts, but this matter is reviewed each year.

(iii) Qualification possible this year if there is significant breakdown in controls and/or an actual fraud (has the Goose Green fraud continued into 20X2?).

(b) **Areas to consider to establish extent of fraud/loss and why**

Area	Why consider
• How long the particular clerk has worked at the Goose Green (GG) branch.	• To establish how long the fraud is likely to have gone on.
• Relationships between staff at the GG branch.	• Possibility of collusion.
• Other branches with poor control environments (all?).	• To establish general likelihood of fraud at other branches.
• Relationships between staff at the GG branch (especially the sales ledger clerk) and staff at other branches.	• Could the fraud have been 'sold' to staff at other branches?
• Whether the GG branch manager runs other branches.	• Could indicate other branches where fraud might be undetected.
• How the fraud was discovered (chance or management control).	• If by management control, then provides some comfort that other frauds would be detected and therefore, generally, fraud less widespread.
• Recoverability of the amount from the clerk.	• To establish actual monetary loss.
• Likelihood of false claims from credit customers (ie, having heard of the fraud, customers claim to have settled their accounts).	• To establish any knock-on monetary loss.
• Adequacy of fidelity insurance.	• Is the loss recoverable?

CHAPTER 3

Professional standards

Introduction

Examination context

TOPIC LIST

Summary and Self-test

Technical reference

Answer to Interactive question

Answers to Self-test

Introduction

Learning outcomes

1 **Legal and other professional regulations, ethics, accepting and managing engagements and current issues**

Students will be able to understand and advise on the regulatory, professional and ethical issues relevant to those accepting, managing and carrying out assurance engagements. Students will be able to understand the processes involved in accepting and managing assurance engagements and how quality assurance processes mitigate the risks to those conducting the engagement.

- Explain the standard-setting process used by national and international (IAASB) bodies and the authority of the national and international standards ☐

- Explain, in non-technical language, significant current assurance issues being dealt with by the national standard-setting body and the IAASB including developments in the use of data analytics ☐

- Explain the principles behind different auditing requirements in different jurisdictions and describe how national and international bodies are working to harmonise auditing requirements, including requirements to report on internal controls ☐

Syllabus links

Some auditing standards were introduced in your lower level Assurance paper. In this paper, you will both build on the knowledge you have gained at the lower level, and be introduced to more standards. As this is an open book exam, you should also have a copy of ISAs (UK) to refer to when reading through this Study Manual. The Technical reference pages will direct you to the exact places in the standards where the requirements discussed in the chapter can be found.

Examination context

While the content of auditing standards will impact on your exam, the details of who issues them and how they are issued are likely to be of less importance, hence the fact that there are few interactive and other questions in this chapter. Ethics, which are covered in the next chapter, are likely to be far more heavily examined in the context of professional standards.

1 The need for professional standards

The benefits of assurance were revised in Chapter 1. A fundamental feature of assurance is that it is provided by independent professionals to particular standards. Users expect assurance providers to be independent and objective (which we shall consider in the next chapter) and competent. They expect an appropriate amount of work to be done to support the conclusion being given. Assurance services are carried out in the public interest. It is important that they are carried out within a context of professional and ethical standards.

In relation to audit, readers **want assurance** when making comparisons of financial statements that **the reliability of the financial statements does not vary from company to company**. This assurance will be obtained not just from knowing each set of financial statements has been audited, but knowing that each set of financial statements has been audited to **common standards**.

Hence there is a need for audits to be **regulated** so that auditors follow the same standards. Auditors have to follow rules issued by a variety of bodies. Some obligations are imposed by governments in law, or statute. Some obligations are imposed by the professional bodies to which auditors are required (by law) to belong.

Figure 3.1: Auditing rules

2 The International Auditing and Assurance Standards Board (IAASB)

Section overview

- International standards are developed by IAASB, a subsidiary of the International Federation of Accountants

- International standards are designed to provide services of a consistently high quality, but they do not override local regulations – although countries are encouraged to develop local systems to comply with these international standards

- A sub-committee of IAASB works on a particular area and develops an exposure draft which is publicised

- The exposure draft is revised as a result of comments made by interested parties and sometimes re-exposed

- When the amendments have been finalised, an international standard is published

2.1 The International Federation of Accountants (IFAC)

IFAC was set up by the professional bodies representing accountants from around the world. It has 163 member organisations from 119 countries. Members from the UK are as follows:

- ACCA (Certified accountants)
- CIMA (Management accountants)
- CIPFA (Public sector accountants)
- ICAEW
- ICAI (Ireland)
- ICAS (Scotland)

IFAC has established the IAASB – the International Auditing and Assurance Standards Board – to issue professional standards on its behalf.

2.2 The forum of firms

The forum of firms was set up by the largest accountancy practices to co-operate on standard setting and other matters.

2.3 The International Auditing and Assurance Standards Board (IAASB)

IAASB was set up by IFAC, which nominates a majority of its members – others are nominated by the forum of firms – to issue professional standards. It replaced its predecessor body the International Auditing Practices Committee (IAPC). It issues the following standards:

- International Standards on Auditing (ISAs)

- International Standards on Assurance Engagements (ISAEs) (applicable to assurance engagements dealing with matters other than historical financial information)

- International Standards on Review Engagements (ISREs) (applicable to the review of historical financial information)

- International Standards on Related Services (ISRSs) (applicable to other, non-assurance engagements)

- International Standards on Quality Control (ISQCs) (applicable to all engagements carried out under any of the IAASB's standards)

IFAC itself issues Statements of Membership Obligations (SMOs) to assist its members in ensuring high quality performance. SMO1 *Quality Assurance* is to be applied to quality assurance review programmes by members carrying out audits of financial statements.

An explanation of the workings of the IAASB, the authority of the ISAs and so on are laid out in the *Preface to the International Standards on Quality Control, Auditing, Review, Other Assurance and Related Services*.

The *Preface* restates the mission of IFAC as set out in its constitution: "The development and enhancement of an accountancy profession with harmonised standards able to provide services of consistently high quality in the public interest".

In working toward this mission, the Council of IFAC established the International Auditing Practices Committee, precursor to IAASB, to develop and issue, on behalf of the Council, standards and statements on auditing and related services. Such standards and statements improve the degree of uniformity of auditing practices and related services throughout the world.

Within each country, local regulations govern, to a greater or lesser degree, the practices followed in the auditing of financial or other information. Such regulations may be either of a statutory nature, or in the form of statements issued by the regulatory or professional bodies in the countries concerned.

National standards on auditing and related services published in many countries differ in form and content. The IAASB takes account of such documents and differences and, in the light of such knowledge, issues ISAs which are intended for international acceptance.

The *Preface* also lays out the authority attached to ISAs in general.

Authority of International Standards on Auditing

International Standards on Auditing (ISAs) are to be applied in the audit of historical financial information.

In exceptional circumstances, an auditor may judge it necessary to depart from an ISA in order to more effectively achieve the objective of an audit. When such a situation arises, the auditor should be prepared to justify the departure.

ISAs do **not** override the local regulations referred to above governing the audit of financial or other information in a particular country.

- To the extent that ISAs **conform** with local regulations on a particular subject, the audit of financial or other information in that country in accordance with local regulations will automatically comply with the ISA regarding that subject.

- In the event that the local regulations **differ from**, or conflict with, ISAs on a particular subject, member bodies should comply with the obligations of members set forth in the IFAC Constitution as regards these ISAs (ie, **encourage changes** in local regulations to comply with ISAs).

Application to public sector

Considerations Specific to Public Sector Entities are set out at the relevant points in the text of the ISA. Where there are no specific public sector considerations, the ISA is applicable in all material respects to the public sector.

2.4 Working procedures of the IAASB

The working procedure of the IAASB is to select subjects for detailed study by a **subcommittee** established for that purpose. The IAASB delegates to the subcommittee the initial responsibility for the preparation and drafting of accounting standards and statements.

As a result of that study, an **exposure draft** is prepared for consideration by the IAASB. If approved, the exposure draft is widely distributed for comment by member bodies of IFAC, and to such international organisations that have an interest in auditing standards as appropriate.

The comments and suggestions received as a result of this exposure are then considered by the IAASB and the exposure draft is **revised** as appropriate. Provided that the revised draft is approved it is issued as a definitive **International Standard** and becomes operative.

2.5 Clarity Project

IAASB completed the Clarity Project in 2009, during which they reissued existing ISAs, redrafted so as to make the requirements within them clearer.

Some of the purposes of the project were:

- eliminating ambiguity in ISAs
- improving the overall readability of ISAs

In June 2016 a revised set of ISAs (UK) were issued, incorporating the IAASB's standards, augmented where necessary with additional material to address specific UK statutory requirements. The ISAs listed in the technical knowledge grid in the introduction to this Study Manual are those issued by the FRC. Unless specified otherwise all references to ISAs in this Study Manual are to ISAs (UK).

2.6 So where are we now?

International Accounting Standards (IAS) should have been adopted by all EU listed companies for accounting periods commencing on or after 1 January 2005.

International Standards on Auditing (ISAs) should have been adopted for the audit of all EU financial statements for periods starting on or after 1 January 2005.

In June 2016 the FRC issued a whole series of revised ISAs (UK) including ISA (UK) 700 *Forming an Opinion and Reporting on Financial Statements* which is based on the equivalent IAASB ISA. Examples of auditor's reports are provided in the FRC's Bulletin (October 2016) *Compendium of Illustrative Auditor's Reports on United Kingdom Private Sector Financial Statements for periods commencing on or after 17 June 2016.* The auditor's report in the UK will be discussed in Chapter 13.

The system in the UK works as follows:

Figure 3.2: UK system for auditing standards

3 The Financial Reporting Council (FRC)

Section overview

- Supervision of accountancy related issues in the UK is provided by the Financial Reporting Council

- The FRC issues auditing standards in the UK; this was formerly the role of the APB

- The FRC adopts International Standards on Auditing, augmented for UK issues and styled ISAs (UK)

- The FRC has not adopted other assurance standards issued by the IAASB

3.1 The Financial Reporting Council (FRC) structure

The FRC was established in 1990 to promote good financial reporting in the UK through the setting of accounting standards and the review of published financial statements.

In July 2012 the reform of the FRC was approved by Parliament and it currently has the following core structure and responsibilities under the overarching FRC Board:

- Codes and Standards Committee – responsible for actuarial policy, audit and assurance, corporate governance, and accounting and reporting policy.

- Conduct Committee – responsible for audit quality review, corporate reporting review, professional discipline, professional oversight, and supervisory inquiries.

There is also an Executive Committee that provides day to day oversight of the work of the FRC.

The FRC is continuing the process of 're-branding' documents and other publications issued by the former APB and other bodies under the old structure. You will therefore see references in the text to APB pronouncements where these still exist and are in force.

The full structure of the FRC is shown in Figure 3.3.

Figure 3.3: Structure of Financial Reporting Council

3.2 The FRC and auditing standards

The FRC issues auditing standards. It:

- amends International Standards on Auditing for any specific UK factors and then issues these as ISAs (UK)

- can issue auditing standards in its own right without having to gain the approval of all the professional accounting bodies

- has strong representation from outside the accounting profession

- has a commitment to openness, with agenda papers being circulated to interested parties and an annual report being published

The FRC issues the following standards and guidance for auditing:

- Auditing standards
- Ethical standards for auditors
- Practice notes
- Bulletins
- Standards for reviews of interim financial statements performed by the auditor of the entity
- Audit quality – thematic reviews

We are primarily concerned with the auditing standards. The scope of these is as follows: 'Quality Control Standards and Auditing Standards for audits of financial statements include objectives for the auditor, together with requirements and related application and other explanatory material. It is necessary to have an understanding of the entire text of a Standard, including its guidance, to understand its objectives and to apply its requirements properly.'

Interactive question: The Financial Reporting Council

Requirement

What are the main functions of the Financial Reporting Council and by what bodies are those functions carried out?

See **Answer** at the end of this chapter.

4 Internal controls

Section overview

- Internal control is an important issue given prominence by the UK Turnbull Report and the US Sarbanes-Oxley Act

- The issue of providing assurance on internal control is important, particularly as little assurance is given on the effectiveness of internal control by the audit

- The APB issued a Briefing Paper on providing assurance on internal control in 2001, which sets out the key issues

- Knowledge of the business will be an important factor in providing assurance on internal controls

- Assurance may be provided on the different stages of the process: identifying the risks, the design of the system, the operation of the system

- Reports providing assurance on the effectiveness of internal controls should mention the inherent limitations of internal control systems to avoid an expectations gap arising in relation to this issue

Internal control is an important issue in business. It has been given particular prominence in the UK by the investigations into corporate governance in the 1990s, notably the Turnbull Report which concentrated on the risks facing companies and the need for directors to manage those risks. In September 2014 the FRC issued *Guidance on Risk Management, Internal Control and Related Financial and Business Reporting,* which incorporates the findings of the Sharman Inquiry into going concern and liquidity risk. The guidance stresses that risk management and internal control should be part of the day-to-day management and governance of a business rather than a separate exercise.

In addition, it has been given prominence by the Sarbanes-Oxley Act in the US, and the requirements that places on chief executive officers to give more certification that the financial statements produced are true, by implication, that the systems supporting them are strong and capable of preventing error.

The auditors' responsibilities with regard to internal control were discussed in the previous chapter and in your earlier studies in relation to Assurance. Due to the limitations of the assurance given in relation to internal control as part of an audit, provision of additional or alternative assurances in respect of internal control has become an important issue.

In July 2001, the APB issued a Briefing Paper on the issue of providing assurance in the effectiveness of internal control. Briefing Papers are not directly examinable, but we shall look at the issues raised in that Briefing Paper as a way at looking at this important issue.

4.1 Providing assurance on internal control

The Briefing Paper draws a clear distinction between two areas of assurance:

- Assurance on the **design** of internal control systems
- Assurance on the **operation** of the internal control system, in accordance with the design.

These are two very distinct issues, and the two assignments should be approached very differently.

4.2 Process of internal control

The Briefing Paper recognises the following process in relation to internal controls:

Figure 3.4: Internal control

Figure 3.4 also illustrates the points of the process where assurance services can be given:

- Risk identification
- Design of system
- Operation of system

In order to carry out an engagement in relation to the internal controls, the practitioners will require sufficient **knowledge of the business** that they can **identify and understand** the events, transactions and practices which will impact on the system of internal control.

4.3 Providing assurance on the operation of the system

The practitioner should establish whether the engagement relates to a period of time or a point of time. The practitioner will only be able to provide a **high level of assurance** on this point if the entity has a detailed description of the design of their system of internal control.

The **report** arising from such an assignment need not be extensive, but is likely to be narrative. This is because practitioners are likely to include such issues as:

- Isolated control failures
- Observation about the abilities of staff involved in operating the system of control
- Potential weaknesses observed which were not contemplated within the design

4.4 Providing assurance on the design and operation of the system

In such an engagement practitioners will consider two issues:

- The design of the system in addressing a set of identified risks
- The operation of the system (discussed above)

Such an engagement will involve significant **discussions with management** at the outset, to establish matters such as:

- The desired balance between prevention and detection controls
- The balance between costs and benefits
- The importance of specific control objectives

The outcome of these discussions will necessarily be included in the assurance **report**, to provide a context for their conclusions. The following things will also be included in the report:

- The applicable risks
- Any framework for design used by either the directors or the practitioners
- A description of the design of the system of internal control

The **level of assurance** given by the practitioners will **depend on several factors**, including the nature of the entity, the knowledge of the business the practitioner possesses and the scope of the engagement. It is likely that the report in this instance would be quite long.

4.5 Providing assurance on the applicable risks and the design and operation of the system

This engagement would include consideration of all three stages of the internal controls process identified above. The identification of risks is likely to involve a **high degree of judgement** as there are no universally recognised criteria suitable for evaluating the effectiveness of an entity's risk evaluation. This means that practitioners are **unlikely to be** able to provide a **high level of assurance** in this area.

The starting point for the practitioner would be the entity's business objectives. The key considerations will include the following:

- The completeness of the applicable identified risks
- The probability of a risk crystallising
- The materiality of the likely impact of the risk
- The time period over which crystallisation is anticipated

In their **report**, the practitioners would have to outline the business objectives of the entity, a description of the risk identification process and the applicable risks.

4.6 Inherent limitations

Internal control systems have inherent limitations, a key one of which is the chance of staff colluding in fraud to override the system. **Any assurance report on internal control** systems should **include a mention of these inherent limitations**, in order to prevent an unnecessary expectations gap.

4.7 Reports

The nature of the individual reports has been touched on above. The discussion paper also includes an example report; however, as it is difficult to issue a standard report for assurance services, which are largely dependent on the scope and nature of the individual assignment, this has not been reproduced here.

5 Current issues

Section overview

- The key current issue for UK standard setters is harmonisation, particularly with European-wide requirements in relation to audit

5.1 Harmonisation

Harmonisation is the process of aligning international standards for auditing so that companies are audited in a comparable way globally.

The EU Directive and Regulation of April 2014 introduced the following with regards to audit:

- Improving the quality of audit and reporting
- Mandatory re-tendering after 10 years
- Change of auditor at least every 20 years
- Ban on providing non-audit services (including tax advice) to public interest entities (PIEs)
- Cap on fees for non-audit services

Taken together these provisions required changes to be made to Ethical and Auditing Standards and to the UK Corporate Governance Code.

5.2 Professional scepticism

Definition

Professional scepticism: *Auditing Standards* define **professional scepticism** as "an attitude that includes a questioning mind, being alert to conditions which may indicate possible misstatement due to error or fraud, and a critical assessment of audit evidence."

In March 2012 the FRC published a briefing paper on professional scepticism. It recognises the difficulty in applying a sceptical approach to audit when the culture of audit firms encourages close working relationships with clients. It also emphasises the role of audit committees in communicating to shareholders the extent of scepticism employed in carrying out the audit work.

The paper comments on the skills auditors use in making judgements based on evidence, and concludes that no opinion can be expressed on the truth and fairness of financial statements until:

- there has been sufficient inquiry and challenge
- management's assertions have been thoroughly tested
- audit evidence has been critically appraised and deemed to be sufficiently persuasive
- alternative treatments for items in financial statements have been considered

5.3 Big data

Big data is a broad term for data sets that are large or complex. Big data presents both a major challenge to, and an opportunity for, existing standards and training within the audit and assurance profession. Big data technology allows the auditor to monitor very large or complete sets of data, rather than samples, on a more frequent (possibly continuous) basis, and to mine unstructured sets of data, such as email, to identify anomalies for further investigation.

Some accountancy firms are currently investing in data analytics to provide a better quality audit, and to reduce risk and liability for the auditor. The International Auditing and Assurances Standards Board (IAASB) has set up a Data Analytics Working Group (DAWG) to monitor the various applications of data analytics and the relationship to the audit, such as the effect on risk assessments, testing approaches, analytical procedures and other audit evidence.

The objectives of the Data Analytics Working Group (DAWG) are as follows:

- "Explore emerging developments in the effective and appropriate use of technology, including data analytics, to enhance audit quality; and

- Explore how the IAASB most effectively can respond to these emerging developments via new or revised International Standards on Auditing or non-authoritative guidance (including Staff publications) and in what timeframe".

The increasing use of technology in the audit will need to be reflected in auditing standards, so that audit data analytics techniques are incorporated into the framework.

DAWG issued a 'Request for Input' in September 2016 and the FRC has responded with reference to its own 'Audit Quality Thematic Review' which was published in January 2017. This review looked at how and to what extent audit firms are using data analytics in the audit of financial statements, with a particular focus on audit quality.

The use of data analytics as part of the audit approach is discussed further in Chapter 10.

5.4 Future of Audit

Recent corporate collapses (Carillion plc, BHS, Quindell and others) have given rise to criticism of external auditors. Rachel Reeves MP commented that 'audits appear to be a colossal waste of time and money, fit only to provide false assurance' (Parliament UK, 2018). The FRC has recently highlighted a decline in the quality of external audit work and there has been much debate about the future of audit including:

- levels of non-audit services provided by audit firms, and the separating of the external audit and advisory practices of firms

- lack of competition, with the Big Four auditing 98% of the top 350 London listed companies, and smaller firms complaining that the costs of preparing audit tenders are prohibitively expensive, which prevents them from entering the audit market for listed companies

- the nature of audit work and whether more needs to be done to assess the risks to businesses over time periods greater than 12 months

- the business models of external audit firms

- the frequency of rotation of audit firms

- the role of FRC in regulating the work of external auditors and conflicts of interest within the FRC.

Michael Izza, the Chief Executive of the ICAEW has blogged

"At a time when the profession is under such scrutiny, for the trend in improving audit quality to be reversed at the four largest firms is frankly not good enough. It overshadows all the progress that has been made in improvements in audit quality over the last decade. I know that this view is shared by the senior partners of all the firms concerned and that they will be working hard to quickly address the issues highlighted by the FRC and to raise standards within their own organisations.

… the events of last week with the publication of the FRC's enquiries into the audits of Quindell and BHS – has reinforced my view that the profession is at a watershed moment. The trust that investors and others place in us to get things right has been brought into question. We not only need to regain that trust but, in my view, we also have to ask ourselves whether or not the services we provide are still fit for purpose. If we have a situation whereby politicians, regulators and society expect something more from us, and the product and service that we delivered is no longer regarded as sufficient, we need to engage to see whether or not that can be changed."

In response to the criticism of auditors, the following reviews have been announced:

- Sir John Kingman is undertaking a government commissioned independent review of the role and powers of the FRC

- The Competitions and Market Authority is reviewing the audit market

- The FRC, the ICAEW and the Audit Quality Forum are planning to review the effectiveness of the existing model for auditing

Michael Izza has blogged as follows.

"These reviews will shape the future of the profession, and it is absolutely critical that we get them right. The eyes of the whole business world will be on what happens. If we cannot demonstrate the value of audit, people may start to ask why we need audits, or an audit profession, at all. I know that we do – trust and confidence are the lifeblood of business. But this means we cannot regard these enquiries as adversarial or as challenges. They are opportunities to change. We must embrace them."

Summary and Self-test

Summary

Self-test

Answer the following questions.

1 Auditing is regulated by the government in the UK.

$\square$ True

$\square$ False

2 The Financial Reporting Council issues auditing standards which auditors are required to follow.

$\square$ True

$\square$ False

3 Why are professional standards important?

4 Which of the following is a UK auditor required to follow?

$\square$ International Standards on Auditing

$\square$ International Standards on Auditing (UK)

$\square$ The FRC's *Ethical Standard*

Exam-style question

5 Discuss the advantages and disadvantages of accounting and auditing standards to auditors and the consequences of such standards being enforceable by statute. **(4 marks)**

Now, go back to the Learning objectives in the Introduction. If you are satisfied you have achieved these outcomes, please tick them off.

Technical reference

Answer to Interactive question

Functions	Committee
• Actuarial policy	Codes and Standards Committee
• Audit and assurance	
• Corporate governance	
• Accounting and reporting policy	
• Audit quality review	Conduct Committee
• Corporate reporting review	
• Professional discipline	
• Professional oversight	
• Supervisory enquiries	
• Day to day oversight of the work of the FRC	Executive Committee

Answers to Self-test

1 False. It is regulated by RSBs and the FRC.

2 True. Auditors face discipline by their RSB if they do not.

3 It is in the public interest that assurance services are carried out to professional standards.

4 Auditors in the UK are required to comply with ISAs (UK) and the FRC's *Ethical Standard* (which we shall look at in the next chapter).

Exam-style question

5 The major **advantages** of accounting standards and auditing standards can be summarised as follows:

(a) **Accounting standards**

   (i) They reduce the areas of uncertainty and subjectivity in accounts.

   (ii) They narrow the areas where different accounting policies can be adopted.

   (iii) They increase the comparability of financial statements.

   (iv) They codify what is considered in most circumstances to be best accounting practice.

   (v) They give an indication of the interpretation of the concept 'true and fair' in many circumstances.

(b) **Auditing standards**

   (i) They give a framework for all audits around which a particular audit can be developed.

   (ii) They help to standardise the approach of all auditors to the common objective of producing an opinion.

   (iii) They assist the court in interpretation of the concept of 'due professional care' and may assist auditors when defending their work.

   (iv) They increase public awareness of what an audit comprises and the work behind the production of an auditor's report.

   (v) They provide support for auditors in a dispute with clients regarding the audit work necessary.

The possible **disadvantages** include the following:

(a) **Accounting standards**

   (i) They are considered to be too rigid in some areas and too general in others, making their application difficult in some circumstances.

   (ii) They can be onerous for small companies to adopt.

   (iii) Their proliferation could be said to increase proportionately the number of qualified auditor's reports thereby reducing the impact of such qualifications.

   (iv) They can create divisions within the profession of those who agree and those who disagree with a particular standard.

   (v) They would be difficult to change once they become statutory as alterations to company law can take years rather than months to enact.

(b) **Auditing standards**

    (i)   It may appear that they impinge on, rather than assist, professional judgement.

    (ii)   They are considered by some to stifle initiative and developments of new auditing methods.

    (iii)   They may create additional and unnecessary work and thus raise fees, particularly on the audit of small companies.

If either type of standard were to be enforceable by statute it would mean that there would be government intervention in areas currently controlled solely by the profession itself. This might ultimately lead to a diminished role in self-regulation. To be enforceable by statute the standards would have to be applicable to all circumstances and thus need to be very general and broad in their instructions. This might reduce their usefulness to the auditors. Auditors might spend unnecessary time ensuring that they have complied with the law rather than considering the quality of their service to their clients.

Finally, it should be considered whether full statutory backing for standards would force auditors into narrow views and approaches which might gradually impair the quality of accounting and auditing practices.

Note: A legal opinion on truth and fairness, accounting standards and the law in the **Foreword to Accounting Standards** strengthens the legal backing for accounting standards and UITF pronouncements. A legal opinion commissioned by the FRC endorsed the opinion in the Foreword.

CHAPTER 4

Professional ethics

Introduction

Examination context

TOPIC LIST

Summary and Self-test

Technical reference

Answers to Interactive questions

Answers to Self-test

Introduction

Learning outcomes

1 **Legal and other professional regulations, ethics, accepting and managing engagements and current issues**

   Students will be able to understand and advise on the regulatory, professional and ethical issues relevant to those accepting, managing and carrying out assurance engagements. Students will be able to understand the processes involved in accepting and managing assurance engagements and how quality assurance processes mitigate the risks to those conducting the engagement.

   - Identify and advise upon the legal, professional and ethical issues that may arise before accepting or during a specified assurance engagement

   - Recognise the professional and ethical issues that may arise during an assurance engagement, explain the relevance and importance of these issues and evaluate the relative merits of different standpoints taken in debate

   - Judge when to raise legal and ethical matters arising from assurance work with senior colleagues for review and possible referral to external parties

   - Discuss the purposes and consequences of UK laws and other regulatory requirements surrounding assurance work

Syllabus links

This topic was covered in detail in Assurance.

Examination context

As this is an important practical area, you can expect it to be examined regularly.

1 The need for professional ethics

Section overview

- The importance of professional ethics is that in order for accountancy services to be meaningful, the public must trust accountants

- Trust is built by the knowledge that accountants are bound by a professional code of ethics

- Independence and objectivity (key features of the Code of Ethics) are fundamental to the provision of assurance services

The accountancy profession has a paradoxical image. On the one hand accountants are seen as pillars of society, providing reliable financial information in their working lives and acting as treasurer for the PTA or the local church in their spare time.

The other side of the coin is the image of aggressive tax schemes, financial scandals and money laundering.

Yet accountants believe that financial information is important. It is necessary for governments, shareholders, trading partners, management and any number of other stakeholders, that the financial and other reports and information provided by accountants are reliable and can be used by others as they go about their daily lives. So the work that accountants and other assurance providers do has benefit for the public interest.

It follows from this that, if the profession is to survive and thrive, and if its members are to maintain their position there has to be a code of conduct so that the public are able to feel that they can trust accountants.

The profession needs a code of professional ethics.

When a good deal of the profession's income comes from audit and other assurance services, where the users of those services are seeking to gain additional confidence in the reliability of information, it is no exaggeration to say that the profession's income actually depends on accountants' reputation for ethical behaviour.

You have already studied professional ethics in relation to assurance services in your earlier studies for your Assurance paper. The following summary is therefore revision, except in the case of the FRC's Ethical Standard, which you have not yet looked at in detail.

2 Code of Ethics

Section overview

- The International Ethics Standards Board (IESBA) is one of the standard setting boards of IFAC

- IESBA issues a Code of Ethics for Professional Accountants, with which you should be familiar

- The IESBA Code has been used as the basis for developing UK codes, in particular, compliance with the ICAEW code ensures compliance with the IESBA Code

2.1 IESBA Code of Ethics - fundamental principles

The fundamental principles are:

- **Integrity** - to be straightforward and honest in all professional and business relationships.

- **Objectivity** - to not allow bias, conflict of interest or undue influence of others to override professional or business judgements.

- **Professional competence and due care** - to maintain professional knowledge and skill at the level required to ensure that a client or employer receives competent professional service based on current developments in practice, legislation and techniques and act diligently and in accordance with applicable technical and professional standards.

- **Confidentiality** - to respect the confidentiality of information acquired as a result of professional and business relationships and should not disclose any such information to third parties without proper and specific authority unless there is a legal or professional right or duty to disclose, nor use the information for the personal advantage of the professional accountant or third parties.

- **Professional behaviour** - to comply with relevant laws and regulations and should avoid any action that discredits the profession.

2.2 Code of Ethics - threats to objectivity and independence

The IESBA *Code of Ethics*, the ICAEW *Code of ethics* and the FRC *Ethical standard* all work on the basis that an assurance firm's integrity, objectivity and independence are subject to various threats and that the firm must have safeguards in place to counter these threats.

Prior to the restructuring of the FRC in July 2012, Ethical Standards were issued by the Auditing Practices Board (APB) and were referred to as the APB Ethical Standards for Auditors. They were then collected into a single document, the FRC *Ethical Standard*, in 2016.

The FRC's approach is to stress that the perceptions of 'an objective, reasonable and informed third party' are more important than the firm's own view.

The FRC's list of threats includes the management threat, which is not covered by either the IESBA or ICAEW documents.

The threats are as follows:

- **The self-interest threat**

    All firms face the self-interest threat, simply because the client pays the fee, and to lose a client may be painful.

    The risk is increased for audit engagements, because, although technically the auditor is appointed by and reports to the shareholders, in practice the appointment depends on the client's management. The auditor may be tempted to allow inappropriate accounting treatments in order to keep the client.

- **The self-review threat**

    It may be difficult for the firm to maintain its objectivity if any product or judgement made by the firm needs to be challenged or re-evaluated at a later date.

    Examples might be brand or company valuations or aggressive tax schemes. If the firm has valued a client's new subsidiary at a price which is questioned when it comes to the audit, there may be some embarrassment, or the temptation to gloss over the differences in values.

    Where the auditor also carries out accounting work on behalf of the client, this may seem innocent enough. Indeed there may be perceived ethical advantages, because the accountant should be able to prepare the accounts 'properly'.

There will be a self-review threat where the accountant prepares financial statements and then acts as auditor, effectively reviewing his own work. The auditor may not want to report mistakes that he, as accountant, had made. Where accounts are prepared by auditing firms, another department always carries out the audit to remove this threat. In some jurisdictions, auditors are not allowed to prepare financial statements for a client, removing this threat completely.

But consider the position where the use of different accounting policies may give very different results, or where different interpretations can be placed on treatments required by accounting standards.

- **The management threat**

  A management threat arises when the audit firm undertakes work that involves making judgments and taking decisions, which are the responsibility of management.

- **The advocacy threat**

  The advocacy threat occurs where the professional adopts a stance arguing for or against the client's point of view, rather than taking a balanced (objective) position.

  The advocacy threat is difficult to deal with because, surely, the professional adviser wants to give the client the best possible support.

  In a tax case, for example, is it not the tax consultant's job to win on behalf of the client at all costs?

- **The familiarity or trust threat**

  This recognises that, if the professional gets to know the client too well, objectivity may be threatened because the auditor becomes too trusting of the client and professional scepticism is impaired.

  This is also quite a difficult area. As we shall see in Chapter 8 the auditor needs to understand the client's business well. Changing the engagement partner may or may not enhance objectivity, but if it does, it may open up greater audit risks due to lack of familiarity with the client's business.

- **The intimidation threat**

  This threat may range from the effective hijacking of the auditor's professional qualification by clients with criminal tendencies – something which the UK Government is concerned about as demonstrated by the anti-money laundering regime they have introduced – to the bullying behaviour of a dominant personality who insists on getting his (or her) own way. The situation may go as far as threatening the auditor with removal if a modified auditor's report is produced.

2.3 Code of Ethics – safeguards against the threats

There are a number of general safeguards against the threats which come from the environment in which the professional accountant operates:

- Training
- ICAEW also offers support systems for its members and students – a local and central counselling service and helpline.

The quality control systems in place at engagement, firm and profession levels including:

- Planning, supervision and review procedures
- Hot and cold file reviews
- Regulatory inspections

Procedures envisaged under the FRC *Ethical Standard* include:

- The overall control environment at the firm which ensures a professional approach towards ethical issues
- The segregation of duties between those engaged on audits and those providing non audit services
- Rotation of engagement partners and staff
- Consulting the ethics partner
- Procedures for evaluating the integrity of potential new clients
- The formal process of reviewing the appropriateness of the firm's continuing in office before its name is allowed to go forward for reappointment
- Staff recruitment procedures
- Regular completion of 'fit and proper' and independence declarations by partners and staff
- Staff training, development and performance appraisal
- Monitoring and evidencing the firm's own systems

Interactive question 1: Fundamental principles

Requirement

Set out the ethical fundamental principles which should be followed by members of the profession.

See **Answer** at the end of this chapter.

3 FRC Ethical Standard

Section overview

- The FRC Ethical Standard (ES) applies to the audit of financial statements and other public interest assurance engagements
- Part A contains overarching principles of integrity and objectivity, and independence
- Part B is divided into six sections:
    - Section 1 focuses on compliance, threats and safeguards
    - Section 2 focuses on relationships between accountants and clients
    - Section 3 focuses on long association between accountants and clients
    - Section 4 focuses on the 'benefits' of the professional relationship, such as fees and remuneration
    - Section 5 focuses on providing other services to audit clients
    - Section 6 relates to the audit of small entities

3.1 The FRC Ethical Standard

- Introduction
- Part A *Overarching Principles and Supporting Ethical Provisions*

- Part B
  - Section 1 *General Requirements and Guidance*
  - Section 2 *Financial, Business, Employment and Personal Relationships*
  - Section 3 *Long Association with Engagements and with Entities Relevant to Engagements*
- Section 4 *Fees, Remuneration and Evaluation Policies, Gifts and Hospitality, Litigation*
- Section 5 *Non-Audit/Additional Services*
- Section 6 *Provisions Available for Audits of Small Entities*

The Introduction and Part A cover the fundamental concepts of integrity and objectivity, and independence.

The concept of independence is what is really at the heart of the standards.

Definitions

Integrity: "Being trustworthy, straightforward, honest, fair and candid; complying with the spirit as well as the letter of applicable ethical principles, laws and regulations; behaving so as to maintain the public's trust in the auditing profession; and respecting confidentiality except where disclosure is in the public interest or is required to adhere to legal and professional responsibilities."

Objectivity: "Acting and making decisions and judgments impartially, fairly and on merit (having regard to all considerations relevant to the task in hand but no other), without discrimination, bias, or compromise because of commercial or personal self-interest, conflicts of interest or the undue influence of others, and having given due consideration to the best available evidence."

Independence: "Freedom from conditions and relationships which, in the context of an *engagement*, would compromise the integrity or objectivity of the *firm* or *covered persons*."

(FRC ES 2016, I23)

The new standard introduces the 'Third Party Test' to evaluate whether the ethical outcomes required have been met from the perspective of "an objective, reasonable and informed third party".

3.1.1 Section 1 *General Requirements and Guidance*

Section 1 sets out the requirement for the audit firm to have policies and procedures to deal with the rules in the standard which need to be documented and communicated to all concerned with the engagement.

The main topics covered by section 1 are summarised below.

Compliance

This includes having appropriate policies and procedures in place to support and monitor ethical behaviour.

It sets out requirements for partners and staff to report:

- Family and other personal relationships
- Financial interests
- Decisions to join

in an entity relevant to an engagement by the firm which might be perceived as casting doubts about the firm's independence.

It then requires a firm to:

- Monitor compliance

- Have systems to ensure that actual or possible breaches are promptly communicated to the engagement partner

- Evaluate the implications of identified possible or potential breaches

- Report specific circumstances as required by ES

- Prohibit management decision taking on behalf of the audited entity

- Establish an enforcement mechanism, to ensure that compliance actually happens, through disciplinary procedures etc

- Empower staff to communicate about ethical issues

The ethics partner

Section 1 requires all firms except the very smallest to appoint an ethics partner, who will be a senior partner with a good deal of authority within the firm, and who will be available for consultation on ethical matters for engagement partners and other matters of judgement that arise.

The ethics partner should be consulted when judgments are being taken about whether the safeguards in place in the firm are sufficient to counter potential threats.

For firms with three partners or less, this function is expected to be covered by regular discussions between the partners.

In the case of firms that undertake engagements for public listed entities (PIEs) the ethics partner should have direct access to the firm's non-executive directors, where such roles exist, or to the senior governance body.

Overall conclusion about compliance

Just as the engagement partner should reach and document his technical conclusion about the audit, he or she should similarly reach and document a conclusion about the firm's compliance on ethics matters. This conclusion should be made at the end of the audit process, but before the auditor's report is signed.

Communication with those charged with governance

The audit engagement partner should ensure that those charged with governance of the audited entity are appropriately informed on a timely basis of all significant facts and matters that bear on the auditors' objectivity and independence.

Section 1 also covers threats and safeguards, which we have already discussed in this chapter in sections 2.2 and 2.3.

3.1.2 Section 2 *Financial, Business, Employment and Personal Relationships*

This section can be summarised relatively simply:

- If you are tempted to take a financial interest in an audited entity – do not do it.

- If you are tempted to go into a business venture jointly with an audited entity – do not do it.

- If staff move from the audit firm to the audited entity there should be disclosure during the process.

- If a former director/employee of an audited entity who was in a position to exert significant influence over the preparation of the financial statements joins the audit firm, he should not be assigned to a position where he can influence the conduct/outcome of the audit (eg, the audit opinion) or its affiliates for two years following leaving the audit client.

Financial interests

Section 2 recognises that financial interests can be direct – owning shares in or making loans to an audited entity – or indirect where there is some intermediary like an investment trust, and whilst there are some minor relaxations in the rules where the interest is both indirect and immaterial to both the auditor and the client, nevertheless the prohibition on such interests should be regarded as absolute.

You may wonder what the issue is here, but consider the case of a 'Big 4' firm which audits a major listed company and where the firm's pension scheme has a holding in a unit trust which invests in, among others, the audited entity.

Joint business ventures

You may think that it is common sense not to allow joint ventures with audit clients, but consider the following situations:

Worked example: Joint business ventures

You have an audit client Technofix Ltd which installs computer systems and another audit client Shoppa Ltd which is looking for some new IT equipment.

Consider the following possibilities:

- You simply put Technofix and Shoppa in touch with each other and say you hope that everything will work to mutual advantage.

- Technofix offers your firm a commission if the deal is successful.

- Technofix provides the equipment and your IT arm agrees to install Shoppa's new accounting software on it as a separate exercise.

- Your firm and Technofix jointly agree to supply the complete system including installation, software and implementation.

- Your firm manages the whole contract, although the equipment is supplied and installed by Technofix.

'Recommending' the services of a client tends towards an advocacy threat because the accountant is promoting the client, which could affect objectivity.

Accepting a commission from a client constitutes a self-interest threat. The danger is that the firm will recommend Technofix because of the economic benefit to the firm rather than because it is the best professional advice that they could give Shoppa. Regardless of whether this is the case or not, it might seem to an objective, reasonable and informed third party that the firm had acted in its own interests and therefore independence is threatened.

The more involvement in the deal that the firm has, the more of a self-interest threat is created. If the IT arm of the firm install the equipment, the firm earns additional fee income and the objectivity of the audit might be threatened by the provision of other services and the overall increase in the firm's dependence on Shoppa Ltd for fees. In addition, the IT system will support the financial reporting system which the auditing arm of the firm might be seeking to rely on and will certainly be assessing as part of the audit, so there is also a self-review threat.

Partners, staff or client staff moving between the audit firm and its audit client

The objective of this part of the statement is to prevent the auditor's independence and objectivity being questioned, because former auditors join a client, or former clients join the auditor.

Where a partner – who could be:

- the engagement partner;

- the partner who carries out an independent review of the audit files; or

- another partner involved on the audit (known as a key audit partner or partner in the chain of command).

is appointed a director or takes on some other key management position at the client, within two years of being involved in the audit, the firm shall resign as auditors.

The firm shall not accept re-appointment as auditor until a two-year period, commencing when the former partner ceased to have the ability to influence the conduct and outcome of the audit, has elapsed or the former audit partner ceases employment with the former audited entity, whichever is the sooner.

So the firm needs procedures and rules so that:

- partners and any other members of the audit team intending to join a client know they must inform the firm of their intentions.

- if someone gives notification, they should be moved off the audit immediately.

- a review shall be carried out on any audit work performed by the resigning team member in the current audit, and, where appropriate, the most recent audit.

- if someone joins the firm from a senior position at the client, they should not be allowed to work on the audit for two years.

Similarly the rules are extended to cover situations where close family members and other people connected with those involved with the audit are employed by, or have financial dealings with, an audit client.

3.1.3 Section 3 *Long Association with Engagements and with Entities Relevant to Engagements* 3

Audit firms are required to have policies in place to monitor the length of time that key member of staff are associated with recurring engagements. Where there is long association the firm should consider threats to integrity, objectivity and independence and apply safeguards so that threats are reduced to an acceptable level. If safeguards cannot be applied then the association should not continue.

Where an engagement partner has held this role for 10 years, the 'third party test' should be applied – the standard talks about giving "careful consideration to whether an objective, reasonable and informed third party would consider the audit firm's objectivity and independence to be impaired". The obvious implication is that partners should be 'rotated' after acting for the same client for 10 years, but that it might be possible to make a case for them remaining in place.

For PIEs Article 17 of EU Audit Regulation imposes more stringent rules for long association:

- Key audit partners responsible for statutory audits should not hold that position for more than five years.

- Once they have ceased to act they should not take up the position again until another five years have elapsed.

- Seven years – engagement quality control reviewers, key partners involved in the audit and senior staff for listed clients.

The five year term for a listed client engagement partner may be extended for an additional period of up to two years if the client's audit committee considers that this is necessary to safeguard the quality of the audit. In these circumstances alternative safeguards need to be introduced in order to minimise any threats.

Where the term has been extended this fact and the reasons for it must be disclosed to the shareholders as soon as possible and again in each additional year to which the extension applies. If the audit client refuses to make this disclosure then the engagement partner may not continue in this role.

Clearly the firm needs to have procedures in place to ensure that the length of time partners and other senior members of staff are associated with the audited entity can be monitored and appropriate action taken.

3.1.4 Section 4 *Fees, Remuneration and Evaluation Policies, Gifts and Hospitality, Litigation*

Again there are some relatively straightforward rules for you to understand:

- 'Contingent' fees for audit work are banned

Definition

Contingent fees: Fees where the amount of the fee is dependent on some event taking place or some other condition being met. An example might be that the audit fee would be increased if the client's bankers agree to extend available borrowing facilities.

- The audit engagement partner shall ensure that sufficient partners and staff are assigned to the audit irrespective of the audit fee to be charged.

- Audit fees should not be influenced or determined by the provision of non-audit services to the audited entity.

- Fees for audit and non-audit services for a listed client should not exceed 10% of the firm's fee income.

- The limit for non-listed clients is 15%.

- Fees for non-audit services (see below) for a listed client should not exceed 70% of the average fees paid by the client and any group companies, if applicable, in the last three consecutive financial years.

- Audit staff should not be assessed, or have their performance appraisal or their pay related to their ability to cross sell the firm's products.

- There should be a firm's policy on the extent to which gifts, hospitality etc may be accepted from audited entities.

- The firm should resign as auditor where there is actual or potential litigation between the firm and the audited entity.

The fee percentages are based on expected regular levels of fee income and relate to the whole firm or unit within the firm where an 'objective, reasonable and informed third party' might consider the firm/partner's objectivity to be impaired.

Where fees amount to 5%–10% (listed clients) or 10%–15% (non-listed), this fact needs to be disclosed to the ethics partner and those charged with governance at the client and appropriate safeguards adopted where necessary; for non-listed clients an external hot review needs to be undertaken (listed clients will be hot reviewed anyway).

The standard also recognises that in its early years a new firm may find the fee percentage limits difficult to comply with and gives a two year grace period providing external hot reviews are conducted.

Similar 'objective, reasonable and informed third party' considerations apply to the firm's policy on gifts and hospitality and whether there are overdue fees outstanding.

3.1.5 Section 5 *Non-Audit/Additional Services*

For a very long time – probably throughout the history of the accountancy profession in the UK – clients have come to accountants for a range of services. Because, until comparatively recently, all companies required an audit, audit was at the core of the services provided. It also made a good deal of sense for the auditors to provide any assistance needed with accounting matters and to 'do the tax'.

You should bear in mind the following:

- In many jurisdictions, notably France, Germany and the US, tax work tends to be handled by lawyers rather than accountants.

- The range of services offered by accountants in the UK has expanded to include actuarial services, brand valuations, IT services and many others.

- Tax services can include controversial tax 'schemes'.

- The increase in the audit threshold to exempt the vast majority of small companies from audit has meant that those clients who do require an audit may well be of a size to have their own, in-house accounting experts.

Section 5 sets out a clear general approach to non-audit services provided by the auditor based on:

- What an objective, reasonable and informed third party would think about the impact on the firm's objectivity and independence.

- The need for the firm to have procedures to monitor and deal with potential threats.

- The need for the client to have 'informed management' as defined below, where the audit firm concludes it can provide non-audit services.

- It is never appropriate for the audit firm to find itself in a position where it undertakes, or is perceived as undertaking, a management role.

This approach states that the firm should:

- Consider the impact of the provision of non-audit services

- Establish safeguards to counter any threats (which may include resignation or refusal to accept appointment as auditor or provider of the non-audit services)

- Consult with the Ethics Partner where there is any doubt

- Communicate with 'those charged with governance'

- Document the rationale for the decisions taken

Section 5 specifically prohibits the provision of the following non-audit services to public interest entities (PIEs):

- Tax services relating to the preparation of tax forms, payroll tax, customs duties, public subsidies, tax inspections, calculation of direct and indirect tax, and the provision of tax advice

- Services involving management or decision making

- Accounting and bookkeeping

- Payroll

- Designing and implementing internal controls that relate to the preparation of financial statements

- Valuation services relating to actuarial or litigation support

- Legal services with respect to the provision of general counsel, negotiation on behalf of the audited entity, and acting in an advocacy role in the resolution of litigation

- Internal audit

- Investment strategy

- Underwriting shares

- Human resources

For non-listed audit clients, the following are examples of what non-audit or additional services might entail.

Audit related services

This is work carried out by members of the engagement team that is closely related to the audit work. Audit related services are as follows:

- Reporting required by law or regulation to be provided by the auditor

- Reviews of interim financial information

- Reporting on regulatory returns

- Reporting to a regulator on client assets

- Reporting on government grants

- Reporting on internal financial controls when required by law or regulation

- Extended audit work that is authorised by those charged with governance performed on financial information and/or financial controls where this work is integrated with the audit work and is performed on the same principal terms and conditions

Only the above services may be described as audit related in communications with those charged with governance.

Internal audit

The firm should not undertake internal audit work, where its external audit opinion is based on significant reliance on its internal audit role.

The main threats to an auditor's objectivity and independence when undertaking internal audit work are the self-review threat and the management threat.

The self-review threat is unacceptably high where substantially all of the internal audit work is outsourced to the firm, and the firm places significant reliance on internal audit work when performing the external audit.

The management threat is unacceptably high if the audit firm makes decisions relating to the following:

- The scope and nature of internal audit services provided to the entity
- Designing or making changes to internal controls
- Taking responsibility for risk management
- Evaluating cost effectiveness of activities, systems and controls
- Pre-implementation work on non-financial systems

IT

The firm should not undertake work on IT systems which would be important to any significant part of the accounting system on which the auditors would place significant reliance.

Valuation and actuarial valuation services

The firm should not undertake valuation services for an unlisted audited entity where the valuation would both:

- involve a significant degree of subjective judgment
- have a material effect on the financial statements

For a listed audited entity, valuation services should not be provided where the valuation would:

- have a material effect on the financial statements

Tax

The firm should not undertake tax services which "would involve acting as an advocate for the entity in the resolution of an issue" where the outcome of the tax work is dependent on a future or contemporary audit judgement.

This rule, when it was first discussed, was thought to be especially tricky for the smaller firm, and it may prove to be so, but it is important to note that:

- the rule does nothing to prevent the usual discussions on points of detail with inspectors of taxes or the provision of information if the case goes to the commissioners
- most tax issues are neither material nor dependent on future or contemporary audit judgments
- where the matter progresses to the commissioners, the conditions of the ESPASE may well apply

For listed companies the audit firm shall not prepare current or deferred tax calculations for the purpose of making accounting entries that are material to the financial statements.

Transaction related services

Transaction related services are 'one-off' engagements such as due diligence work.

Restructuring services

These are non-audit services provided to an audited entity in connection with a planned change in its equity or debt financing structure, its corporate structure or its operating structure.

An audit firm may not provide restructuring services where to do so would:

- involve taking on a management role
- require the firm to act as advocate for the audited entity
- give rise to a self-review threat

When a listed audit entity is in distress, there is further limitation to the restructuring services that can be provided. In essence the audit firm can only act in an advisory capacity in such circumstances.

Accounting services

The provisions dealing with accounting services were also expected to prove controversial for smaller practitioners, but in the event this seems unlikely due to:

- the increase in the audit threshold
- the acceptability of appropriate safeguards
- the impact of the ESPASE

Nevertheless firms will need to remember:

- providing accounting services for listed audit clients is banned
- the auditors must never find themselves undertaking a management role

3.1.6   Section 6 *Provisions Available for Audits of Small Entities*

Section 6 applies where the client qualifies as a small company under the Companies Act 2006 and covers three issues dealt with by the ethical standard:

- Fee dependence
- Non-audit services
- Partners joining an audit client

Fee dependence

Where it is expected that the total fees for audit and other services receivable from a small entity will regularly exceed the 10% threshold but will not regularly exceed 15% section 6 exempts the audit firm from the requirement in section 4 for an external independent quality control review. The expectation should be disclosed to the ethics partner and to those charged with governance of the audited entity.

Non-audit services

For small entities the restrictions on the provision of non-audit services are waived, but:

- there needs to be 'informed management'
- the audit firm needs to extend its cycle of cold reviews
- the departure needs to be mentioned in the auditor's report for which suggested wording is provided

Partners joining audit client

For small entities the provisions concerning partners joining audit clients are waived provided there is no threat to the audit team's integrity, objectivity and independence and disclosure is made in the auditor's report.

3.2 Informed management

In the FRC's *Ethical Standard*, the concept of 'informed management' is regarded as a crucial safeguard where there are potential conflicts of interest posed by the provision of non audit services and where the provisions of section 6 apply.

'Informed management' is defined as follows:

- Objective and transparent analyses need to be provided for the client
- The client must have the genuine opportunity to decide between alternative courses of action
- There should be a member of management designated to receive the results of non-audit services and make necessary judgments and decisions
- That member must have the capability to make independent judgments and decisions on the basis of the information provided

3.3 It is all about timing

Knowing what the threats are is all very well, knowing what you are supposed to do about them is even better, but how are you supposed to detect the threats in the first place?

Section 1 has some suggestions.

The impact of any threats needs to be assessed:

- On appointment or reappointment as auditor
- When planning the engagement
- When forming the opinion
- When considering appointment or reappointment for non-audit services
- When potential threats are reported

At all times it is the perceptions of third parties which matter and this means that the consideration of potential problems cannot be restricted to the particular engagement currently under consideration.

The auditor has to ask how the ethics of the situation look in the context of:

- Past engagements?
- Other engagements currently on hand?
- Potential future engagements?

Interactive question 2: Fee income

Aitken and Waterman have been asked by a long-standing client, Lewis plc (a quoted company) to perform a special assignment. This would take the total fees received by Aitken and Waterman from this client to £55,000. Gross practice income is £500,000.

Requirement

Comment and reach a conclusion on the above situation.

See **Answer** at the end of this chapter.

Interactive question 3: Threats to objectivity

Your firm is the auditor of Alpha Ltd and Beta Ltd.

(1) It provides quarterly VAT services to Alpha Ltd, which involves completing the VAT return for submission by management from information extracted from the company's records.

(2) It is also the auditor of Beta Ltd's largest customer.

Requirement

What potential threats to objectivity do each of these situations pose to your firm, and what safeguards should be in place to address them?

See **Answer** at the end of this chapter.

4 ICAEW *Code of Ethics*

Section overview

- The ICAEW Code covers independence and objectivity (as we saw in the context of the FRC Ethical Standard in section 3)

- Accountants are required to keep information obtained in the course of professional work confidential

Many of the independence issues covered by the ICAEW *Code of Ethics* are also covered by the FRC *Ethical Standard* in section 3, so we shall concentrate on issues of confidentiality here.

4.1 ICAEW *Code of Ethics* section 140 Confidentiality

Due to the nature of their work, Chartered Accountants find themselves in a privileged position in that they gain access to books and records and have access to information and explanations from the directors of the company that they would otherwise not be party to.

This is particularly true of the Companies Act auditor, but does apply to all members. So the Institute's guidance is designed to reinforce to all members that information that comes into their possession as a result of the work they are completing should remain confidential.

Section 140 states that the principle of confidentiality is not only to keep information confidential, but also to take all reasonable steps to preserve confidentiality. The professional accountant should assume that all unpublished information is confidential, however it is gained. The professional accountant should not disclose information received in confidence except in the circumstances set our below and should not use confidential information to their own personal advantage or the advantage of third parties.

Disclosure of information

Section 140 identifies three circumstances where the professional accountant is or may be required to disclose confidential information:

- Where disclosure is permitted by law and is authorised by the client or the employer, for example where the auditor has uncovered a fraud and the client is in agreement that the matter should be referred to the police

- Where disclosure is required by the law. Examples include:

  - Reporting directly to regulators, such as the Financial Conduct Authority, on regulatory breaches in respect of financial service and investment businesses or the Charity Commission in respect of charities

  - The reporting of suspected money laundering to NCA

  In making such a report, an auditor is not deemed to have broken the confidence of the client. It is normally addressed by setting out the auditor's right to disclose in the engagement letter.

- Where there is a professional duty or right to disclose, when not prohibited by law. In this case the *Code of Ethics* states that a professional accountant may disclose confidential information to third parties if the disclosure can be justified in 'the public interest'.

Difficult judgements are required by auditors as to whether the 'public interest' overrides the duty of confidentiality. Usually, the auditors should take legal advice on the matter.

ISA (UK) 240 *The Auditor's Responsibilities Relating to Fraud in an Audit of Financial Statements*, ISA (UK) 250A *Consideration of Laws and Regulations in an Audit of Financial Statements* and ISA (UK) 250B *The Auditor's Rights and Duty to Report to Regulators of Public Interest Entities and Regulators of Other Entities in the Financial Sector*, also provide guidance on this issue.

ISA (UK) 240 and ISA (UK) 250A&B

What the ISAs require is that when the auditors become aware of suspected or actual frauds or instances of non-compliance which should be reported to the relevant authority, they should:

- report to management
- report to those charged with governance
- report to regulatory and enforcement authorities, where appropriate

Obviously, if they suspect management of being involved in the non-compliance, etc they should report the matter directly to those charged with governance or, if appropriate, to a higher authority such as the audit committee.

Anti-money laundering legislation in the UK requires auditors to report suspected money laundering activity. In doing so auditors should be mindful of the offence of 'tipping off' possible suspects and prejudicing any investigation.

Auditors should also consider whether (having taken legal advice) any matters should be reported in the public interest.

In addition, professional accountants may also be entitled to disclose confidential information for the purpose of defending themselves.

In the UK, ISA (UK) 250B has specific guidance on reporting to regulators of financial institutions.

Improper use of information

A professional accountant acquiring or receiving confidential information in the course of his or her professional work should neither use, nor appear to use, that information for his or her personal advantage or for the advantage of a third party.

Examples of particular circumstances are:

- on a change in employment, professional accountants are entitled to use experience gained in their previous position, but not confidential information acquired there.

- a professional accountant should not deal in the shares of a company in which the member has had a professional association at such a time or in such a manner as might make it seem that information obtained in a professional capacity was being turned to personal advantage ('insider dealing').

- where a professional accountant has confidential information from Client 1 which affects an assurance report on Client 2 he cannot provide an opinion on Client 2 which he already knows, from whatever source, to be untrue. If he is to continue as auditor to Client 2 the conflict must be resolved. In order to do so normal audit procedures/enquiries should be followed to enable that same information to be obtained from another source. Under no circumstances, however, should there be any disclosure of confidential information outside the firm.

Informants

The majority of confidentiality issues relate to the professional accountant's treatment of confidential information belonging to the client or employer. However, the accountant may also be approached in confidence with information about alleged illegal or improper acts on the part of employees or management of the business for which the informant works. This information must be treated sensitively, particularly as it is likely that the informant has approached the accountant on the basis that he is someone that the informant can trust. In this situation the professional accountant should:

- advise the informant to pass on the information to his employer in accordance with company procedures

- protect the identity of the informant to the extent that this is possible

- take care in the way that this information is used, if at all

4.2 ICAEW *Code of Ethics* section 220 Conflict of Interest

Situations are frequently perceived by clients as 'conflicts of interest' where in reality they involve no more than concerns over keeping information confidential. Hence the issues of confidentiality covered above and conflicts of interest are related.

4.2.1 General principles: conflict of interest

Section 220 states that firms should have in place procedures to enable them to identify whether any conflicts of interest exist and to take all reasonable steps to determine whether any conflicts are likely to arise in relation to new assignments involving both new and existing clients.

If there is no conflict of interest, firms may accept the assignment. If there is a conflict of interest, but it is capable of being successfully mitigated by the adoption of suitable safeguards, firms should record those safeguards.

There is nothing improper in a firm having two clients whose interests are in conflict provided that the activities of the firm are managed so as to avoid the work of the firm on behalf of one client adversely affecting that on behalf of another.

Where a firm believes that a conflict can be managed, sufficient disclosure should be made to the clients or potential clients concerned, together with details of any proposed safeguards to preserve confidentiality and manage conflict. If consent is refused by the client then the firm must not continue to act for one of the parties.

Where a conflict cannot be managed even with safeguards, then the firm should not act.

4.2.2 Conflict between the interest of a professional accountant or his firm or a client

A self-interest threat to the objectivity of a professional accountant or his firm will arise where there is or is likely to be a conflict of interest between them and the client, or where confidential information received from the client could be used by them for the firm's or for a third party's benefit.

The test to apply is whether an objective, reasonable and informed observer would perceive that the objectivity of the member or his firm is likely to be impaired. The member or his firm should be able to satisfy themselves and the client that any conflict can be managed with available safeguards.

Safeguards might include the following:

- Disclosure of the circumstances of the conflict
- Obtaining the informed consent of the client to act
- The use of confidentiality agreements signed by employees
- Establishing information barriers
    - Ensuring that there is no overlap between different teams
    - Physical separation of teams
    - Careful procedures for where information has to be disseminated beyond a barrier and for maintaining proper records where this occurs
- Regular review of the application of safeguards by a senior individual not involved with the relevant client engagement
- Ceasing to act

Interactive question 4: Confidentiality

You are in the middle of an audit with a tight deadline, the manager is due to visit you at the client tomorrow and you need to be home early to meet the builders at your new flat. You are considering taking the sales ledger and the cash book home with you to finish the trade receivables section ready for the manager to review tomorrow.

Requirement

What must you consider before you remove any client files from their offices?

See **Answer** at the end of this chapter.

Summary and Self-test

Summary

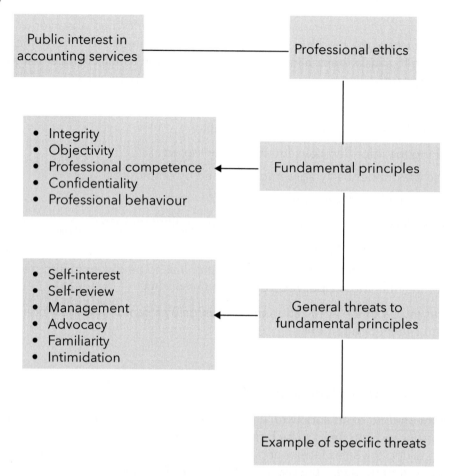

Self-test

Answer the following questions.

1   What are the six general threats to integrity and objectivity?

    (i)   ....

    (ii) ....

    (iii) ....

    (iv) ....

    (v)   ....

    (vi) ....

2   Give three examples of when auditors are entitled to make a disclosure in breach of the duty of confidence.

    (i)   ....

    (ii) ....

    (iii) ....

Exam-style questions

3   As auditor of Northend Ltd you prepare quarterly management accounts for the company, and these are passed on to the company's bankers. Northend Ltd's overdraft is close to its limit and the bank manager has contacted you to discuss the high level of bad debts disclosed in the latest management accounts.

    What considerations will determine the extent to which you divulge information to the bank manager? **(2 marks)**

4   Three situations have arisen with audit clients of your firm.

    (i)   Due to cash flow difficulties, overdue fees from Doe Ltd have built up to include all bills submitted by your firm in the last twelve months.

    (ii) The engagement partner of Ray Ltd has acted for the company for many years.

    (iii) To express his gratitude for the quality of service he has received from your firm, the managing director of Mee Ltd has invited all partners and staff involved with his affairs for a golf day and dinner at an exclusive club one weekend.

    State the threats to objectivity that these matters represent and how the threats could influence objectivity. **(4 marks)**

5   Your firm has been invited to tender for the audit of East Ltd. Your firm has not previously acted in any capacity for this company but does act for West Ltd, which is East Ltd's major competitor.

    Identify and explain the principal ethical issue relating to this situation, and state the procedures you would implement to address this issue. **(3 marks)**

6   Examples of situations when the auditors' independence may be impaired include the following.

    (i)   Providing taxation services to the company and its directors.

    (ii) Providing accountancy services, including preparing periodic management accounts and annual financial statements.

    (iii) Providing management consultancy, including advice on new computer systems and systems of internal control.

(iv) Preparing confidential reports to the company's bank and other lenders on the financial position of the client. The conclusions of these reports are not made available to the audit client.

Requirement

Describe how each of the situations listed above may compromise auditors' independence, and the ways in which an audit firm can minimise the effect which the provision of other services has on independence. **(13 marks)**

7 You have recently come across the following professional issues.

(i) During the audit of a listed company on which you were involved, you overheard the finance director on the telephone to a family friend requesting him to buy shares on his behalf, prior to an announcement about a new product which you know is likely to increase the share price significantly. The finance director is a chartered accountant.

(ii) During a night out at the pub following your exams one of your fellow students told you in strictest confidence that he had tampered with his degree certificate on his computer to improve the classification. He explained that he had done this to satisfy the minimum requirements to secure a job at his firm, one of your main rivals. He boasted about how easy it was with new computer technology currently available.

(iii) One of the audit clients you recently worked on was so impressed with your courtesy towards his staff members that he wanted to make you a gift of tickets to the World Cup football final, along with an overnight stay in a hotel.

Requirement

Set out the problems inherent in each of the above situations and the action that you should take. **(10 marks)**

8 You are a sole accountancy practitioner. The following situations have arisen.

(i) At the request of Ace Ltd (an audit client) you have agreed to provide advice on the preparation of a tender for a very large contract. Subsequently, client Black & Co (a partnership for whom you prepare accounts and provide a wide range of advice) also asks for your assistance in preparing a tender for the same contract.

(ii) Whilst carrying out the final audit of the accounts of Club Ltd (deadline one month after the reporting date), you discover a substantial trading debt due from another client, Diamond Ltd. Although it has not been made public, you are aware that Diamond Ltd is in serious financial difficulties and the bank is considering appointing a receiver. The directors of Club Ltd have made no allowances for irrecoverable or doubtful receivables against the amount due from Diamond Ltd.

Requirement

Explain the action you would take in each of the above circumstances. **(10 marks)**

Now, go back to the Learning outcomes in the Introduction. If you are satisfied you have achieved this outcome, please tick it off.

Technical reference

Answers to Interactive questions

Answer to Interactive question 1

Members should:

- behave with integrity in all professional and business relationships

- strive for objectivity in all professional and business judgements

- not accept or perform work beyond own competence (unless obtain adequate advice and assistance)

- carry out work with due care, skill and diligence and follow expected technical and professional standards

- respect the confidentiality of information acquired

- act professionally and comply with relevant laws and regulations

Answer to Interactive question 2

- Total fee income received from Lewis plc > 10% of gross practice income of firm as a whole; therefore there is a risk that perception will be that objectivity impaired

- But FRC's *Ethical Standard* (section 4) deals with total fees which 'regularly exceed' the threshold and this is a 'one off' assignment

- Need to determine whether regular fees will exceed 5% threshold

Conclusion

Assignment may be accepted. Ethics partner should be consulted and those charged with governance informed of the situation.

Answer to Interactive question 3

Threats to objectivity and safeguards:

Alpha Ltd

- Self-interest threat
- Self-review threat
- Firm may be susceptible to pressure for fear of losing work
- Lack objectivity when checking VAT
- Different staff should be used for VAT work and audit

Beta Ltd

- Self-interest threat
- Advocacy threat
- Either company may be uncomfortable with arrangement and exert pressure
- Beta could exert pressure re your knowledge of customer
- Separate audit partners
- Separate audit teams

Answer to Interactive question 4

The auditor must obtain the client's permission before removing any files from the client's offices.

Answers to Self-test

1 (i)   Self-interest
   (ii)   Self-review
   (iii) Management
   (iv)   Advocacy
   (v)   Intimidation
   (vi)   Familiarity

2 (i)   Reporting of suspected money laundering
   (ii)   Reporting of terrorist offences
   (iii) Defending oneself against negligence charges

Exam-style questions

3 **Disclosure of information**

   - Whether Northend Ltd's permission has been obtained to discuss matters freely with bank

   - Extent to which information has already been divulged by the bank to Northend Ltd's management

   - Terms of engagement with Northend Ltd and/or bankers for preparation of management accounts

   - Duty/responsibility to bankers

4 **Threats**

Threat	How influence objectivity
(i) Self-interest	• Auditor may worry that fees will not be paid if report is qualified or going concern doubts disclosed
(ii) Familiarity	• Partner may be reluctant to upset or be too reliant on representations from 'friend'
(iii) Self-interest	• Partners and staff may be reluctant to appear ungrateful or hope for further hospitality

   General

   - Proper audit may not be carried out
   - Inappropriate opinion may be given

5 **Principal ethical issue**

   - Confidentiality
   - East and West may perceive a threat in respect of disclosure/use of information
   - Conflict of interest

   Procedures to address

   - Procedures to ensure staff are aware of confidentiality issues and such issues have been brought to attention of staff (eg, Chinese walls)

   - Staff to certify awareness of these procedures

   - Obtain informed consent of clients

   - Use of different partners and teams

   - Independent review of arrangements for ensuring confidentiality maintained

6   (i)   **Taxation services**

Many audit firms prepare tax computations for their client companies and this should not normally compromise independence.

Where taxation services are provided to the company, a conflict of interest could arise in dealing with the tax affairs of the directors (eg, if any of the directors are also shareholders, they may have preferences as to dividends or bonuses, which are not in the best interests of the company's tax or cash flow position).

There may also be independence issues in relation to tax advisory work. For example, the firm may have difficulty in giving an independent view on the acceptability of a scheme to the Revenue or Customs and Excise if the firm designed the scheme itself in the first place.

As a safeguard, a tax manager (or partner) independent of the audit function should be assigned to deal with individual director's tax affairs.

(ii)   **Accountancy services**

For many audit clients it is common to provide a range of accountancy services including participation in the preparation of accounting records. For listed or other public interest clients, an audit firm should not participate in the preparation of the company's accounts and accounting records.

Preparing periodic management accounts may draw the auditor, inadvertently, into performing management functions.

Safeguards for non-listed companies include the following:

- The client accepting responsibility for the records as its own

- The auditor not assuming an operational role

- Conducting appropriate audit tests on records processed/maintained by the auditor

(iii)   **Management consultancy**

An auditor's independence may be compromised if a course of action is recommended to an audit client. For example, if the auditor advises on a new computer system which is then found to be unreliable, the auditor may be reluctant to report the weaknesses to management.

As a safeguard auditors should lay the facts before the directors and let them make the decision. It is important that the auditor is not seen to be acting as part of the management function.

The additional guidance on best practice has also now provided that services involving the design and implementation of financial information technology systems (FITS) should not be provided unless:

- management accept overall responsibility in writing

- management do not rely on the FITS work as the primary basis for determining the adequacy of internal controls and financial reporting systems, and

- the design specifications are set by management.

In any case separate engagement teams are likely to be necessary to mitigate the potential threat to independence.

(iv) Preparing confidential reports

Auditors are not prevented from producing confidential reports for banks and other lenders, provided they have obtained the client's authority to do so.

A 'clean' confidential report recently issued to a lender may be borne in mind when forming the audit opinion. This may increase pressure not to qualify the audit opinion (to add credibility to the confidential report) when qualification is justified.

A partner other than the audit engagement partner should be responsible for the confidential reports. Unless confidentiality is absolutely necessary, the client should be made aware of the reports to lenders. The quality of these reports may be enhanced by consideration of management's views on matters included.

7 (i) Share purchase for FD

Problems

- This constitutes insider dealing which is a criminal offence, as the financial director is benefiting financially from an inside knowledge of the business.

- All chartered accountants and trainees, whether in business or practice, are required to comply with the *Code of Ethics*. This states that members should act with integrity at all times and not act to bring the profession into disrepute.

Action

- Inform the audit partner but do not approach the finance director directly yourself.

(ii) Exam certificates

Problems

- The student is guilty of obtaining an employment position under false pretences and by deception. This is not appropriate behaviour for a future chartered accountant.

- It is unlikely that the firm would have taken the student if it had known the class of degree.

Action

- No duty of confidentiality to his friend.

- Encourage the friend to admit to his employer.

- If not, the matter should be discussed with your own partner, who would make contact with the staff partner of the other firm.

(iii) Accepting a gift from an audit client

Problems

- Firm's independence on the audit may be called into question; need to consider.

- Size and availability to all employees of the client company. (Generally gifts from clients should only be accepted if value modest and available to all employees.)

- Whether own firm's regulations may prohibit this.

Action

- Discuss with partner and only accept if firm's permission is given.

8   (i)   **Tender preparation**

Additional service

When agreeing to provide any additional services to an audit client it is important to recognise that the independence of the audit may appear to be compromised even though the auditor considers he is able to be objective in executing his work. In general, additional services of an advisory nature are permitted provided no executive function is taken on which might conflict with the office of auditor.

Ace Ltd

The decision to provide advice and assistance in connection with the tender is not unethical provided it is made clear to the directors that any tender ultimately remains their responsibility. The directors should be sent a supplementary engagement letter, distinguishing the nature of an audit from other work and clarifying the extent of the advice to be given.

Black & Co

Independence may also be affected by a conflict of interest between two clients. With Ace Ltd and Black competing by tender for the same contract, it is likely that detailed inside information of both businesses would be obtained which would be of considerable value to the competitor.

Although there is, in theory, nothing improper in having two clients whose interests are in conflict, it must be possible to manage the activities of the firm so that the work on behalf of one client does not adversely affect that on behalf of the other. However, in this case the auditor is a sole accountancy practitioner so safeguards such as 'Chinese walls' which could be put in place in a large firm are unlikely to be feasible.

To advise both clients would not therefore appear to be independent. It would be difficult to be objective and avoid influencing one or other of the tenders unfairly.

It would be preferable to advise only one of the two clients – probably Ace Ltd as already agreed – and thereby avoid conflict. However, the knowledge of Black & Co's business may be seen to impair objectivity, and Black & Co might well object to assistance being provided to Ace Ltd.

It may therefore be best to advise neither client but to explain the predicament to both and suggest that each consults another independent firm of accountants.

(ii)   **Confidentiality**

To inform the directors of Club Ltd that the accounts will not give a true and fair view unless an allowance for doubtful receivables is made against the debt due from Diamond Ltd would be a breach of confidentiality. It could also have the undesirable effect of precipitating the collapse of Diamond Ltd since the directors of Club Ltd would take steps to obtain payment from Diamond Ltd as soon as possible.

To ignore the information about Diamond Ltd's financial position (since it is not publicly available) and give an unqualified auditors' report, in a situation where the accounts are known (by the auditor) not to give a true and fair view, would be *prima facie* a breach of an auditor's statutory duty under the Companies Act 2006 and in breach of section 140 Confidentiality of the Code of Ethics.

If the auditor is to continue to act for Club Ltd the conflict must be resolved. To do so normal audit procedures should be followed and enquiries made to enable the information about Diamond Ltd to be obtained from another source. It may be possible to delay forming an opinion until the situation crystallises. Under no circumstances must there be any disclosure of confidential information outside the firm.

Note: Notice how practical this question is. Your answer should not merely be a repetition of the ethical guide but should apply it to the specific circumstances given. Part (2) is really 'unanswerable' and what is required is simply a sensible discussion of the possibilities. In any question on ethics, try to use common sense and come up with practical suggestions, and bear in mind that there may be no 'right' answer.

CHAPTER 5

Quality control

Introduction

Examination context

TOPIC LIST

Summary and Self-test

Technical reference

Answers to Interactive questions

Answers to Self-test

Introduction

Learning outcomes

1 Legal and other professional regulations, ethics, accepting and managing engagements and current issues

Students will be able to understand and advise on the regulatory, professional and ethical issues relevant to those accepting, managing and carrying out assurance engagements. Students will be able to understand the processes involved in accepting and managing assurance engagements and how quality assurance processes mitigate the risks to those conducting the engagement.

- Identify the sources of liability (including professional negligence) arising from an assurance engagement and their impact upon the conduct of the engagement

- Formulate the approach suitable for management of the assurance engagement

- Explain the principles and purposes of quality control of assurance engagements

- Demonstrate how the assurance function within an organisation can be monitored

- Demonstrate how quality control processes improve the quality of assurance work

- Describe how quality can be monitored and controlled through procedures external to the organisation

Syllabus links

Your understanding of quality control issues will be necessary at the Advanced stage.

Examination context

This is an area of the syllabus that is likely to be examined in conjunction with other issues such as client acceptance or ethics. It has featured as a part of long questions and also as short form questions.

1 The need for quality standards

- Quality control procedures are essential to ensure that an acceptable job is carried out by the assurance firm and assurance engagement risk is reduced to an acceptable level

- An engagement could go wrong due to client-based problems, or assurance firm based problems, for example that the engagement team has insufficient knowledge of the business or are badly directed and supervised

- Audit quality is monitored by the Monitoring Committee of the FRC (listed or public interest entities) or by ICAEW under their Practice Assurance scheme

- There are six key elements of a quality control system (which we shall look at in turn in the next sections of this chapter):
    - Leadership
    - Ethical requirements
    - Acceptance and continuance of client relationships/specific engagements
    - Human resources
    - Engagement performance
    - Monitoring

The main reason the end user wants to have an assurance report prepared is to reduce the risk of making a wrong decision. As a result someone is prepared to pay an assurance firm a fee.

As you know (and we shall look at this in more detail in Chapter 9) the amount of work the firm does is dictated by the need to reduce **assurance engagement risk** to acceptable levels. If the firm does not do this, it has not carried out a job which is acceptable when judged against professional standards.

The firm should ensure that the quality of its work does not fall short by implementing its own quality control procedures. ISA (UK) 220 *Quality Control for an Audit of Financial Statements* requires that those procedures should provide reasonable assurance that:

- professional standards and legal and regulatory requirements have been met; and
- the auditor's report is appropriate.

The ultimate aim of any quality control procedures is to improve the quality of work conducted by firms and by the profession as a whole. Relevant findings from quality control reviews are fed back into firms' processes and methodologies in order to foster continuous improvement. They are also used to guide future regulatory developments by the standard setting and other bodies.

1.1 What could go wrong?

Worked example: Need for quality

Take a moment to think about what the areas of risk are for the firm. The list you came up with might look something like this.

The terms 'auditor' and 'audit' are used here, because audits are a common form of assurance engagements but the same principles will apply to any assurance engagement.

Let us start, as it were, from the bottom up.

The client

- Could be incompetent
- Could be negligent
- May mislead the audit team

The individual auditor

- May not have adequate understanding of the client's business
- May not perform the right work to an adequate standard
- May not record the work done adequately

The supervisor

- May not have an adequate understanding of the client's business
- May not brief and direct the staff properly
- May not carry out sufficient supervision so that the wrong work is done by the audit team
- May fail to deal with issues raised adequately
- May fail to communicate the issues arising to the engagement partner

The engagement partner

- May have insufficient knowledge of the client and its environment
- May fail to pass knowledge of the business on to the audit team
- May select the wrong team for the audit
- May not adequately brief and supervise the team
- May not consult sufficiently with colleagues and outside experts
- May not review the work carried out by the team with sufficient care
- May fail to deal with issues raised adequately
- May not draw the correct conclusions from the evidence available

1.2 The consequence of quality failure

As we have seen assurance engagements, including audits, do not offer the end user absolute assurance about the subject matter of the assurance report. At best, they offer **reasonable assurance**, a **high** level of assurance.

As a consequence, the firm needs to have quality systems and procedures primarily to ensure that its work is of a sufficiently high standard so that failures simply do not happen.

In the event of a complaint, the firm will have a defence, providing it has followed suitable procedures.

ICAEW firms carrying out audit work have been subject to regulatory inspections for some time, and although inspections of listed company audit files have moved to the Monitoring Committee of the Financial Reporting Council, regulatory reviews of non-listed audits remain the responsibility of the ICAEW.

In June 2004 the ICAEW membership approved the introduction of a scheme called 'Practice Assurance' which means that all aspects of a firm's work are subject to periodic review by consultants acting for ICAEW.

During this review, which is designed to be constructive rather than disciplinary in tone, the consultants working on behalf of ICAEW will examine files and procedures in all the firm's departments. They will compare what they find with standards set out by ICAEW, and, where appropriate, make recommendations for improvement.

Clearly, if a firm's working practices were found to be inadequate, there could be disciplinary consequences, but the overall thrust of the scheme is intended to be supportive – in effect to provide the firm with access to consultancy. All members of the ICAEW who hold a practising certificate will be included in the programme of visits.

Audit failures revealed by such visits may result in disciplinary action being taken against the firm. This can lead to fines or, possibly, suspension of the firm's authorisation to carry out audits.

The consequences of failure can be catastrophic, as Andersens found out following the Enron affair, but even a complaint which is successfully defended can absorb huge amounts of time and expense. It really is sensible to avoid getting into the situation in the first place.

1.3 Approach to quality control

If you look carefully at the bullet points in the worked example above, you should see that if you were to devise counter-measures against the threats listed, these measures could be listed under a small number of categories:

- Procedures for ensuring only suitable clients are taken on

- Procedures for ensuring only suitable clients are retained

- Procedures for ensuring that the firm's partners and staff have the necessary knowledge and competence

- Guidance on ethics

- Communication skills

- Briefing and supervision skills

- Professional scepticism and judgement

- Monitoring

ISQC (UK) 1 *Quality Control for Firms that Perform Audits and Reviews of Financial Statements and other Assurance and Related Services Engagements* lists the following as elements of a firm's quality control system:

- Leadership responsibilities for quality within the firm
- Ethical requirements
- Acceptance and continuance of client relationships and specific engagements
- Human resources
- Engagement performance
- Monitoring

ISQC (UK) 1 also requires that the firm documents its policies and procedures and communicates them to the firm's personnel.

In other words, ISQC (UK) 1 deals with the sort of procedures you would expect in a straightforward, logical way. We will look in more detail at the elements in the rest of the chapter.

The elements it lists are fairly self-explanatory – human resources incorporates issues dealing with staff recruitment, training and appraisal.

In the exam you are not expected to regurgitate lists but the above approach should convince you that you have an understanding of the issues involved.

We will now look at the elements of a quality control system which affect the way the engagement is carried out – 'Engagement performance' under ISQC (UK) 1. We will, on the whole, look at the procedures which affect an audit and which are dealt with by ISA (UK) 220 *Quality Control for an Audit of Financial Statements* because these are broadly applicable to all assurance engagements.

Interactive question 1: Benefits of quality control procedures

Requirement

Your manager has been asked to brief your department on the new quality control procedures that the firm has introduced. Your manager has asked you to prepare a list of the benefits of quality control procedures in a firm, which he can use as part of his presentation.

See **Answer** at the end of this chapter.

2 Leadership

Section overview

- The ISQC (UK) points out the importance of quality being an established part of the culture of the firm

- This must be instigated by the leaders of the firm, that is, the partners

It is important that the culture of the firm is that quality is essential in performing assurance engagements. This should be led by the leaders of the firm, that is, the partners.

In practical terms, the people directing the firm and its resources should ensure that:

- commercial considerations do not override the quality of work performed;

- the firm's policies in relation to staff promotion, remuneration and performance review incorporate the importance of quality work; and

- Sufficient resources are allocated to the development, documentation and support of quality control policies and procedures.

3 Ethics

Section overview

- The firm should have policies and procedures designed to ensure that ethical requirements are met

We saw in the previous chapter how important ethics are to assurance providers, as they underpin the public trust required to make assurance services viable.

The firm must put together policies and procedures to ensure that it meets ethical requirements.

Worked example: Policy in respect of employees' shareholdings

Freshfields & Co is a large accountancy practice. It has a number of assurance clients. At the beginning of every year it circulates a memorandum to all staff employed in the assurance division requesting that they disclose any shareholdings in a list of named assurance clients. It further emphasises the need for disclosure of such shareholdings should they arise in the year. Every staff member joining the assurance department during the year is also asked to make the disclosure.

4 Acceptance of engagements

Section overview

- The firm should also have policies and procedures designed to ensure that only appropriate clients are accepted in the first place and retained

The firm should also have policies and procedures designed to ensure that only appropriate clients are accepted in the first place and retained. We shall look in more detail at acceptance issues in Chapter 6. The engagement partner should carry out similar considerations as he did when he accepted the client every year when bearing in mind whether to retain the client.

5 Human resources

Section overview

- As part of the firm's overall culture of quality control, it should have policies and procedures to ensure that it employs and retains staff with the capabilities, competence and commitment to ethical principles necessary to perform the engagements

- There should be policies on recruitment, career development, performance evaluation and promotion

- It is also important to allocate staff to assurance engagements appropriately

As part of the firm's overall culture of quality control, it should have policies and procedures to ensure that it employs and retains staff with the capabilities, competence and commitment to ethical principles necessary to perform the engagements. This means it should have policies on all aspects of employing professional staff. The ISQC (UK) lists the following:

- Recruitment

- Performance evaluation

- Capabilities, including time to perform assignments

- Competence

- Career development

- Promotion

- Compensation (that is, how staff are remunerated)

- The estimation of personnel needs (for instance, self-appraisal as well as appraisal by others)

These will cover matters such as professional education (for trainees), continuing professional development (for everyone), practical work experience and coaching by more experienced staff.

ICAEW members are required to certify that they have carried out appropriate professional development annually as part of their membership. For members in practice, the ISQC (UK) puts professional development on the agenda of firms as well, as part of their overall quality control procedures.

Another important matter in relation to human resources is the allocation of staff to engagement teams. Firms are required to have policies to ensure the following:

- Clients are informed of the identity and role of the engagement partner.

- The engagement partner has the capabilities, competence, authority and time to perform the role.

- The responsibilities of the partner in respect of the engagement are clearly defined and communicated to that partner.

The engagement partner should ensure that he allocates appropriate staff to the engagement team. Staff need the following:

- Understanding of/practical experience with similar engagements
- Understanding of relevant professional and legal requirements in relation to the client
- Appropriate technical knowledge
- Knowledge of the relevant industry
- Ability to apply professional judgement
- Understanding of the firm's quality control procedures and policies

You can see that the types of training and appraisal discussed above will be important as ongoing monitoring of the staff member's abilities and, therefore, capability to be assigned to particular engagements and in what capacity.

6 Engagement performance

Section overview

- Key issues are supervision, direction, review, consultation and resolution of disputes

6.1 Direction

This is largely the responsibility of the engagement partner who controls how the assurance engagement should be conducted, but this duty will be delegated to the most senior team member on site at the engagement, who will direct the engagement in accordance with the overall strategy.

The engagement partner is responsible for ensuring team members know:

- What work they are supposed to be doing
- The nature of the entity's business
- Any risks relevant to the engagement
- Problems that might arise during the engagement
- The detailed approach to the engagement

6.2 Supervision

ISA (UK) 220 *Quality Control for an Audit of Financial Statements* lists four features of supervision:

- Progress tracking

- Considering the competence and capabilities of individual members of the audit team

- Addressing significant matters arising during the audit

- Identifying matters for consultation or consideration by more experienced engagement team members during the audit engagement

Good supervision can be a difficult skill to master:

- If it is too close it can stifle initiative and waste the time of supervisor and assistant alike
- If it is too loose, mistakes may be made or time wasted in ineffective work

The partner has overall responsibility for supervising the audit, but will normally delegate supervisory duties to a manager or supervisor who will similarly delegate to the 'senior' or 'in charge' who is responsible for the day-to-day management of the engagement.

6.3 Review

Work performed by staff is reviewed by other more senior staff or the engagement partner.

The purpose of the review is to consider whether the work done is in line with the audit strategy and whether:

- the work has been performed in accordance with professional standards and regulatory and legal requirements;
- significant matters have been raised for further consideration;
- appropriate consultations have taken place and the resulting conclusions have been documented and implemented;
- there is a need to revise the nature, timing and extent of work performed;
- the work performed supports the conclusions reached and is appropriately documented;
- the evidence obtained is sufficient and appropriate to support the report; and
- the objectives of the engagement procedures have been achieved.

The engagement partner must be satisfied that sufficient appropriate audit evidence has been obtained to support the conclusions in the auditor's report.

6.3.1 Engagement quality control review

For listed entities, and those other entities determined by the firm, an engagement quality control review is conducted by a suitably-qualified partner or other person in the firm not otherwise involved in the engagement or by an external consultant. The purpose of this independent review is not to re-perform the other reviews in the audit process but to provide an additional safety check about the validity of the firm's opinion on the financial statements.

The following matters need to be considered:

- The evaluation of independence in relation to the engagement that has taken place
- Whether appropriate consultation has taken place on contentious issues
- Whether the documentation selected for review reflects the work performed in relation to the significant judgements and supports the conclusions reached
- Significant risks identified and responses to those risks
- Judgements made during the engagement, for example, in relation to materiality and significant risks
- The significance of corrected and uncorrected misstatements
- The matters to be communicated to the client

6.3.2 'Hot' review

A hot review is a review carried out by a partner not otherwise involved in the engagement or an external consultant before the auditor's report is signed. It is not necessarily the same as an engagement quality control review.

6.4 Documentation and review

You should remember from your studies for the Assurance paper that ISA (UK) 230 *Audit Documentation* requires that audit documentation should contain the following:

What would be necessary to provide an experienced auditor, with no previous connection with the audit, with an understanding of the nature, timing and extent of audit procedures, the results of audit procedures, and the audit evidence obtained, and significant matters arising during the audit and conclusions reached thereon.

One of the key purposes of the documentation of audit procedures is to enable the reviews described in section 6.3 to be carried out. Adequate documentation is also essential to allow the firm to implement overall monitoring of quality (see section 7.1).

6.5 Consultation

When difficult or contentious issues arise, the assurance team must consult properly on the matter and the conclusions drawn as a result of consultation must be properly recorded.

Any differences of opinion must be resolved prior to the assurance report being issued. This may mean that a person independent of the engagement (such as the quality control reviewer) may have to be involved in resolving the difference of opinion.

7 Monitoring

Section overview

- The firm must have policies in place to ensure that their quality control procedures are adequate and relevant, that they are operating effectively and are complied with

- Management of the assurance firm (that is, the partners) should receive an annual report on the outcome of monitoring activities

- The most important issues will be systematic or repetitive deficiencies

The ISQC (UK) states that firms must have policies in place to ensure that quality control procedures are adequate and relevant, that they are operating effectively and are complied with. The firm might have a compliance or quality department which carries out such reviews.

Monitoring might take place by ongoing evaluation of the system and also by periodic review of selected engagement files to assess whether policies and procedures were put into place during the engagement.

The partners in the firm (the management board) should receive at least an annual report of the results of monitoring of quality control procedures. Key issues will be systematic or repetitive deficiencies that require corrective action.

Where monitoring reveals a problem with an individual, then remedial action should be taken with that individual, and possibly, additional quality control reviews might be required on that person's work to ensure that corrective action is taken.

The people checking compliance with quality control standards should liaise closely with the training department or partner to ensure that any misunderstandings or problems with controls are corrected during on-the-job training.

7.1 Monitoring (or 'cold' review)

Cold reviews are designed to be a continuing part of the quality control process and take place after the assurance assignment has been completed.

They are usually conducted either:

- as a process, whereby partners in a firm review each other's work;
- by a team specifically constituted to conduct such reviews – usually under the direction of a partner, but the work is usually carried out by suitably qualified and experienced managers; or
- by a suitably qualified external consultant.

The review team should also develop appropriate courses of action where failures are identified, including the following:

- Communication of the findings within the firm
- Additional training and professional development
- Changes to the firm's policies and procedures
- Disciplinary action against those who repeatedly fail to comply with the firm's standards.

Interactive question 2: Quality control issues on an engagement

You are an audit senior working for the firm Addystone Fish. You are currently carrying out the audit of Wicker Ltd, a manufacturer of waste paper bins. You are unhappy with Wicker's inventory valuation policy and have raised the issue several times with the audit manager. He has dealt with the client for a number of years and does not see what you are making a fuss about. He has refused to meet you on site to discuss these issues.

The former engagement partner to Wicker retired two months ago. As the audit manager had dealt with Wicker for so many years, the other partners have decided to leave the audit of Wicker in his capable hands.

Requirement

Comment on the situation outlined above.

See **Answer** at the end of this chapter.

8 UK Corporate Governance Code requirements

Section overview

- Audit committees have a role in monitoring the effectiveness of the audit process

The UK Corporate Governance Code requires audit committees of listed entities to review and monitor the external auditor's independence and objectivity and the effectiveness of the audit process, taking into consideration relevant UK professional and regulatory requirements.

Many firms discharge this responsibility by the use of questionnaires conducted with members of the audit committee, executive directors, senior management and internal audit. Participants are asked to rate the external auditor on factors such as:

- Independence and objectivity
- Audit planning and execution
- Conduct and communication
- Audit findings and feedback
- Quality of reports
- Expertise and resourcing
- Business understanding
- Continuity and experience of personnel
- Cost effectiveness/value for money

9 Getting the assurance opinion wrong

Section overview

- Getting the audit opinion wrong could lead to:

    - Being sued for professional negligence
    - Prosecution and fines
    - Disciplinary proceedings from ICAEW
    - Loss of reputation, clients, key staff
    - Assurance firm collapse

- In the context, quality control procedures are important

- Risk is another key issue associated with getting the opinion wrong – are some clients too risky to accept?

- Liability limitation agreements for auditors are acceptable in UK law

Think for a moment about the possible cost of getting the audit opinion wrong:

- If someone can demonstrate that you owed them a duty of care and they suffered loss by relying on the financial statements, they could sue you under the tort of negligence, as you saw previously whilst studying for the Law paper

- You as auditor may not be the only person responsible for their loss – the directors, who are responsible for preparing financial statements which give a true and fair view, probably had a hand in it somewhere – but you could find yourself solely liable

- As a member of the ICAEW you could also face disciplinary proceedings, fines and penalties.

Audit firms must carry professional indemnity insurance, which means that any settlement will be paid out by the insurance company, but there is quite a long list of audit firms which no longer exist – ranging from Spicer and Oppenheim as a result of the British and Commonwealth/Atlantic Computers failure to Andersens, the former auditor of Enron – as a result of the collapse of an audit client.

To some extent the final cost of the settlement is only a part of the overall cost. Lawyers do not come cheap, particularly good corporate lawyers, and the time of partners and staff taken up with defending such an action can also represent a huge cost.

There is a further substantial, but intangible cost, resulting from the damage to a firm's reputation following its involvement with a client collapse. This is the loss of other clients and often key members of staff who no longer want to be associated with the firm.

Remember that many assurance firms operate as partnerships whose partners have unlimited and joint and several liability (which you also will remember from your law studies). If one partner gets it wrong, all the partners could be found liable.

Clearly in this context, quality control policies and procedures, which help to ensure that the wrong opinion is not given, are very important. However, it is not just a question of quality. As you saw in your studies for Assurance, and as we shall look at in more detail in the next chapter, it is a question of risk. Increasingly, assurance firms are concluding that there are some clients which are too risky to take on, leaving companies required to have an audit under the law unable to appoint an auditor.

This situation has needed resolution. One way of trying to restrict liability has been to look at the business vehicles through which many assurance firms operate. As a result, many have incorporated in a limited way, becoming Limited Liability Partnerships (LLPs), which were introduced into UK law back in 2001.

However, there has also been a need to review the whole concept of who is to blame when things go wrong. The profession has favoured a scheme of 'proportional liability', whereby the assurance provider only pays for its share of the blame when things go wrong.

9.1 Possibilities for limitation of liability

Companies Act 2006 makes provision for auditors to agree limits on their liability to companies in respect of statutory audits. For such an agreement to be valid it must:

- cover only one financial year
- be approved by a resolution of the company's shareholders.

The arrangements are only effective to the extent that they are 'fair and reasonable' in the particular circumstances. This means that the Court could override the contractual agreement and amend the liability to a level set by the Court.

The Act does not specify the manner in which liability may be limited. This means that the contractual limits could be set in a variety of ways, for example:

- Based on the auditor's proportionate share of the responsibility for any loss;

- Purely by reference to the 'fair and reasonable' test;

- A cap on liability, which could be either a monetary amount or on the basis of an agreed formula; or

- Some combination of the above methods.

One related development is that the National Association of Pension Funds, which represents a substantial body of institutional investors who carry a great deal of voting power in large companies, has issued the following policy statement:

"Investors should consider voting against resolutions which propose any form of liability limitation other than proportionate liability unless there are compelling reasons why that is not appropriate, and why the directors feel that another form of liability limitation would survive a court's judgement of what is fair and reasonable in all the circumstances".

This provision in the Companies Act has disappointed mid-tier firms, as they believe that this could reduce their chances of competing for audits with larger firms, as they would have to negotiate lower caps as their resources are smaller. The Act theoretically gives the Government power to intervene if this appears to be the case, but we will have to wait and see what the outcome is in practice.

9.2 Criminal offence

While the liability limitation provisions could be seen as reducing the risks facing audit firms, Companies Act 2006 also includes the criminal offence of knowingly or recklessly causing an auditor's report on company accounts to include any matter that is misleading, false or deceptive in a material particular.

The penalty for the offence is a fine although an earlier draft of the law included the possibility of imprisonment.

Members of the profession are worried about the risk here that an honest mistake could attract a criminal penalty but the government's view is that 'recklessness' has a very high hurdle and would only catch an auditor who is "aware that an action or failure to act carried risks, that they personally knew that the risks were not reasonable ones to take, and that, despite knowing that, they went ahead".

Summary and Self-test

Summary

Self-test

Answer the following questions.

1   Compliance with quality control policies and procedures as required by ISQC (UK) 1 will constitute a good defence against allegations that the firm has been negligent.

☐ True
☐ False

2   The ICAEW's practice assurance scheme is primarily disciplinary.

☐ True
☐ False

3   Which **one** of the following statements about formal leadership is incorrect? Partners should ensure that:

- Commercial considerations do not override the quality of work performed.
- Sufficient resources are allocated to developing quality controls polices and procedures.
- Staff prioritise quality control procedures over ethical considerations for listed clients.
- The firm's policies in relation to remuneration should reflect the importance of quality.

4   Explain an ICAEW member's responsibility with regards to CPD.

5   List four items the engagement partner should ensure the assurance team are aware of prior to commencing an engagement.

(i)   ....

(ii) ....

(iii) ....

(iv) ....

6   Define hot review.

Exam-style questions

7   You are about to start work on an assignment. What would you expect the role of your senior to be in terms of supervising you and explaining your role on the audit?   **(2 marks)**

8   A qualified senior and yourself are due to start work on an assignment. He will review your work before the file is passed on to the manager.

    What aspects will he be considering when he is reviewing your work?   **(2 marks)**

9   Your firm has recently been appointed as auditor of Jog Ltd ('Jog'), a company operating within the sports and leisure sector. Your audit manager has arranged a meeting with the company's finance director for early next week and she has asked you to assist her, in advance of this meeting, with the audit planning for the year ending 30 June 20X6. Your audit manager has also asked you to carry out some preliminary analytical procedures on the year-end financial statements of Jog when these become available.

    Jog's business can be split into the following three divisions:

- Sports equipment retail outlets: 35 sports equipment retail outlets located in 'out of town' retail parks
- Fitness clubs: 15 fitness clubs, each offering a fully equipped gym together with yoga, aerobics, and circuit training classes
- Machine manufacture: a manufacturing unit in which running machines and rowing machines are assembled using components sourced from overseas.

Further information:

Sports equipment retail outlets

The retail outlets are all located close to major towns and cities throughout the whole of the UK. Each outlet stocks a standard range of products which are supplied from a central warehouse operated by Jog. Salaries for the core staff at the outlets are paid by Jog's head office by direct bank transfer. Each outlet is run on a day-to-day basis by a manager who is responsible for hiring casual staff to cover peak periods. These casual staff members are generally paid using cash from the till.

Jog received some bad publicity during the year following its inclusion in a television documentary which revealed that one of its non-UK sports shoe suppliers was making its employees work long hours for very low wages. In an attempt to manage this adverse press attention, Jog has now had to source these products from alternative suppliers based in the UK.

Fitness clubs

Jog's 15 fitness clubs are all located directly above existing Jog retail outlets. Each club has its own on-site manager and is operated independently of the adjacent retail outlet. Customers of the fitness clubs pay by one of three methods: on a 'pay per session' basis over the fitness club counter; by monthly direct debit paid into Jog's head office bank account; or by annual subscription to head office. Customers are then issued with a membership card which enables them to gain access to the club.

The company operates a bonus incentive scheme for the managers at both its retail outlets and fitness clubs. The size of the bonus is linked to the profitability of their individual operation.

Machine manufacture

During the year Jog started to manufacture its own running machines and rowing machines. It sources the machine components from China and Taiwan. These components are assembled in the UK at Jog's factory for sale both in Jog's own stores under their own 'Jog' brand and also to independent sports shops under the 'Iron Champ' brand. The latter accounts for approximately 80% of Jog's total production of both running and rowing machines. Sales to independent sports shops achieve a gross profit margin of 50%, whereas sales to Jog's own shops are made to that division at cost plus 10%.

Jog is invoiced by its non-UK component suppliers in their respective local currency. The components are sent by sea, which means that Jog's typical lead time for components from the placing of an order to delivery in the UK is three months. Jog is required to pay its suppliers 50% with order and 50% upon receipt of the components in the UK.

Quality control

In line with your firm's system of quality control, procedures were conducted prior to accepting Jog as an audit client, to ensure that it was appropriate to accept such an appointment. Your audit manager has asked you to consider the other objectives of a system of quality control and why they may be particularly relevant to Jog.

Requirements

(a) and (b) omitted until later chapter

(c) (i) State the objectives of a system of quality control within an audit firm.

   (ii) Identify, with reasons, which of the above objectives are likely to be particularly relevant to your audit of Jog.   **(8 marks)**

Parts (a) and (b) of this question will be included in Chapter 7. Note that much of the information given in the question relates to these parts, but has been left in so that you can use any relevant information for the purposes of answering Part (c)(ii).

Now, go back to the Learning outcomes in the Introduction. If you are satisfied you have achieved these outcomes, please tick them off.

Technical reference

Answers to Interactive questions

Answer to Interactive question 1

The benefits of quality control procedures include:

- Standard of all audit work completed is high and consistent
- Registered auditors are regarded as professionals who follow standards
- Quality of the work completed can be measured against a standard
- Individuals within firms know if the work they have completed is acceptable

Answer to Interactive question 2

Several quality control issues are raised in the scenario:

Engagement partner

An engagement **partner** is usually appointed to each audit engagement undertaken by the firm, to take responsibility for the engagement on behalf of the firm. Assigning the audit to an experienced audit manager is not sufficient.

The lack of an audit engagement partner also means that several of the requirements of ISA (UK) 220, about ensuring that arrangements in relation to independence and directing, supervising and reviewing the audit, are not in place.

Conflicting views

In this scenario the audit manager and senior have conflicting views about the valuation of inventory. This does not appear to have been handled well, with the manager refusing to discuss the issue with the senior.

ISA (UK) 220 requires that the audit engagement partner takes responsibility for settling disputes in accordance with the firm's policy in respect of resolution of disputes required by ISQC (UK) 1. In this case, the lack of engagement partner may have contributed to this failure to resolve the disputes. In any event, at best, the failure to resolve the dispute is a breach of the firm's policy under ISQC (UK) 1. At worst, it indicates that the firm does not have a suitable policy concerning such disputes as required by ISQC (UK) 1.

Answers to Self-test

1 True

2 False, although disciplinary action may be taken as a result of a review if required.

3 Staff prioritise quality control procedures over ethical considerations for listed clients.

4 Every member is required to certify that he/she has carried out appropriate professional development annually.

5 Four from:

   (i) What work they are supposed to be doing
   (ii) The nature of the entity's business
   (iii) Any risks relevant to the engagement
   (iv) Problems that might arise during the engagement
   (v) The detailed approach to the engagement

6 A hot review is a review carried out by a partner not otherwise involved in the engagement or an external consultant before the auditor's report is signed.

Exam-style questions

7 **Supervision**

- Inform you of your responsibilities

- Explain the objectives of the work you are carrying out

- Explain the nature of the entity's business

- Highlight possible accounting and auditing problems which may affect the procedures you carry out

8 **Review of work**

- Work properly conducted in accordance with plan/programmes
- Working papers to a standard/evidence recorded
- Conclusions valid
- Matters identified for further consideration
- Working papers headed, initialled, dated

9 (c) **Objectives of quality control**

The objectives of an audit firm's system of quality control are to ensure that the auditor performs the right work to a high standard and adequately records the work done. It involves selecting the appropriate team, supervising staff, consulting sufficiently with colleagues and outside experts and reviewing the work carried out by the team with sufficient care.

A system of quality control will also ensure that the auditor draws the correct conclusions from the evidence available, forms the appropriate audit opinion and deals adequately with issues raised including reporting to management.

Quality control is also designed to protect the auditor from risks arising as a result of incompetence or negligence of the client's staff and will protect the firm from the risk of litigation.

Objectives relevant to the audit of Jog

Jog operates out of many locations and because it has a number of diverse activities, the audit firm may not have staff with relevant expertise. It is therefore particularly important that a team with appropriate skills and experience is selected for the audit and that the work is supervised closely.

As Jog is a new audit client and because its business is diversified it is particularly important that the audit team has an adequate understanding of the business. The risks arising from the client's staff being incompetent or negligent are particularly relevant to Jog as the auditor does not yet know the client very well.

CHAPTER 6

Accepting engagements

Introduction

Examination context

TOPIC LIST

Introduction

Learning outcomes

1 **Legal and other professional regulations, ethics, accepting and managing engagements and current issues**

   Students will be able to understand and advise on the regulatory, professional and ethical issues relevant to those accepting, managing and carrying out assurance engagements. Students will be able to understand the processes involved in accepting and managing assurance engagements and how quality assurance processes mitigate the risks to those conducting the engagement.

   - Discuss the issues which underlie the agreement of the scope and terms of an assurance engagement (new or continuing)

   - Explain the main ways in which national legislation and other regulations affect the scope and nature of the audit and the appointment and removal of auditors (including the relationship between the law and auditing standards)

   - Understand and explain the legal requirements for appointment and removal of auditors

   - Identify the professional and ethical matters a firm should consider when accepting appointment as assurance providers

   - Understand the need to clarify the terms of engagement in writing and understand and explain the issues involved

   - Discuss the process by which an auditor obtains an engagement

Syllabus links

Many of the considerations set out in this chapter have already been introduced in the Assurance paper. In this paper, you are required to consider the matters at a higher level, and be able to explain and discuss the matters in more detail.

Examination context

You may be asked to apply the principles discussed in this chapter to a scenario question in the exam.

1 Tendering

Section overview

- An assurance firm might be invited to accept an engagement or to tender for an engagement
- A tender is in effect a 'bid' for an engagement
- The firm will set out the reasons why it is best placed to provide the engagement and the fee at which it can do it
- Lowballing may occur during a tender process, and while this is not ethically wrong, it may require ethical safeguards to be put in place

An assurance firm might obtain an engagement by the following methods:

- Being approached by a potential client and being asked to accept the engagement
- Being approached by an existing client and being asked to accept the engagement
- Being approached by a potential or existing client and being asked to tender for the engagement

In practice, the most common method of obtaining an audit is by tender. In a tender process, several assurance firms are in effect asked to 'bid' for the engagement, by setting out the attributes their firm possesses that makes them the best placed to carry out the engagement, and, sometimes very importantly, by indicating the level of fee that they are likely to charge. The company seeking auditors then considers the bids (which may be written or presented orally or both) and invites the successful party to accept the audit.

Although the price of the proposed engagement can be very important, it is not the only consideration for the company in a tender process. Other important considerations are as follows:

- The quality of the service the prospective auditors are likely to provide
- The knowledge of the business they possess
- The experience of the industry they have
- The proposed personnel on the audit team
- References obtained about the audit firm

An issue to consider briefly in the context of tendering is lowballing. Lowballing is the name given to the practice of charging less than the 'market rate' for the audit. In other words, say five comparable-sized firms were tendering for an audit, it is likely that their proposed fees would be similar. If one were significantly lower than the others, then it might be that the firm was quoting at a low rate in order to obtain the engagement on those grounds, in other words, lowballing.

The ICAEW *Code of Ethics* states that a firm may quote any fee it considers acceptable. In other words, the practice of lowballing is not unethical in itself. However, ethical safeguards should be considered as lowballing does increase the self-interest threat of not being able to complete the audit to the appropriate standards in a commercial way.

The Code of Ethics suggests that the basis for fee computation should be disclosed to and discussed with the client/potential client as soon as possible, so this would probably be incorporated into a tendering document. It states that fees should be determined with reference to the following:

- The seniority and professional experience of the persons necessarily engaged on the work
- The time expended by each
- The degree of risk and responsibility which the work entails

- The nature of the client's business, the complexity of its operation and the work to be performed

- The priority and importance of the work to the client

- Together with any expenses properly incurred

Giving the client such details about the basis of the fee will help the client determine if he is getting value for money, particularly in comparison with other tenders.

2 Risk analysis

Section overview

- Firms carry out risk analysis prior to accepting engagements

- This is in order to ensure that the risk of giving an inappropriate opinion on the engagement is not too high

- Matters to consider are whether the directors appear to have integrity, the company has a good financial record and prospects, the attitude to internal control and the nature of the client's transactions

As you learnt in Assurance, assurance firms will carry out a risk analysis before accepting clients. This is partly to determine what fee they think is appropriate for the engagement (the higher risk the client, the greater the benefit that the firm will want from undertaking the engagement) but also to lay foundations for understanding the risks associated with the engagement if it is taken on and the amount of work that will have to be undertaken to reduce assurance risk to an acceptable level for that assignment. As noted in Chapter 5, it may be that an engagement is too risky for a firm to risk taking on.

Worked example: Two clients

Imagine two clients of a similar size, in the same industry:

Client A

You have never had to make any adjustments to client A's financial statements, which are produced by their qualified chief accountant and his experienced and competent staff from proprietary software which both you and they know and understand well. The company's chief executive is a stickler for deadlines, but takes a genuine interest in the financial statements so that accurate numbers are produced on time on a regular basis.

Client B

The chief executive of client B is a 'seat of the pants' man, who has little time for accountants and the financial statements they produce. The accounts department is understaffed, those working there are unqualified and using an accounting package on which they have received no formal training. Every year you go through a lengthy process of correcting the trial balance before you can even start to think about analytical procedures and audit work proper. You are always under pressure to finish the engagement on time and there is always an argument about the fee.

Which of these clients presents the higher risk?

Clearly client A is better organised than client B on the accounting front. Client A therefore starts out as a lower risk proposition than client B, based on the firm's experience of client A, its organisational culture and its reliable systems.

After the financial statements for both clients are finalised, however, you may feel more confident about the figures for client B because you had analysed them in more depth.

Another question

Would you prefer to be operating client A or client B if:

- you were a fraudster, hoping to inflate the value of your company so that a venture capital fund would invest, or a bank would continue with finance, or a large multinational would purchase it; or

- you were a money launderer wanting to introduce the profits from your drug smuggling and dealing activities into an otherwise legitimate business.

You could argue that things are so chaotic at client B that no one would notice a few stray transactions.

Or you might think that the auditors have to spend so much time on the detail that they would have quite a good chance of picking something up.

Perhaps the well organised, reliable client A, where the auditors don't seem to do very much detailed checking, might be a better bet.

The most that can be said therefore is that the assessment of risk is something of a balancing act between your judgement of how reliable the information coming from the client is likely to be and the things you can actually do.

The example illustrates that such judgements are not simple, but generally speaking when carrying out risk analysis prior to accepting a client, assurance providers will be seeking to determine:

- Whether the directors/management of the company appear to have integrity: this can be assessed by looking at the accounting policies of the company (are they prudent and conservative or imprudent?) and the qualifications of the finance director it employs, or by obtaining references for key personnel from parties known to the assurance firm, such as bankers or solicitors, or the previous auditors

- Whether the company has a good financial record, resources and outlook: this can be assessed by looking at recent financial performance and reports and by making enquiries (with permission) from its bankers

- Whether the company appears to have good internal control, or, at minimum, a good control environment: this might be indicated by the existence of an internal audit department, or assessed through inquiries of management

- Whether the company has unusual transactions: this can be assessed by reviewing published financial statements

In general terms, if the directors appear to have integrity, the financial record is strong and prospects look good, there is a good attitude to internal control in the company and it has few unusual transactions, then it is lower risk than a company for which those things are not true.

Remember, that if a firm determines that a company is a high risk client, this does not necessarily mean that the firm will not accept the engagement, but this preliminary assessment of risk will be incorporated into the audit procedures when risk assessment identification and procedures are carried out on the engagement.

Another area constituting risk to the auditor, as indicated in the example above, is the risk that the client may be money laundering. As you know, accountants are required to report suspicions of money laundering and failure to report a suspicion is a criminal offence. The auditors are also required to carry out client due diligence with respect to money laundering at the start of an engagement. This was all set out in your manual for Assurance, and you should refer back to it for the details.

3 Acceptance and legal issues

When deciding whether to accept an assurance engagement, the auditors need to consider the following:

- The results of risk analysis (discussed above)

- Whether there are any ethical issues which prevent acceptance (discussed in Chapters 4 and 5)

- Whether the firm has sufficient experience and resources (mainly staff who are appropriately qualified, experienced and available) to undertake the engagement

- For an audit engagement, whether all the legal requirements associated with the appointment of the incoming auditors and the removal or resignation of the outgoing auditors have been met

3.1 Ethical issues

The ICAEW *Code of Ethics* sets out the following points in relation to changes in professional appointment.

3.1.1 Prospective auditors

When a prospective auditor is first approached by a prospective client or nominated, he should explain to the prospective client that he has a professional duty, if asked to act or be nominated, to communicate with the existing auditor. (This may be mentioned in replying to requests to submit tenders.)

The client should give the existing auditor written authority to discuss the client's affairs with the prospective auditor.

The prospective auditor should then write to the existing auditor, seeking information which could influence his decision as to whether or not he may properly accept appointment.

If the existing auditor fails to respond within a reasonable time, the prospective auditor should write to the existing auditor by recorded delivery stating an intention to accept the appointment in the absence of a reply within a specified period. The existing auditor's silence would imply that there were no adverse comments.

Once the prospective auditor has received confirmation that there are no reasons not to act, or has become satisfied that he can properly act, and is prepared to accept nomination/appointment, he should inform the client.

3.1.2 Existing auditor

The existing auditor should get written authority from the client to communicate with the prospective auditor. In the absence of specific instructions by the client an existing auditor should not ordinarily volunteer information, as he is bound by confidentiality.

The existing auditor or adviser should quickly answer the communication from the prospective auditor. However care must be taken in situations where the existing auditor knows or suspects that his or her client is involved in money laundering as it is a criminal offence to 'tip off' a money launderer.

If there are no matters of which the latter should be aware, the existing auditor should write to say that this is the case.

If there are such matters, he should inform the prospective auditor of those factors within his knowledge of which, in his opinion, the latter should be aware. It is not sufficient to state that unspecified factors exist.

Matters may include:

- unlawful acts by the client
- unpaid fees
- differences of opinion between the auditor and the client

The fact that there are issues that should be brought to the attention of the prospective auditor does not preclude him or her from accepting appointment; it merely identifies issues that need to be considered.

This communication between the prospective and existing auditors should also provide evidence to the prospective auditor of both the identity and integrity of the client. This is additionally valuable in the light of new requirements on accountants to verify the identity of clients to guard against money laundering.

3.1.3 Client refuses permission to contact previous auditors

If the client fails or refuses to grant the existing auditor or adviser permission to discuss the client's affairs with the proposed auditor, the existing auditor or adviser should report that fact to the prospective auditor or adviser, who should carefully consider the impact of this on his decision whether to accept the appointment/nomination or not.

3.1.4 Additional work

A professional accountant invited to undertake work which is additional to and related to continuing work carried out by another professional adviser should notify that other professional adviser of the work he has been asked to undertake.

It is generally in the interest of the client that the existing auditor or adviser be aware of the nature of the additional work being undertaken.

The existing adviser will be provided with the opportunity to communicate with the professional accountant to provide information, lack of which might otherwise prevent the additional work from being carried out effectively.

Additionally, such notification could affect the way an existing auditor or adviser discharges his continuing responsibilities to his client.

Notification should always be given unless the client advances reasons which persuade the firm that, in all the circumstances, the existing adviser should not be informed.

An example of such a situation might be where a client disagrees with the proposed audit opinion of its auditors and engages a second accountant to give him a second opinion on the matter. A key danger in this situation is that the second accountant does not have all the information necessary to give an appropriate second opinion, thus communication is vital. Auditors should always be wary of giving second opinions as they may compromise the position of the first auditor, trying to give an appropriate, independent opinion.

3.2 Legal issues

3.2.1 Appointment of auditors by the members

In order to carry out the audit of a company, the auditor first needs to be appointed by ordinary resolution.

The members (ie, shareholders) of a company appoint the auditor at an annual general meeting (AGM), or other general meeting of the company at which the financial statements are put forward for approval by members. The appointment must be made by the end of the 28 days after the last date on which the account must be filed. If an auditor is not appointed within this time, the existing auditor is deemed to be reappointed, subject to certain conditions.

3.2.2 Appointment of auditors by the directors

The exception to the above rule is where the directors appoint the auditor either to:

- fill a casual vacancy, for example when the existing auditor resigns during the year; or
- appoint the first auditor between the date of incorporation and the first AGM or if the company qualifies to require an audit, before the next AGM.

As noted above, however, in both cases the members must then reappoint the auditors at the next AGM, by ordinary resolution.

3.2.3 Appointment of auditors by the Secretary of State

In rare circumstances where no auditor has been appointed at the appropriate time, the company must inform the Secretary of State within one week of the relevant timing expiring and the Secretary of State will then appoint an auditor.

3.2.4 Removal of auditors

If the members of the company wish to remove the existing auditor and appoint a new one, they can do so by ordinary resolution with special notice at a general meeting.

Where this happens the auditors must make a statement of circumstances (see below) and they have certain rights, which include the right:

- to receive notice, attend and speak at the meeting where they would have been appointed, or the proposed new auditor is appointed
- to have a written representation of a reasonable length circulated to all members. Such a representation might explain why they should not be removed as auditors

In practice, it tends to be the directors who decide that they would like the existing auditor removed, but to achieve this they must put up a resolution for the members to vote on.

One of the possible reasons why directors might wish to make this change is because they have had a disagreement in principle with the existing auditor over the accounting treatment of an item in the financial statements, but have no such disagreement with the new auditor. (Finding auditors who are more acquiescent is a process known as 'opinion shopping'). It is to protect the existing auditor (by giving him a right to argue his case) that company law provides for an auditor being removed to make written representation to members and to speak at the meeting at which the resolution is voted on.

3.2.5 Resignation of auditors

If the auditor resigns during his year of office, he must submit written notice to the company at the company's registered office. The auditor must also send a statement of circumstances (see below).

The auditor has certain rights here, which include the right:

- to request that the directors convene a general meeting of the company so that the auditor can explain the circumstances connected with the resignation

- to require the company to circulate the statement of circumstances in advance of:

  - the general meeting requested by the auditor

  - any general meeting at which the auditor's term of office would otherwise have expired or at which it is proposed to fill the vacancy caused by the resignation

On receipt of the auditor's resignation the company must then notify:

- the Registrar of Companies
- anyone entitled to receive a copy of the company's accounts.

As an alternative to resignation the auditor may simply not seek reappointment, or the company may decide against reappointment. In either of these two circumstances, the auditor is still required to prepare a statement of circumstances or confirm in writing that there are no circumstances of which members should be aware.

3.2.6 Statement by auditor ceasing to hold office as auditor

An auditor who ceases to hold office as auditor of a non-PIE company is required to deposit at the company's registered office:

- A statement of the circumstances connected with his ceasing to hold office which he considers should be brought to the attention of the members or creditors of the company; or

- A statement that there are no such circumstances if he considers this to be the case.

This requirement is waived under revised s.519 of Companies Act 2006 where:

- The auditor's term of office has come to an end or;

- The auditor ceases to hold office during their term of office for exempt reasons, for example the auditor ceases to practise as an auditor.

There are no such exemptions in Companies Act 2006 for an auditor who ceases to hold office as auditor of a public interest company. That auditor must deposit a 'statement of reasons' connected with his ceasing to hold office at the company's registered office. There is no option to deposit a statement that there are no circumstances.

This makes it very difficult for an auditor who thinks something is wrong at a company, but is not sure, to walk away quietly without telling the members.

Interactive question 1: Disagreement with directors

You have recently had a serious disagreement with the directors of one of your major audit clients who, as a result, have threatened to recommend another firm of auditors for appointment at the next AGM.

Requirement

What statutory rights do you have if they carry out their threat?

See **Answer** at the end of this chapter.

4 Terms of an audit engagement

Section overview

- As part of engagement acceptance, the assurance providers will negotiate the terms of the engagement. For assurance engagements, this will include:

    - The scope of the engagement
    - The subject matter of the engagement
    - The criteria by which the subject matter is being judged
    - The level of assurance required and therefore the type of opinion to be given
    - The timings associated with the engagement
    - Any restriction in liability
    - The fee for the engagement

With regard to audits, the scope of the engagement is determined by law and professional standards, but the auditors must ensure that these terms are understood by the client. In addition, the following matters will need to be agreed:

- The fee or the basis by which the fee will be determined

- The limited liability agreement, that is, the cap on the auditors' liability for the engagement (discussed in the previous chapter)

4.1 Audit engagement letters

You were introduced to the concept of an engagement letter in your studies for Assurance. Engagement letters are required under ISA (UK) 210 *Agreeing the Terms of Audit Engagements*. As you may remember, it is a requirement of this standard that the terms of the engagement are put in writing.

The form and content of an engagement letter will vary, but should cover the following matters:

- The objective and scope of the audit of financial statements (including reference to applicable legislation, regulations, financial reporting framework and auditing standards)

- Management's responsibilities (including responsibility for the financial statements and the company's system of internal control)

The auditor's responsibilities

- The form and content of reports and communications that will arise from the audit

- The fact that due to the test nature and other limitations of an audit, there is an unavoidable risk that some material misstatement may remain undiscovered

- The fact that auditors are entitled to unrestricted access to records, documents and other information requested in connection with the audit

The expectation that management will provide written representations

The letter may also cover practical matters, such as arrangements relating to planning, using the work of experts, liaising with the internal audit department, the fee and restriction of auditor liability.

4.2 Recurring audits

When the audit is a recurring audit, it is not necessary to issue a new letter each year. However, the auditors should consider every year whether a new letter is required. The following factors may indicate a new letter is required:

- Indications that the client misunderstands the terms of the engagement

- Revised or special terms of the engagement

- A recent change in senior management or directors
- A significant change in ownership of the company
- A significant change in the nature or size of the company
- Legal or regulatory requirements
- A change in the financial reporting framework adopted in the preparation of the financial statements
- A change in other reporting requirements

4.3 Changes in engagement

If the auditor is asked to change the engagement to one which provides a lower level of assurance then he should consider the appropriateness of doing so. Obviously, if the audit is a statutory audit, the auditor must provide an appropriate audit as required by law, that is one giving reasonable assurance on the truth and fairness of the engagement.

If the terms are changed, the auditor and the client must agree the terms. If the auditor and the client cannot agree, the auditor should withdraw from the existing arrangement.

4.4 Disclosure of the terms of agreement

The Companies Act 2006 makes provision for potential future regulations requiring disclosure of the terms of the audit engagement. Currently there are no such regulations in place.

Interactive question 2: Engagement letter

Mr Angry of Gonzo Animations Ltd has approached your audit firm to undertake the audit of his company. When the partner held the initial meeting with Mr Angry, the client refused to sign the engagement letter as he said that it was merely a means of the firm abdicating its responsibility for the audit.

Requirement

Your partner has asked you to draft a letter to the client explaining the need for a letter of engagement.

See **Answer** at the end of this chapter.

Summary and Self-test

Summary

Self-test

Answer the following questions.

1 Define lowballing.

2 List four issues that ICAEW states should be referred to when determining fees

  (i)   ....

  (ii)   ....

  (iii) ....

  (iv)   ....

3 Why do firms undertake risk analysis?

4 If the client refuses the existing auditor permission to communicate with the prospective auditor, the prospective auditor should decline the appointment.

  ☐ True

  ☐ False

5 An auditor can be appointed by which of the following methods?

  ☐ Ordinary resolution by shareholders

  ☐ By directors to fill a casual vacancy

  ☐ By directors to appoint first auditor

  ☐ By Secretary of State

6 If a client requests that an auditor reduce the level of assurance offered on a statutory audit, an auditor may agree and reduce procedures accordingly.

  ☐ True

  ☐ False

Exam-style questions

7 Acer Ltd is a client of your firm and is seeking funding in order to expand the business. The directors have prepared profit and cash flow forecasts for the next three years ending 30 June 20X9 in support of the request for funding. The company's bankers require this information to be reviewed by independent accountants and the board of directors has requested that your firm undertakes this review.

  Set out the matters that you would include in the engagement letter in relation to the respective responsibilities of the directors and the reporting accountant.   **(2 marks)**

8 **Wrapper Ltd**

  Your firm, which has six partners, has been invited by Mr Packer, the managing director and majority shareholder of Wrapper Ltd, to accept appointment as auditor of the company and also provide assistance with the preparation of the financial statements and the corporation tax computation.

  The principal activity of Wrapper Ltd is the production of paper carrier bags, serviettes, coffee cups and lids which are sold to customers operating in the fast food sector. Wrapper Ltd was incorporated on 1 October 20X4 and the financial statements will cover the 15 month period to 31 December 20X5. Although the company's revenue and assets are below the thresholds for statutory audit purposes, the company's bankers require the annual accounts to be subjected to a full audit.

Mr Packer started the business using a combination of money inherited from his grandfather and a bank loan. The loan agreement includes a covenant specifying that the company's debt equity ratio should not exceed parity (ie, 1:1).

The accounting records are computerised and the company uses software which was developed by IT Systems Ltd, a company owned by Mr Packer's brother. The software has been customised to integrate inventory control with receivables and payables. IT Systems Ltd also provides support for the company's computer systems. The accounting records are maintained by Mrs Carlton, assisted by Mrs Biggs who works one day a week and is responsible for payroll processing.

Requirements

(a) State, with reasons, the matters to be considered and procedures to be performed prior to your firm accepting and commencing the audit of Wrapper Ltd for the period ending 31 December 20X5. **(8 marks)**

(b) Identify, from the information provided above, the factors which should be taken into account when assessing the risk of misstatement in the financial statements of Wrapper Ltd and explain why such factors should be taken into account when conducting the audit. **(10 marks)**

(18 marks)

9 The directors of Harmony Ltd ('Harmony') have approached you with a view to your firm accepting appointment as its auditor for the year ending 31 July 20X6. Harmony manufactures satellite navigation systems which it supplies to many of the major motor car manufacturers with UK-based factories.

Harmony has a wholly-owned subsidiary undertaking located overseas which manufactures 'high-end' audio systems for locally based motor car manufacturers. The subsidiary, which is of a similar size to Harmony, is located in a country where there is no audit requirement for companies whose shares are not publicly held. Harmony prepares consolidated financial statements.

The shareholders of Harmony are actively involved in the day to day running of the business and that of the wholly-owned subsidiary.

The directors of Harmony have told their existing auditors that they will not be re-appointed at the company's forthcoming annual general meeting. They have not given them a reason for this, but the existing auditors suspect that it is due to a dispute that arose during the audit of last year's financial statements. At 31 July 20X5 Harmony was carrying inventory totalling £375,000 in respect of a cancelled order for a satellite navigation system from a motor car manufacturer that had gone into liquidation. During September 20X5, modifications were made to the inventory, at a cost of £75,000, to enable them to be sold to another customer for £195,000 that same month. The directors of Harmony were concerned at the effect that any allowance to reduce inventory to NRV in the financial statements would have on their distributable profits for the year. The directors accordingly insisted on including the inventory in the financial statements at £375,000, which gave rise to a modified auditor's report.

In addition to your appointment as auditor, the directors of Harmony have also requested:

(i) That you, as the proposed engagement partner, attend the company's monthly board meetings; and

(ii) That your firm be appointed to provide internal audit services to Harmony.

Your firm has seven partners in total and has an office in each of three cities in the South of England.

Requirements

(a)   Outline the reasons for and against the subsidiary of Harmony having an audit on its own basis despite being owner-managed.   **(6 marks)**

(b)   Set out the key issues specific to Harmony that may prevent you from accepting the appointment solely as its external auditor, and state what action you could take to resolve these issues.   **(6 marks)**

(c)   Discuss the potential threats to objectivity caused by the provision of the additional services requested by Harmony and describe what safeguards could be put in place to mitigate those threats.   **(8 marks)**

(20 marks)

Now, go back to the Learning outcomes in the Introduction. If you are satisfied you have achieved these outcomes, please tick them off.

Technical reference

Answers to Interactive questions

Answer to Interactive question 1

Rights:

- To receive notice of the resolution to appoint another auditor
- To have written representations circulated to all members, or read out at the meeting
- To attend the meeting
- To be heard at the meeting

Answer to Interactive question 2

ABC & Co Chartered Accountants
123 High Street
Bristol
BS6 7HJ
5 April 20X2

V Angry Esq
Gonzo Animations Ltd
Muppet Road
Bath
BA18 9LL

Dear Mr Angry

Engagement letters

We are required by International Standards on Auditing (UK) to send you a formal engagement letter before conducting the audit. All firms of auditors should abide by this procedure.

The letter is there as much to protect the client, as it is the auditor, and we would suggest that legal advice is taken prior to you accepting the terms.

Purpose of engagement letter

The purpose of the letter is to:

- define clearly the extent of the our responsibilities, and your responsibilities.

- minimise the possibility of any misunderstanding between ourselves and Gonzo Animations Ltd.

- provide written confirmation of our acceptance of appointment, the scope of the audit and the form of the report.

We believe that it is important for both parties to clearly understand their roles within the external audit function.

Contents of engagement letter

The contents of the letter are set out below, together, where necessary, with the justification of the inclusion of the section.

- Our respective relevant statutory and professional responsibilities (to avoid misunderstanding).

- An explanation of the scope of the audit (so that we inform you of what we will do). This covers a number of issues.

  - The audit will be carried out in accordance with the International Standards on Auditing (UK) issued by the Financial Reporting Council.

- We need to obtain an understanding of the accounting system in order to assess its adequacy as a basis for the preparation of the financial statements.

- We need to obtain relevant and reliable evidence sufficient to enable us to draw reasonable conclusions therefrom.

- The nature and extent of our procedures will vary according to the assessment of the accounting system and, where we wish to place reliance upon it, the system of internal control.

- We will endeavour to plan the audit so that we have a reasonable expectation of detecting material misstatements in the financial statements or accounting records resulting from fraud, error or non-compliance with law or regulations but that the examination ought not to be relied upon to disclose all frauds, errors or instances of non-compliance which may exist (as some may be immaterial).

- Due to the test nature and other inherent limitations of an audit, together with the inherent limitations of any system of internal control, there is an unavoidable risk that even some material misstatement may remain undiscovered.

- An explanation that management representations may be required in writing during the audit (this will only be in the case of audit areas where we have to rely on your representations).

- The fact that we may send a letter of comment, adding value to the audit, by outlining ways in which we discussed the business may be improved.

- Other matters such as:

  - Our billing arrangements

  - Any arrangements in the future concerning the involvement of:

    - other auditors and experts
    - internal auditors
    - previous auditors

  - Management's responsibility to detect and prevent fraud

  - Your complaints procedures

  - A proposed timetable for the engagement (which will vary each year).

I hope this clarifies the need for the letter. Except for the timetable, we will only send out such letters in future where absolutely necessary.

Yours sincerely

Mr A Accountant

Answers to Self-test

1   Lowballing is the practice of charging less than the market rate for assurance services.

2   Four from:

   (i)   The seniority and professional experience of the persons necessarily engaged on the work

   (ii)   The time expended by each

   (iii)   The degree of risk and responsibility which the work entails

   (iv)   The nature of the client's business, the complexity of its operation and the work to be performed

   (v)   The priority and importance of the work to the client

   (vi)   Together with any expenses properly incurred

3   • To ensure that the assurance provider believes an appropriate conclusion can be drawn.

   • To assist in determining an appropriate fee (that reflects the risk of the assignment).

4   False. Not necessarily, although this might be an indicator that the auditor should have concerns about director integrity.

5   All of them.

6   False. A statutory audit provides a reasonable level of assurance.

Exam-style questions

7   **Directors**

  Responsible for:

   • Forecasts including the assumptions on which they are based.

   • Cooperating with the reporting accountant by making available records, documents and personnel.

  Reporting accountant

   • Forecast is properly prepared on the basis of the assumptions made.

   • Provide negative assurance that nothing has come to reporting accountant's attention to cause them to believe that the assumptions do not provide a reasonable basis for the forecast.

8   **Wrapper Ltd**

  (a)   **Matters/procedures prior to acceptance of audit**

     (i)   Check adequacy of resources to enable:

       • Work to be completed to a high standard on a timely basis/use of competent staff

       • Provision of tax/accountancy services without compromising independence (ie, safeguards can be put in place) eg:

         –   Use of separate personnel to perform accountancy and tax

         –   Review by an independent partner/senior staff member with appropriate expertise if tax computation prepared by audit team

         –   Review of the audit by an audit partner who is not involved in the audit engagement

(ii) Establish/document existence of informed management – to ensure auditor does not take management role

(iii) Consider relationships/familiarity threat – to ensure independence/objectivity not impaired

(iv) Consider potential conflicts of interest (eg, competing clients) – to ensure act in the best interest of clients

(v) Consider integrity of client – to reduce risk of misstatements due to fraud/misrepresentation

(vi) Client identification procedures – to reduce exposure to money laundering/comply with money laundering requirements

(vii) Send letter of engagement – to ensure client understands nature and scope of the work to be undertaken/narrow expectations gap

(b)

Factors	Why taken into account
• New client	• Lack of familiarity – may not identify events and transactions which have an impact on the financial statements/higher detection risk
• Start-up	• Going concern risk
	• Doubts/material uncertainty will require disclosure in the financial statements
	• Lack of going concern status will require financial statements to be prepared on a break-up basis
• Lack of prior year figures	• Lack of comfort/corroboration from use of analytical review procedures
	• Require more extensive use of tests of details (substantive tests)
• Bank covenant	• Risk that profits may be overstated in order to preserve the debt equity ratio
• Trading with IT Systems Ltd	• Need to ensure complete disclosure of related party transactions
• Customised accounting software	• May not be reliable, resulting in errors
• Lack of segregation of duties	• Misstatements may not be prevented or detected and corrected on a timely basis/higher control risk
	• Determine the audit approach which is likely to be substantive based

9 (a) **Arguments for Harmony's subsidiary having an audit**

An audit requires all similar-sized companies to be treated the same, regardless of ownership. It provides assurance that the company has complied with the Companies Act and accounting standards. Many would consider that an external audit is a fair price to pay for limited liability.

There are more stakeholders in a company than simply its shareholders who can use the assurance generated by the audit work. The tax authorities can place more reliance on the financial statements and an audit affords some measure of protection to creditors that the company is not trading whilst insolvent. It also means potential investors can place similar reliance on the financial statements whether or not the company is listed.

Arguments against Harmony's subsidiary having an audit

Harmony's shareholders are actively involved in the management of the subsidiary and therefore an audit will be of little value to them. The auditor's report will be addressed to shareholders and therefore contribute little to their knowledge and understanding of the business. Furthermore, an audit can cause unnecessary red tape and expense.

(b) The audit of Harmony will include the results of the subsidiary, which are material as the subsidiary is the same size as Harmony. The audit firm must consider whether it has adequate resources to audit the overseas subsidiary itself and whether it has the required level of competence. Harmony should appoint a local audit firm and undergo an audit of its subsidiary voluntarily. This local firm would use the firm's UK audit packs and the UK firm would review the work of the local auditor in detail.

The dispute with the previous auditors may also cast doubt over the integrity of management and whether accepting the appointment will put the firm at risk of management intimidation. In an attempt to resolve this issue, permission should be sought to speak with the outgoing auditors and enquire of them whether there are any other issues of which the incoming auditor should be aware.

The engagement partner assigned must ensure that members of the audit team have appropriately consulted on difficult or contentious issues. It is also recommended that an independent second partner review of the audit file is undertaken in the first year, before the auditor's report is signed.

(c) **Threats to objectivity**

In some cases, for example when management representations are discussed, it may be desirable for the auditor to attend board meetings. However, an auditor must not under any circumstances make management decisions. Attending board meetings is allowed if the auditor is acting in an advisory capacity only or is reporting the results of audit work.

Safeguards

To safeguard against this threat, the auditor should ensure that there is 'informed management' at the company. The auditor should inform the directors that they alone are responsible for decision-making and he should get their written confirmation of agreement to this. In the interests however of being 'seen to be independent' it may be best to decline the offer of attendance at monthly board meetings.

Threat to objectivity

The provision of internal audit service causes a self-review threat to the external auditor as the external audit staff members may overlook errors made by their internal audit colleagues or may place too much reliance on their work.

Safeguards

The external audit firm can only act as internal auditor if the external auditor does not place significant reliance on the work or relies on it only after rigorous and objective assessment of the work completed by the internal auditors. Additional safeguards include separate engagement partners, separate engagement letters and different teams for the two respective roles.

Finally, the directors must confirm in writing that they are responsible for the overall system of internal control including the work of internal audit, and that they are responsible for acting on the recommendations of internal audit.

CHAPTER 7

Planning

Introduction

Examination context

TOPIC LIST

Summary and Self-test

Technical reference

Answers to Interactive questions

Answers to Self-test

Introduction

Learning outcomes

2   Planning engagements

Students will be able to plan assurance engagements in accordance with the terms of the engagements and appropriate standards.

- Assess the impact of risk and materiality on the engagement plan, including the nature, timing and extent of assurance procedures, for a given organisation

- Discuss the benefits and limitations of analytical procedures (including data analytics) at the planning stage

- Specify and explain the steps necessary to plan, perform, conclude and report on the audit of the financial statements of a non-specialised profit oriented entity in accordance with the terms of the engagement including appropriate auditing standards

Syllabus links

You have studied these matters for your Assurance paper, so much of the technical detail covered here is revision. It is important at this Professional stage to be able to explain and apply the techniques outlined in the chapter.

Examination context

A question which deals with planning in the exam is also very likely to deal with risks, which we shall look at in more detail in the next chapter, hence the question practice given in this chapter is limited and more practice will be given in the next chapter.

1 The need to plan

Section overview

- Audits are planned so that auditors know what to do so that the appropriate conclusion can be drawn

- It is a requirement of ISA (UK) 300 *Planning an Audit of Financial Statements* that audits are planned

Audits (and other assurance engagements) are planned because if they are not:

- time might be wasted doing the wrong work
- the really important work might not be done at all
- ultimately, the wrong conclusion might therefore be drawn

Planning an engagement is a key aspect of the quality control associated with that audit. If an audit is planned, then the right work is done, it is easier to supervise and review that work, and therefore it adds to the quality of the whole engagement.

In addition, as you know from your studies for Assurance, audits are planned because it is a requirement of auditing standards. ISA (UK) 300, *Planning an Audit of Financial Statements* requires audits to be planned so that they can be carried out 'effectively'.

Much of the material we look at in this chapter, you have covered in your lower level studies. In this area, you need to be able to apply your knowledge to the scenarios presented in the exam.

In summary, planning helps the auditor know:

- what to do
- how much to do
- where to focus resources
- what the important matters that need dealing with

Interactive question 1: The need to plan

Requirement

State the reasons why auditors need to plan audits.

See **Answer** at the end of this chapter.

2 Overall audit strategy and audit plan

Section overview

- The key planning document is called the overall audit strategy

- It covers matters such as materiality, risk, audit approach, use of experts/internal audit, timings, team, budget and deadlines

- Many audit firms have 'audit packs' containing example audit strategies and plans, but care should be taken when using them

- The other key document in audit planning is the audit plan

2.1 Key planning documentation

As you know from your studies for Assurance, the key planning document is called an overall audit strategy. This covers the main general areas of planning: materiality, risk, audit approach, use of experts and internal audit, timing, team, budgets and deadlines.

The technical details of many of these issues will be covered in later chapters.

Most audit firms have 'audit packs' which have a specific planning section and set out the key areas that auditors must consider when planning an audit. However, care should be taken when using any standard forms, as there is a risk that matters particular to the client might be forgotten. It is important to tailor the plan to the client, not the other way around. Identifying key issues relating to the client and then adjusting the audit approach will be necessary. This is why understanding the business (Chapter 8) and risk assessment (Chapter 9) are very important.

The overall audit strategy should be updated as necessary during the course of the engagement.

As you also know from your earlier studies, the other key document in audit planning is the audit plan, which is more detailed that the audit strategy, and sets out the nature, timing and extent of planned audit procedures (including risk assessment procedures) to fulfil the requirements of the overall audit strategy and auditing standards.

The audit plan should be updated as necessary during the course of the engagement.

2.2 Automating the audit process

Many audit firms use some form of automated process during the planning stage of the audit and when carrying out audit fieldwork, with the aim of improving audit quality and reducing costs.

During the planning stage, automation can help with bringing information forward from the previous audit and populating checklists, identifying resource requirements, generating working paper templates and identifying information required from the client prior to any site visit.

During the fieldwork phase automated templates help to ensure that all areas are covered in sufficient detail, enable electronic sign-off to take place and can feed into the auditor's report and into any report to management on deficiencies identified.

As with audit packs, it is important that any generic documentation is customised to fit the specific audit needs of each client.

3 Materiality

Section overview

- An item is material if its omission or misstatement could influence the economic decisions of users taken on the basis of the financial statements

- Items might be material by value or nature

- Materiality is a matter of auditor judgement

You learnt about materiality and the principles of ISA (UK) 320 *Materiality in Planning and Performing an Audit* in your studies for Assurance. The following is therefore revision.

Definitions

Material: Information is **material** if its omission or misstatement could influence the economic decisions of users taken on the basis of the financial statements. Materiality depends on the size of the item or error judged in the particular circumstances of its omission or misstatement. Thus, materiality provides a threshold or cut-off point rather than being a primary qualitative characteristic which information must have if it is to be useful.

Performance materiality: An amount or amounts set by the auditor at less than materiality for the financial statements as a whole to reduce to an appropriately low level the probability that the aggregate of uncorrected and undetected misstatements exceeds materiality for the financial statements as a whole or, if applicable, for a particular class of transaction, account balance or disclosure.

Auditors should consider materiality when determining the nature, timing and extent of audit procedures.

Items might be material due to their:

- Amount/value/quantity
- Nature/quality

The Standard does not specify a methodology for determining materiality for the financial statements as a whole. In practice, however auditors will set a computed level of materiality, often based on the following ranges:

Revenue:	0.5%–1%
Profit before tax:	5%–10%
Gross assets:	1%–2%

In addition, some matters might be material by nature, for example:

- The £1 that turns a profit into a loss might be considered very important by some companies/shareholders

- The £1 that changes the thresholds the company operates in (for example, becoming a medium-sized rather than small company) might also be very important

- Some matters are automatically material, such as matters relating to directors, or related parties because these matters have to be disclosed in financial statements regardless of their value

Performance materiality should be set so that misstatements which are in themselves immaterial, but which in aggregate could cause the financial statements to be materially misstated, are unlikely to remain undetected. In other words the probability of such misstatements remaining undetected should be reduced to an acceptably low level. Performance materiality can be one or more amounts, and it should be revised as the audit progresses, if the auditor becomes aware during the audit of information that would have caused a different amount to be set in the first place.

Auditors should always bear in mind that materiality is a matter of professional judgement. Materiality is also important at the completion stage of an audit, when the auditors are evaluating the effect of discovered misstatements. We shall look at this in Chapter 12.

4 Analytical procedures

Section overview

- Analytical procedures must be used in risk assessment
- The benefits of analytical procedures in planning are the 'overall' perspective, the use of information outside of the accounting records and the comparison of different elements of the financial statements
- The limitations of analytical procedures in planning are:
    - Substantial knowledge of the business is required for results to be meaningful (therefore experienced staff may be required to carry them out)
    - They can be performed mechanically
    - The relevant information may not be available

You looked at analytical procedures in some detail in your studies for Assurance. You should be able to explain what analytical procedures are and carry out basic analytical procedures.

ISA (UK) 315 *Identifying and Assessing the Risks of Material Misstatement through Understanding of the Entity and Its Environment* states that the auditor should use analytical procedures in risk assessment in order to obtain an understanding of the entity and its environment. We shall look at this in detail in the next chapter.

In this syllabus you are required to be able to discuss the benefits and limitation of analytical procedures at the planning stage.

Interactive question 2: Benefits and limitations of analytical procedures

Analytical procedures must be carried out at the planning stage of an audit to help identify risk areas requiring extra work.

Requirement

Set out the benefits and limitations of using analytical procedures to identify risk areas during audit planning.

See **Answer** at the end of this chapter.

These are the ratios students need for applying analytical procedures.

Heading/Ratio	Formula	Purpose
Performance		
Return on capital employed	$\dfrac{\text{Profit before interest and tax}}{\text{Equity} + \text{net debt}}$	Effective use of resources
Return on shareholders' funds	$\dfrac{\text{Net profit for the period}}{\text{Share capital} + \text{reserves}}$	Effective use of resources
Gross profit percentage	$\dfrac{\text{Gross profit} \times 100}{\text{Revenue}}$	Assess profitability before taking overheads into account
Cost of sales percentage	$\dfrac{\text{Cost of sales} \times 100}{\text{Revenue}}$	Assess relationship of costs to revenue
Operating cost percentage	$\dfrac{\text{Operating costs / overheads} \times 100}{\text{Revenue}}$	Assess relationship of costs to revenue

Heading/Ratio	Formula	Purpose
Net margin/operating margin	$\dfrac{\text{Profit before interest and tax} \times 100}{\text{Revenue}}$	Assess profitability after taking overheads into account
Short-term liquidity		
Current ratio	Current assets : Current liabilities	Assess ability to pay current liabilities from current assets
Quick ratio	Receivables + Current Investments + cash : liabilities	Assess ability to pay current liabilities from reasonably liquid assets
Long term solvency		
Gearing ratio	$\dfrac{\text{Net debt}}{\text{Equity}}$	Assess reliance on external finance
Interest cover	$\dfrac{\text{Profit before interest payable}}{\text{Interest payable}}$	Assess ability to pay interest charges
Efficiency		
Net asset turnover	$\dfrac{\text{Revenue}}{\text{Capital employed}}$	Assess revenue generated from asset base
Inventory turnover	$\dfrac{\text{Cost of sales}}{\text{Inventories}}$	Assess level of inventory held
Inventory days	$\dfrac{\text{Average inventory} \times 365}{\text{Cost of sales}}$	Assess the average inventory-holding period
Trade receivables collection period	$\dfrac{\text{Trade receivables} \times 365}{\text{Revenue}}$	Assess ability to turn receivables into cash
Trade payables payment period	$\dfrac{\text{Trade payables} \times 365}{\text{Credit purchases}}$	Assess ability to pay suppliers

Worked example: Analytical procedures

A distribution and warehousing company is seeking to increase its overdraft and the bank has requested to review its audited financial statements. The company's contracts cover periods of between three and five years. Invoicing takes place after the service has been provided and terms of trade require payment in 30 days. Revaluation of land and buildings has occurred during the financial year. The company owns its own vehicles and trailers.

The following information has been extracted from the financial statements for years ended 31 May:

Extracts from the statement of profit or loss

	Draft 20X8 £'000	Actual 20X7 £'000
Revenue	25,417	23,867
Cost of sales	(21,895)	(20,924)
Gross profit	3,522	2,943
Administrative expenses	(2,205)	(2,011)
	1,317	932
Loss on sale of vehicles and trailers	(232)	–

	Draft 20X8 £'000	Actual 20X7 £'000
Profit from operations	1,085	932
Finance cost	(345)	(302)
Profit before tax	740	630

Extracts from the statement of financial position

	£'000	£'000
Non-current assets		
Property, plant and equipment	7,987	6,528
Current assets		
Trade receivables	3,156	2,681
Non-current liabilities		
Borrowings – bank loan	3,000	2,500
Current liabilities		
Trade payables	1,553	1,922
Borrowings:		
Overdraft	499	454
Bank loan	500	250

From this information the auditor may wish to highlight the following factors, and to consider the audit risk that they pose:

- Revenue has increased by 6.5% which may be indicative of overstatement due to early recognition of income or cut off errors.

- There has been a significant increase in the gross margin from 12.3% to 13.8%. This may be indicative of inflated sales or unrecorded purchases.

- There is a significant loss in sales of vehicles which may be indicative of inappropriate asset lives and consequently overstatement of carrying amounts.

- The revaluation of land and buildings may have been undertaken in order to inflate the assets figure.

- There has been an increase in trade receivables days from 41 to 45 days. This is greater than the normal terms of trading of 30 days and may be indicative of overstatement. This may be due to inclusion of sales invoices relating to the next accounting period or unrecoverable debts.

- There has been a reduction in payables days from 33.5 to 25.9 days, which may be indicative of understatement. This may be due to a failure to record all supplier invoices relating to the period.

5 Going concern

Section overview

- The question of whether an entity is a viable going concern is an important consideration for the auditor at the planning stage of the audit

- A number of indicators can alert the auditor to possible problems with the going concern assumption

- In times of economic uncertainty, additional doubts over going concern may be highlighted

- There are specific risks that need to be borne in mind at the planning stage of the audit

ISA (UK) 570 *Going Concern* deals with the assumption of going concern as applied to the preparation of financial statements. The auditor's responsibility is to obtain sufficient appropriate audit evidence about the appropriateness of management's use of the going concern assumption. The risks of the client not being a going concern will need to be considered and planned for at the planning stage.

A list of possible symptoms of going concern problems is given in ISA (UK) 570 *Going Concern* . It is reproduced here.

- **Financial indications**

    - Net liability or net current liability position

    - Fixed-term borrowings approaching maturity without realistic prospects of renewal or repayment, or excessive reliance on short-term borrowings to finance long-term assets

    - Indications of withdrawal of financial support by creditors

    - Negative operating cash flows indicated by historical or prospective financial statements

    - Adverse key financial ratios

    - Substantial operating losses or significant deterioration in the value of assets used to generate cash flows

    - Arrears or discontinuance of dividends

    - Inability to pay creditors on due dates

    - Inability to comply with terms of loan agreements

    - Change from credit to cash-on-delivery transactions with suppliers

    - Inability to obtain financing for essential new product development or other essential investments

- **Operating indications**

    - Management intentions to liquidate the entity or to cease operations
    - Loss of key management without replacement
    - Loss of a major market, key customer(s), franchise, license, or principal supplier(s)
    - Labour difficulties
    - Shortages of important supplies
    - Emergence of a highly successful competitor

- **Other indications**

    - Non-compliance with capital or other statutory requirements

    - Pending legal proceedings against the entity that may, if successful, result in claims that the entity is unlikely to be able to satisfy

    - Changes in law or regulation or government policy expected to adversely affect the entity

    - Uninsured or underinsured catastrophes when they occur

ISA (UK) 570 also says that the auditors have to discuss the going concern issue with the client's management, with an emphasis on the following:

- To test the assumptions they have made to ensure they are justified

- To obtain written representations from management about the things they are intending to do in the future to ensure that the going concern basis is appropriate

- To review that disclosures made in the financial statements relating to going concern are sufficient to give a true and fair view in the UK.

If, in making their assessment, the directors have used a period of less than a year from the date of approval of the financial statements and have not disclosed that fact in the financial statements, the auditors should do so in the auditor's report.

In the present circumstances of economic uncertainty, the availability of credit and the costs of borrowing may be factors that the auditor identifies as specific events or conditions that raise doubts over going concern. If events or conditions have been identified that may cast significant doubt on the entity's ability to continue as a going concern, the auditor shall perform additional audit procedures that may include the following:

- Analysing and discussing cash flow, profit and other relevant forecasts with management

- Analysing and discussing the entity's latest available interim financial statements

- Reading the terms of debentures and loan agreements and determining whether any have been breached

- Reading minutes of the meetings of shareholders, those charged with governance and relevant committees for reference to financial difficulties

- Inquiring of the entity's legal counsel regarding the existence of litigation and claims and the reasonableness of management's assessments of their outcome and the estimate of their financial implications

- Confirming the existence, legality and enforceability of arrangements to provide or maintain financial support with related and third parties and assessing the financial ability of such parties to provide additional funds

- Evaluating the entity's plans to deal with unfilled customer orders

- Performing audit procedures regarding subsequent events to identify those that either mitigate or otherwise affect the entity's ability to continue as a going concern

- Confirming the existence, terms and adequacy of borrowing facilities

- Obtaining and reviewing reports of regulatory actions

- Determining the adequacy of support for any planned disposals of assets

6 Risk factors

Section overview

- A number of potential risk factors need to be considered at the planning stage of the audit:

    - Management manipulation of the accounting records
    - Inappropriate or unauthorised journal entries
    - Incorrect revenue recognition

- Audit data analytics (ADA) can be a useful tool for identifying risks at the planning stage

We shall now consider some of the specific risk factors that auditors need to be aware of during the planning stage of the audit.

6.1 Management override

ISA (UK) 240 uses this term to refer to the unique ability of management to manipulate the accounting records and therefore produce misleading financial statements. Reasons for management override are many and varied, for example financial gain, tax avoidance, or the enhancement of personal or business performance. The risk of management override is present in every audit assignment.

Auditors need to assess the risk of management override during the planning stage of the audit, and to design appropriate audit procedures in response. Those procedures should include:

- Testing journal entries to ensure they are appropriate
- Review of accounting estimates to judge whether management bias has been applied
- Scrutinising significant and unusual transactions

6.2 Journals

Fraudulent activities can be perpetrated by inappropriate or unauthorised journal entries, especially in organisations where internal controls are poor. When selecting journal entries for testing, auditors should include:

- Entries made to unrelated, unusual or seldom-used accounts
- Journals put through by individuals who do not normally make journal entries
- Journals recorded at the end of the period or after closure, with little or no explanation or description
- Journals made without account numbers
- Round number entries

Auditors may also wish to look at journals made outside normal office hours and postings to and from suspense accounts.

6.3 Revenue recognition

Auditors should be aware of the risks of material misstatement due to incorrect revenue recognition. The risk of this is greater in organisations where management reward is linked to revenue or profit. Revenue may be misstated by, for example, premature recognition or recording fictitious revenue.

Audit procedure in response to the risks relating to revenue recognition may include:

- Analytical procedures including revenue streams and month by month comparisons
- Customer confirmation
- Review sales near the end of the accounting period and any unusual terms and conditions
- Observe goods being despatched
- Sales and revenue cut-off procedures
- Tests of controls over electronic revenue transactions

6.4 Audit data analytics (ADA)

With the growth of big data (see Chapter 3) there is scope for auditors to exploit new sources of data when planning audit engagements. Such data sources include:

- The internet for actual transactions and sites visited
- Cloud computing
- Social media
- Mobile technology and location tracking
- Open data from the public sector

The development of new audit techniques and processes are predicted to have a significant impact on how audits are carried out in future. At the planning stage, ADA methods can be used to identify patterns, correlations and deviations from expected outcomes. This information can be used to enhance the auditor's knowledge about the client and the risks that are specific to the client's environment and activities.

6.5 Cloud computing

Definition

Cloud computing: A model for enabling ubiquitous, convenient, on-demand network access to a shared pool of configurable computing resources (eg, networks, servers, storage, applications, and services) that can be rapidly provisioned and released with minimal management effort or service provider interaction.

(US Department of Commerce, National Institute of Standards and Technology)

Recent years have seen increased adoption of cloud computing services. This is because cloud computing offers greater flexibility for users, but also significant cost savings in comparison with traditional on-site IT storage facilities. Cloud computing offers organisations the ability to access their data quickly from any location in the world, which can be extremely valuable for some entities.

Cloud computing does bring risks as well as advantages. The key risk is that the entity relinquishes control of its data, handing it over to the entity providing the cloud-based service. Data may be in danger of being lost, corrupted or stolen. These risks are not absent from internal, on-site data storage, but where data is held on-site the entity itself at least has the opportunity to put in place sufficient cyber security measures to keep the data secure. Where cloud computing services are used, the security of the data is entirely dependent on controls at another entity (the service provider); it is therefore crucial that proper consideration is given to whether the service provider's controls are reliable.

6.6 Cyber security

Definition

Cyber security: The protection of systems, networks and data in cyberspace.

This definition can be extended to include the protection of data from unauthorised modification, disclosure or destruction, and the protection of the information system from the degradation or non-availability of services – in other words, system failure.

The widespread use of IT/IS throughout the world presents organisations with the increasingly complex challenge of keeping the systems and data they hold safe from a range of constantly evolving risks. This has made cyber security a major issue for most organisations. Cyber security is directed towards protecting IT systems from risks which predominantly feature some degree of human involvement.

Although by no means definitive, the list below details some of the most significant cyber risks an organisation's IT systems might encounter:

- **Human threats**: hackers may be able to get into the organisation's internal network, either to steal data or to damage the system. Political terrorism is a major risk in the era of cyber-terrorism.

- **Fraud**: the theft of funds by dishonest use of a computer system.

- **Deliberate sabotage**: For example, commercial espionage, malicious damage or industrial action.

- **Viruses and other corruptions**: can spread through the network to all of the organisation's computers.

- **Malware**: this terms is used for hostile or intrusive software such as worms, Trojan horses, spyware and other malicious programs.
- **Denial of Service (DoS) attack**: a denial of service attack is characterised by an attempt by attackers to prevent legitimate users of a service from using that service.

In recent years, there has been an alarming rise in the number of so called 'cyber attacks' carried out by hackers and saboteurs, intent on causing maximum disruption to organisational IT systems.

The growth of big data and its use in the business environment poses new risks for businesses and for auditors. Some recent high profile incidents of security breaches have highlighted the reputational risk that organisations face when data is hacked. In addition, the failure to protect personal data can result in fines for breaching data protection legislation.

The ICAEW publication *Audit insights: cyber security* (2014) identifies four areas for businesses to consider to mitigate the risk:

- Consider 'cyber' implications in all business activities, not simply as an IT issue
- Accept the fact that security will be compromised and act accordingly
- Focus on critical information assets and key data
- Get the basics right

On the final point, it is estimated that up to 80% of security breaches could be prevented by having basic protection measures, such as malware, in place. There is also evidence of complacency, where businesses believe that they have adequate security in place and therefore no more needs to be done.

6.6.1 Challenges and recommendations

In this section consideration is given to those challenges – identified by the ICAEW's 2014 report – that organisations face when trying to understand cyber risks, as well as to how organisations can combat these challenges:

- **Communication is a key barrier to common understanding and discussion**. The language of cyber security is often highly technical and difficult for the layperson to fully understand. As a result it is becoming increasingly important for organisations to install a chief information security officer (CISO) to translate such language into a form which is accessible for employees to understand. Organisations need to work with security professionals to build better communication about the articulation and management of cyber risks, and the value of associated security spending.

- **Organisational structures need to define responsibility and accountability for cyber security**. Particularly in larger organisations, in recent years there has been a growth in the number of entities operating information security functions. The challenge for these departments is finding individuals with the specialist skills and expertise to help the organisation protect itself against cyber-attacks.

- **Board-level accountability for cyber risks needs to be determined**, but at present in many organisations it is unclear who is ultimately responsible for managing cyber risks. Accountability for such activity could be assigned to a number of roles including the CEO, chief risk officer, chief information officer and even the HR director. Equally important is the need to ensure that clear lines of responsibility for cyber security are embedded in day-to-day operations throughout the organisation. Furthermore, the board need to regularly consider the organisation's risk tolerance and risk appetite in relation to cyber security and reflect this in risk management strategies.

- **Non-executive directors and audit committees also need to play a part** in tackling cyber security, by ensuring that the executive management put in place adequate provisions to safeguard the organisation. For non-executive directors to be effective they need to have sufficient knowledge and confidence to hold the board to account in a meaningful way.

It is however important to note that the points outlined above in the ICAEW's report do present some challenges for small and medium sized enterprises. Creating new positions such as the chief information security officer role and introducing dedicated information security teams is very often unviable for smaller entities. Due to their size, and simpler business models, the associated costs involved in pursuing best practice in the field of cyber security often mean that smaller organisations lag behind their larger counterparts. Smaller organisations are unlikely to have dedicated IT departments or in-house experts monitoring their exposure to cyber risk. It is common for such organisations to rely on external third parties such as outsource firms providing IT services to put in place measures to address the threats posed by cyber risk. As a result it is likely that to some degree a 'cyber gap' will remain.

6.6.2 IT security controls

Security can be subdivided into a number of aspects.

- **Prevention**: practical measures such as the use of passwords and securing IT assets by keeping doors leading to servers locked when not in use may help to prevent unauthorised access. In practice it is impossible to prevent all threats cost-effectively.

- **Detection**: detection techniques are often combined with prevention techniques: a log can be maintained of unauthorised attempts to gain access to a computer system.

- **Deterrence**: as an example, computer misuse by personnel can be made grounds for dismissal.

- **Recovery procedures**: if the threat occurs, its consequences can be contained.

- **Correction procedures**: these ensure the vulnerability is dealt with (for example, by instituting stricter controls).

- **Threat avoidance**: this might mean changing the design of the system.

6.6.3 Combating IT risks and IT security

There are a number of practical measures that organisations can take in combating IT risks.

- **Business continuity planning**: this means that there should be measures to ensure that if major failures or disasters occur, the business will not be completely unable to function.

- **Systems access control**: this includes protection of information, information systems, networked services, detection of unauthorised activities and security when using the systems.

- **Systems development and maintenance**: this includes security measures and steps to protect data in operational and application systems and also ensuring that IT projects and support are conducted securely.

- **Physical and environmental security**: measures should be taken to prevent unauthorised access, damage and interference to business premises, assets, information and information facilities and prevention of theft.

- **Compliance** with any relevant legal requirements and also with organisational policies in standards. There is no point in having them if they are not enforced.

- **Personnel security**: this covers issues such as recruitment of trustworthy employees, and also reporting of security-related incidents. Training is particularly important, with the aim that users are aware of information security threats and concerns and are equipped to comply with the organisation's security policy.

- **Security organisation**: it should be clear who has responsibility for the various aspects of information security. Additional considerations will apply if facilities and assets are accessed by third parties or responsibility for information processing has been outsourced.

- **Computer and network management**: this includes ensuring continuity of operations and minimising the risk of systems failures, also protecting the integrity of systems and safeguarding information, particularly when exchanged between organisations. Particularly important is protection from viruses.

- **Asset classification and control**: information is an asset, just like a machine, building or a vehicle, and security will be improved if information assets have an 'owner', and are classified according to how much protection they need.

- **Security policy**: a written document setting out the organisation's approach to information security should be available to all staff.

Worked example: Cyber security

One of your audit clients, Derby Ltd (Derby) has outsourced its payroll function. The service organisation that processes the payroll provides Derby with monthly payroll information for its employees. Using this information Derby pays wages and salaries directly into its employees' bank accounts, and pays the relevant payroll taxes to the tax authorities.

The business risks arising from the outsourcing of Derby's payroll function, and the implications for the financial statements, are as follows:

- Loss, theft or misuse of personal data

- Reputational damage

- Fines for late submissions to the tax authorities

- Fines for breach of data protection legislation (these increased significantly under General Data Protection Regulation, which came into force in May 2018)

- Risk of material misstatements in the financial statements due to unrecognised provisions, failure to disclose contingent liabilities or going concern issues, and inappropriate basis of preparation

Summary and Self-test

Summary

Self-test

Answer the following questions.

1 State why audits are planned.

2 Why should care be taken if using a standardised audit pack?

3 Give an example of an item being material by its nature.

4 Analytical procedures should be carried out by an audit junior.

- [ ] True
- [ ] False

Exam-style questions

5 The gross profit percentage in your client's draft financial statements is the same as in the previous year.

What further information would you require in order to use this fact at the planning stage of the audit? **(1 mark)**

6 Described below are situations which have arisen in three audit clients of your firm. The year end in each case is 31 March 20X6.

Jay plc (Jay)

The directors have included the following note to the financial statements for the year ended 31 March 20X6:

"Although the company has incurred significant trading losses and cash outflows during the last two years, the directors believe that the effects of internal restructuring and corporate disposals undertaken will bring about improved results as indicated in the detailed profit and cash flow forecasts for the period to the end of March 20X7. These forecasts indicate that the company will be able to trade within its agreed working capital facility for at least the next 12 months from the date of this report. Considerable progress has been made on the financial restructuring of the company.

On the basis of the above factors the directors consider it is appropriate that the financial statements are prepared on the going concern basis. Should the company fail to meet its forecasts, the going concern basis may prove to be inappropriate. In such circumstances adjustments are likely to have to be made to the net assets shown in these financial statements to reduce assets to their recoverable amounts, to reclassify non-current assets and payables due after more than one year to current assets and current liabilities and to provide for further liabilities that may arise."

Finch plc (Finch)

Finch has included the results of Wren Ltd ('Wren'), a subsidiary, in the consolidated financial statements. Wren is audited by a different firm of auditors who have modified their opinion on Wren's financial statements for the year ended 31 March 20X6 because a fire at the company's premises destroyed the physical inventory count sheets which were the only record of the year end inventory. Wren has included inventory at its estimated cost of £500,000 in the financial statements for the year ended 31 March 20X6.

The consolidated pre-tax profit of Finch is £33.4 million and the pre-tax profit of Wren is £1.2 million for the year ended 31 March 20X6.

Sparrow Ltd (Sparrow)

On 30 April 20X6, the board of directors decided to undertake a restructuring programme which would commence in June 20X6. A provision of £1.8 million in respect of the restructuring costs has been included in the financial statements for the year ended 31 March 20X6.

The pre-tax profit of Sparrow for the year ended 31 March 20X6 is £7.2 million.

Requirements

(a) Discuss what is meant by the concepts of materiality and a true and fair view. **(6 marks)**

(b) Explain why there can be difficulties for auditors regarding materiality and true and fair in relation to the three cases above: Jay, Finch and Sparrow. **(6 marks)**

(12 marks)

7 Your firm has recently been appointed as auditor of Jog Ltd ('Jog'), a company operating within the sports and leisure sector. Your audit manager has arranged a meeting with the company's finance director for early next week and she has asked you to assist her, in advance of this meeting, with the audit planning for the year ending 30 June 20X6. Your audit manager has also asked you to carry out some preliminary analytical procedures on the year-end financial statements of Jog when these become available.

Jog's business can be split into the following three divisions:

- Sports equipment retail outlets: 35 sports equipment retail outlets located in 'out of town' retail parks

- Fitness clubs: 15 fitness clubs, each offering a fully equipped gym together with yoga, aerobics, and circuit training classes

- Machine manufacture: a manufacturing unit in which running machines and rowing machines are assembled using components sourced from overseas.

Further information:

Sports equipment retail outlets

The retail outlets are all located close to major towns and cities throughout the whole of the UK. Each outlet stocks a standard range of products which are supplied from a central warehouse operated by Jog. Salaries for the core staff at the outlets are paid by Jog's head office by direct bank transfer. Each outlet is run on a day-to-day basis by a manager who is responsible for hiring casual staff to cover peak periods. These casual staff members are generally paid using cash from the till.

Jog received some bad publicity during the year following its inclusion in a television documentary which revealed that one of its non-UK sports shoe suppliers was making its employees work long hours for very low wages. In an attempt to manage this adverse press attention, Jog has now had to source these products from alternative suppliers based in the UK.

Fitness clubs

Jog's 15 fitness clubs are all located directly above existing Jog retail outlets. Each club has its own on-site manager and is operated independently of the adjacent retail outlet. Customers of the fitness clubs pay by one of three methods: on a 'pay per session' basis over the fitness club counter; by monthly direct debit paid into Jog's head office bank account; or by annual subscription to head office. Customers are then issued with a membership card which enables them to gain access to the club.

The company operates a bonus incentive scheme for the managers at both its retail outlets and fitness clubs. The size of the bonus is linked to the profitability of their individual operation.

Machine manufacture

During the year Jog started to manufacture its own running machines and rowing machines. It sources the machine components from China and Taiwan. These components are assembled in the UK at Jog's factory for sale both in Jog's own stores under their own 'Jog' brand and also to independent sports shops under the 'Iron Champ' brand. The latter accounts for approximately 80% of Jog's total production of both running and rowing machines. Sales to independent sports shops achieve a gross profit margin of 50%, whereas sales to Jog's own shops are made to that division at cost plus 10%.

Jog is invoiced by its non-UK component suppliers in their respective local currency. The components are sent by sea, which means that Jog's typical lead time for components from the placing of an order to delivery in the UK is three months. Jog is required to pay its suppliers 50% with order and 50% upon receipt of the components in the UK.

Quality control

In line with your firm's system of quality control, procedures were conducted prior to accepting Jog as an audit client, to ensure that it was appropriate to accept such an appointment. Your audit manager has asked you to consider the other objectives of a system of quality control and why they may be particularly relevant to Jog.

Requirements

(a) (i) List, with reasons, the information you would require in order to carry out analytical procedures on the draft financial statements of Jog for the year ending 30 June 20X6.

(ii) Set out the limitations of using analytical procedures at the planning stage of an audit. **(8 marks)**

(b) Identify which of the circumstances outlined above, should be taken into account when planning the audit of Jog. Explain clearly why these matters are important and set out their effect on your proposed audit work. **(24 marks)**

You attempted Part (c) of this question (for 8 marks) in Chapter 5.

(32 marks)

Now, go back to the Learning outcomes in the Introduction. If you are satisfied you have achieved these outcomes, please tick them off.

Technical reference

Answers to Interactive questions

Answer to Interactive question 1

Purpose of planning:

- To enable the audit to be performed in an effective and timely manner

- To ensure that:

    - Appropriate attention is directed to important areas of the audit
    - Potential problems are identified
    - Work is completed expeditiously

- Assists in:

    - Proper assignment of work to the team
    - Co-ordination of work done by others

- Facilitates review.

Answer to Interactive question 2

Benefits:

- Identifies items for attention that detailed tests may miss
- Uses information outside accounting records, for example, budgets
- Allows comparison of data from different sources

Limitations:

- A good knowledge of the business is required to understand results

- Consistency of results may conceal a material error

- There may be a tendency to carry out procedures mechanically, without appropriate professional scepticism

- Requires an experienced member of staff to be done properly

- Reliable data may not be available

Answers to Self-test

1 To ensure that the right work is carried out resulting in the right conclusion being drawn.

2 It is important for the audit plan to be tailored to the client.

3 Examples include:

- Related party transactions
- Directors' transactions
- £1 that makes a company small/medium/large
- £1 that turns a profit into a loss

4 False, as experience and understanding are required to carry out analytical procedures properly.

Exam-style questions

5
- Client's expectation of GP%
- Changes in year that affect GP%

6 (a) **Materiality**

Information is material if its omission or misstatement could influence the economic decisions of users taken on the basis of the financial statements.

Materiality:

(i) Is not capable of mathematical definition

(ii) Can be quantitative (size) or qualitative (nature)

(iii) May be considered in the context of any individual primary statement within the financial statements or of the individual items included within them

(iv) Depends on the size of the item or error judged in the particular circumstances of its omission or misstatement

True and fair

True is generally accepted as meaning in accordance with the facts and fair as meaning objective or unbiased and concerned with the presentational aspects of information including substance over form. True and fair is not defined by statute, however, Counsel's opinion is that financial statements prepared in accordance with GAAP will give a true and fair view. Furthermore, there may be more than one true and fair view for a given set of circumstances.

The concepts of materiality and true and fair require the exercise of professional judgement.

(b) **Jay**

Materiality/true and fair

The difference between the figures prepared on each basis may not be significantly different. However, the effect on the business is so significant that the user needs to be made aware of the situation. The auditor needs to judge whether the disclosures are sufficient for the user to understand the circumstances.

Finch

Materiality/true and fair

Although material to Wren as 42% of pre-tax profits, it is unlikely to be considered material in the context of the consolidated pre-tax profit as it is only 1.5% of consolidated pre-tax profit. Materiality should be considered in the context of the entity on which the auditor is reporting. However, it may be material by nature if a key ratio (eg, current ratio) is affected.

Sparrow

Materiality/true and fair

There is no obligation at the reporting date in respect of restructuring costs. The financial statements therefore do not comply with FRS 102 section 21 *Provisions and Contingencies* as they include a provision in respect of restructuring costs. The amount of the provision for restructuring costs is considered material by size as it is 25% of pre-tax profit, thereby exceeding the commonly used yardstick of 5 – 10% of pre tax profit.

7 (a) **Information required**

Individual statements of comprehensive income and split of the statement of financial position for each division are required. Each division has different profit margins and the split of the statement of financial position figures will enable the calculation of inventory and trade receivable days for each division.

Budget information for each division is required, together with the date from which the machine division commenced trading, so that its figures can be adjusted to take account of a trading period of less than one year. Comparative information by division from Jog's previous financial statements will also be needed. This information will allow actual and budget performance to be compared. This could identify material or significant items, potential misstatements or variations from expected results.

If available, financial information from companies in the same industries could be used to identify where the company has performed well or badly and prompt areas for further enquiry by the auditor.

Limitations of using analytical procedures

One limitation of analytical procedures at the planning stage of an audit is that the auditor needs a good understanding of the business to interpret the results of analytical procedures. If analytical procedures are performed mechanically, a consistency of results from one year to the next may in fact conceal a material error which may not be identified. Effective analytical procedures need to be carried out by experienced members of staff and they rely upon good quality and reliable information being available from the client which may not always be available.

(b) This is a new audit client which means that there is a lack of cumulative prior knowledge which in turn increases the risk of an undetected misstatement in the financial statements. The audit work will include an evaluation of the company's accounting systems and internal controls in addition to consideration of opening balances. Adequate planning will be essential to avoid over-auditing in the first year.

The company operates from 35 locations at which it holds material balances of inventory and non-current assets. The risk of a breakdown in head office controls is higher in multi-site locations. The year-end attendance at inventory counts should cover all material locations and it would be efficient to take the inventory count attendance as an opportunity to inspect material non-current assets and carry out selected cash counts. If the audit approach relies upon controls, it must be ensured that the tests of controls sample covers all material locations.

The company makes cash sales in its retail outlets and fitness clubs and it pays its casual staff in cash. Cash transactions increase the risk of misappropriation of cash and the understatement of revenue in the financial statements. The employment of casual staff may also mean that the company is failing to declare the appropriate amounts of PAYE, which could lead to penalties from the tax authorities. The effect of this on the audit work is that controls over cash must be evaluated and audit effort should be directed to confirming the completeness of recorded sales. In addition, the company's compliance with PAYE regulations should be considered and the wages included in the financial statements should be checked to ensure that this agrees with the company's payroll records.

The company has received adverse publicity over the use of 'sweatshops'. This may damage the reputation of the company which could in turn affect the status of Jog as a going concern. The audit work should attempt to assess the effect of the publicity on Jog's business. The cost implications of the switch by Jog to alternative suppliers in the UK also need to be considered as part of the audit work.

Jog fitness clubs receive annual subscriptions which may cause revenue to be recognised in the wrong accounting year. The company's accounting policy for revenue recognition will need to be considered and audit work should include testing of new subscriptions close to the year end to ensure that an appropriate proportion of income is deferred at the year end.

The company has a profit-related bonus scheme increasing the risk of manipulation of profit by the company's management. Audit work should include checks on income recognition to ensure it has not been accelerated to boost profits. For similar reasons purchase cut-off should be checked to identify any potential suppressed invoices.

The company purchases its machine components in a foreign currency, under payment terms which specify 50% be paid with order. Foreign currency transactions may lead to the incorrect translation of these transactions in the financial statements. The existence of a three-month delivery lead time on these transactions may also give rise to adverse foreign currency exposure. Component payment terms may also lead to cut-off errors arising from incorrect treatment of the first 50% paid with order. The audit work should include sample checks of the company's foreign exchange translation to an independent source such as the FT. The steps taken to minimise the company's exposure to foreign exchange risk needs to be discussed with management. Careful consideration should be given to cut-off for any goods in transit at the year end.

Some of the machines manufactured using imported components are transferred to the company's retail outlets at cost plus 10%. This inter-divisional trading means the value of the retail outlet inventory may contain some unrealised profit. In addition, the practice of adding only 10% onto the cost price, may cause outlets to under price these products, damaging the gross profit margin of the company as a whole. The audit approach should ensure all inter-divisional trading is separately analysed so that any unrealised profit can be identified.

CHAPTER 8

Understanding the entity and its environment

Introduction

Examination context

TOPIC LIST

Summary and Self-test

Technical reference

Answers to Interactive questions

Answers to Self-test

Introduction

Learning outcomes

2 Planning engagements

Students will be able to plan assurance engagements in accordance with the terms of the engagements and appropriate standards.

- Explain, in the context of a given scenario, why it is important to have an understanding of the business when planning an engagement ☐

- Identify ways of gaining an understanding of a client's business; ☐

- Recognise the circumstances under which it may be necessary to bring in expertise (including expertise in cloud computing and cyber security) from other parties to support assurance processes ☐

- Identify the risks arising from error, fraud and non-compliance with law and other regulations and assess their implications for the engagement ☐

Syllabus links

We introduced this topic in Assurance, where you learnt the basic content of ISA (UK) 315 *Identifying and Assessing the Risks of Material Misstatement through Understanding of the Entity and Its Environment*. In this syllabus you need to consolidate and build on this knowledge.

Examination context

Understanding the entity is a key component of risk assessment. Risk assessment is the subject of Chapter 9, which is a big exam topic.

1 Why?

> **Section overview**
>
> - It is important to understand the client's business:
>   - In order to assess risk
>   - In order to comply with auditing standards

You know from your previous studies and from what has already been said in this Study Manual that assessing risk is very important in assurance engagements.

In general terms, it is clearly impossible to be sure how risky a client may be if you do not understand:

- Who they are
- What they do
- How they do it
- Whether there are any special circumstances (like specific laws and regulations) which govern their business
- The integrity and competence of their staff

If you understand a client's business properly you will:

- Be able to assess the skills and competence which the audit team needs
- Be able to plan your audit work so that it is appropriate and efficient
- Be able to assess what controls have been put in place by the client which may reduce the level of control risk
- Be able to assess any significant risks which need special attention
- Be able to perform analytical procedures
- Comply with professional requirements (the reports by the ICAEW, ICAS and ICAI to the UK government about the results of monitoring visits to firms in the last five years have commented, every year, about the need for recording and disseminating knowledge of the business).

Also, assessing risk is compulsory – ISAs (UK) 315 and 330 require it.

Finally, consider **fraud** – understanding the entity may not guarantee that you will uncover a clever, well laid fraud, but not understanding the entity certainly will guarantee that you have very little chance of finding it.

Auditors need to be particularly vigilant during a period of economic downturn and uncertainty, when company directors and accountants may be under pressure to present favourable results by artificially increasing revenues or profits. Whilst a variety of treatments may be permitted by legislation and accepted standards, aggressive earnings management, as this practice is known, is a form of fraud.

2 How?

Section overview

- Understanding of the client's business can be obtained from:
    - External sources of information (such as industry surveys/publications)
    - The firm (permanent files (including previous years' audited financial statements), correspondence files, personnel associated with the engagement in previous years)
    - The client (personnel, correspondence/procedures manuals, watching procedures, current year management accounts)
- Auditors are required to carry out a combination of procedures to understand the business:
    - Inquiries of client personnel
    - Analytical procedures
    - Observation and inspection

It is important to understand where the information comes from.

2.1 External sources

There are reports auditors can look at:

- Credit reference agencies
- Industry surveys
- Industry publications such as trade journals
- The Irish Revenue produces similar information which is available on its website
- Companies House searches.

Remember, for an existing client, assurance staff have a better source of information much closer to home.

2.2 The firm

Remember, the firm should not have taken the client on in the first place if it does not have the competence to service it in line with ethical and professional standards. So, it follows that someone in the firm must know something about the client and its environment. Usually the person who has most knowledge will either be the engagement partner or, for firms dealing with industries where specialist knowledge is required, the industry expert.

It is the firm's responsibility to ensure that audit staff are properly briefed, but it is also the responsibility of each member of the team to ensure he is properly briefed. Team members:

- Read:
    - Last year's file
    - The permanent file
    - The correspondence file
    - The tax file

- Talk to:
    - The partner
    - The manager
    - The tax person
    - Last year's senior
    - The firm's industry specialist

This may appear both obvious and a bit woolly, but it is specifically dealt with in ISA (UK) 315. As you know, there is a requirement for a discussion of the client's business as part of the planning process, and for that discussion to be documented.

You also need to consider your own knowledge and background.

- Have you worked on similar clients before?
- What do you know of the industry?
- How would you expect it to work?

2.3 The client

Then move out to the client:

- Talk to the people responsible for the area you are auditing – the people actually doing the work and their bosses

- Read internal correspondence and minutes of board/committee meetings – you have rights of access, subject to your professional duty of confidentiality

- Read internal audit reports (if there is an internal audit function)

- Observe what goes on around you, how transactions are recorded and how processes are operated

- Look at the website, brochures etc

To be professional, auditors must be wary of ignorance combined with pride. If something is difficult to understand – ask. If it is still difficult, it is possible that you should not be doing the audit, but it is also possible that there is a fraud going on.

You learnt about the specific requirements of ISA (UK) 315 in relation to obtaining the information in your Assurance studies. Remember, you are required to use a combination of the following procedures:

- Inquiry of management and others within the entity
- Analytical procedures
- Observation and inspection

2.4 Summary

Figure 8.1 provides a general summary of how understanding the client's entity can be achieved.

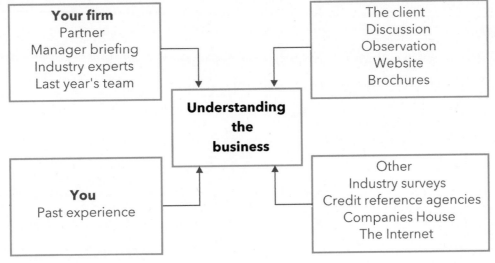

Figure 8.1: Sources of information

Interactive question 1: Sources of information

Requirement

From what sources of information can auditors obtain a knowledge of the entity they are about to audit and the industry in which that entity operates?

See **Answer** at the end of this chapter.

3 What?

Section overview

- The auditors need to understand any aspect of the business which might affect the audit
- ISA (UK) 315 contains a list of potential areas to be understood in paragraph 11

3.1 The basics

If the following nine questions have been answered in sufficient depth, the audit file should contain sufficient evidence that the auditors have satisfied the requirements of ISA (UK) 315 *Identifying and Assessing the Risks of Material Misstatement through Understanding of the Entity and Its Environment.*

- What does the client do?
- What are the characteristics of the industry/environment in which it operates?
- Is it governed by specific laws and regulations, or is it at greater risk than other businesses from the incidence of more general laws and regulations?
- What are the characteristics of its relationships with external parties, shareholders, other stakeholders, trading partners and providers of finance?
- Is it under threat from takeover or lack of finance?
- Are there any dealings with related parties?
- How competent is its management?
- Are suitable systems and controls in place?
- What accounting policies has it adopted?

Figure 8.2 may help.

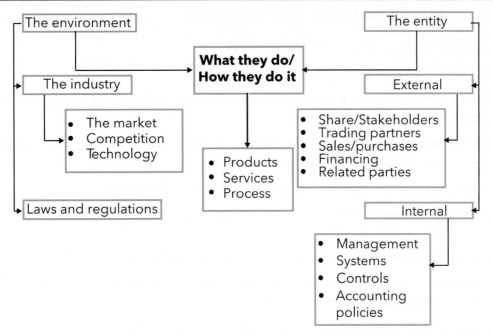

Figure 8.2: What knowledge?

3.2 Laws and regulations

To understand the client, auditors need to have a good understanding of any laws and regulations which have an impact on its operations.

Laws and regulations are considered to be of two types:

- Those which affect the preparation of financial statements
- Those which affect the way the client conducts its business

Clearly the auditor should know about relevant laws and regulations, such as the Companies Act 2006 and IFRSs, which affect the way the financial statements are prepared. The auditor is not expected to be an expert in all the laws and regulations which affect the client, but, it is not quite as simple as this, if a client fails to comply with the laws and regulations which govern its business:

- It will very soon go out of business; and
- This will have a material impact on its financial statements.

It follows, therefore, that if an audit firm has a client in the haulage industry, it cannot simply ignore what the law says about tachographs and vehicle maintenance. If a client runs a restaurant the auditors need to know something of the food hygiene enforcement regime operated by local authorities.

How much knowledge an assurance provider should have and in what depth is another question of risk.

- If the likely impact of non-compliance is assessed as low, auditors will ask management for background information and that will be sufficient.

- If the likely impact is assessed as high, but management has good systems for controlling the risk, auditors will confirm that the systems appear to operate effectively.

- If the risk is high and management appears to do nothing about it…let us simply say it will have a direct impact on audit work.

Paragraph A18 of ISA (UK) 250A gives the following list of indicators of non-compliance:

- **Investigation** by a **government department**

- **Payment of fines or penalties**

- **Payments** for **unspecified services** or loans to consultants, related parties, employees or government employees

- **Sales commissions** or agents' fees that appear excessive in relation to those normally paid by the entity or in its industry or to the services actually received

- **Purchasing** at **prices significantly above** or **below market price**

- **Unusual payments** in **cash**, purchases in the form of cashiers' cheques payable to bearer or transfers to numbered bank accounts

- **Unusual transactions** with companies registered in **tax havens**

- **Payments for goods or services made other than to the country from which** the goods or services **originated**

- **Payments without proper exchange control documentation**

- **Existence** of an **information system** that **fails**, whether by design or by accident, to **provide adequate audit trail** or sufficient evidence

- **Unauthorised transactions** or improperly recorded transactions

- Adverse **media comment**

3.3 Fraud

ISA (UK) 240 *The Auditor's Responsibilities Relating to Fraud in an Audit of Financial Statements* stresses that auditors have no responsibility for the prevention and detection of fraud as such – that is management's job, but fraud can have a material impact on financial statements, so it becomes a part of audit after all!

Remember, the ISA (UK) makes a crucial distinction between two types of misstatements arising from fraud:

- Misstatements arising from fraudulent financial reporting
- Misstatements arising from misappropriation of assets

In understanding the client's business there are some key questions that need to be asked:

- Can the figures be manipulated and if so how?
- Which areas are most susceptible to manipulation?
- Can assets be misappropriated and if so how?
- Which areas are most at risk?

3.4 Service Organisations

Increasingly, companies are outsourcing processes and operations to third party organisations. Some examples of activities that may be outsourced are:

- information processing
- maintenance of accounting records
- facilities management

ISA (UK) 402 *Audit Considerations Relating to an Entity Using a Service Organisation* highlights the issues that must be considered if the auditor discovers during the planning phase of the audit that the client (the user) has outsourced, for example, its payroll accounting function. In broad terms the main requirements are to:

- Obtain an understanding of the services provided by a service organisation, including internal control, specifically:
  - The nature of the services provided by the service organization
  - The nature and materiality of the transactions processed
  - The degree of interaction between the activities of the service organization and those of the company
  - The nature of the relationship between the user entity and the service organization, including the relevant contractual terms
- Consider access to sources of evidence
- Assess the risks arising

The user auditor, in obtaining an understanding of the service organisation's internal controls, may obtain one of the following reports from the auditor of the service organisation:

- A report with the objective of conveying reasonable assurance that includes the service auditor's opinion on management's description of the service organisation's system, control objectives and related controls and the suitability of the design of the controls to achieve the specified control objectives.

- A report as above that also provides the service auditor's opinion on the operating effectiveness of the controls, and a description of the service auditor's tests of the controls and the results thereof.

Interactive question 2: What matters?

Auditors should use their knowledge of the business to assess the risks arising from fraud, error and non-compliance with laws and regulations.

Requirement

What matters should they consider in making this assessment?

See **Answer** at the end of this chapter.

Summary and Self-test

Summary

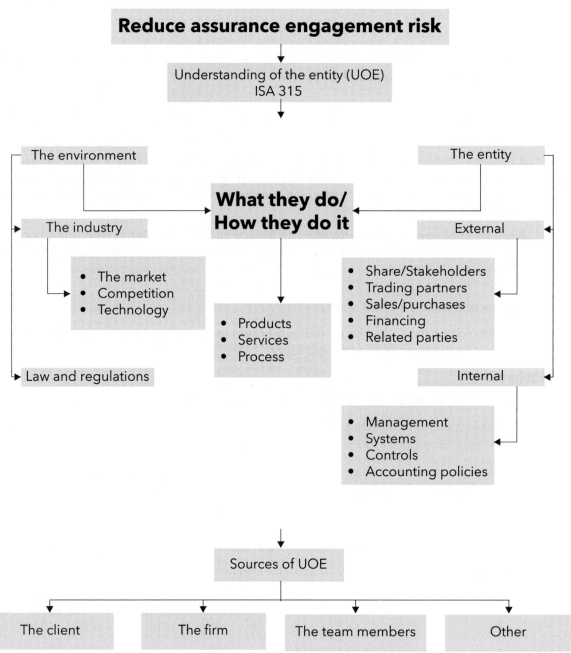

Self-test

Answer the following questions.

1   What key knowledge should an audit firm obtain about its client and why is this understanding of the entity important?   **(3 marks)**

2   G Co is a manufacturing company which has one factory and two warehouse sites. It imports raw materials from Asia.

     What are the key factors the auditors need to consider about G Co and how this may impact their audit?   **(3 marks)**

Now, go back to the Learning outcomes in the Introduction. If you are satisfied that you have achieved these outcomes, please tick them off.

Technical reference

Answers to Interactive questions

Answer to Interactive question 1

- Previous experience with entity and its industry

    - Last year's file/audit team
    - Permanent file
    - Tax file
    - Correspondence file

- Visits to entity's premises and plant facilities

- Discussion with people within entity

- Discussion with other auditors and with legal/other advisers who have provided services to the entity or within the industry (eg, industry specialists)

- Publications related to the industry legislation and regulations that significantly affect the entity, eg, industry surveys

- Industry publications such as trade journals and HM Revenue and Customs publications for the relevant industry

- Documents produced by the entity/entity website

- Companies House searches

Answer to Interactive question 2

Non-compliance (ISA (UK) 250A A18)

- Previous experience

- Incidents which call into question integrity or competence of management or other staff, eg:

    - Investigations
    - Payment of fines/penalties

- Unusual transactions/payments

- Payments for/of

    - Unspecified services/loans
    - Excessive commission

- Unauthorised/improperly recorded transactions

- Accounting system which fails to provide adequate audit trail/sufficient evidence

- Adverse media comment

Fraud/error (ISA (UK) 240 Appendix 3)

- Discrepancies in the accounting records, eg:

    - Incomplete recording of transactions
    - Significant last-minute adjustments

- Conflicting or missing evidence, eg:

    - Missing documents
    - Unexplained items on reconciliations

- Problematic or unusual relationships between the auditor and management, eg:

  - Denial of access to records or delays in producing information
  - Complaints about the conduct of the audit

- Other, eg:

  - Accounting policies at variance with industry norms
  - Frequent, unnecessary changes in accounting estimates

Answers to Self-test

1   **Key knowledge to obtain**

- Nature of the business

- Key personnel and their integrity/competence

- Whether there are any laws or regulations which apply to the entity

- Whether there are any pressures on the directors which may lead them to show the company in a more favourable light than might otherwise be the case – for example

  - Directors' profit related bonuses
  - Cash flow/financing concerns
  - Stock market pressures

- Strength of internal control systems

- Existence of related parties and related party transactions

- Complex account transactions

Why important?

The above knowledge is important in order for the auditor to assess the level of risk associated with the client and the potential likelihood that an incorrect opinion may be given.

2   • As a manufacturing company G Co will hold inventory of raw materials, work in progress and finished goods at the end of the year.

  The auditor will need to consider whether the valuation of work in progress is appropriate given its stage of completion and that only production overheads are included.

- G Co has two warehouse sites.

  The auditor should obtain an understanding as to how G Co ensures all inventory items held are counted only once and how goods moving between sites are dealt with to ensure they are properly recorded.

- G Co imports raw materials.

  Inventory items may well be in transit at the end of the year. The auditor will need to consider when title to the goods passes to G Co in order to assess when the goods should be included in inventory at the year end.

  It is also possible that the raw materials attract import duties and so the auditors should consider whether the cost of raw materials is fairly stated.

CHAPTER 9

Risk assessment

Introduction

Examination context

TOPIC LIST

Summary and Self-test

Technical reference

Answers to Interactive questions

Answers to Self-test

Introduction

Learning outcomes

2   Planning engagements

Students will be able to plan assurance engagements in accordance with the terms of the engagements and appropriate standards.

- Identify the risks arising from, or affecting, a given set of business processes (including risks associated with cloud computing and cyber security) and circumstances and assess their implications for the engagement

- Assess significant business risks (including risks associated with cloud computing and cyber security) identified for their potential impact upon an organisation, in particular their potential impact on performance measurement;

- Identify the components of risk for a specified assurance engagement

- Identify the components of audit risk for a specified audit engagement, including the breakdown of audit risk into inherent risk, control risk and detection risk

- Evaluate the impact of risk and materiality in preparing the audit plan, including the nature, timing and extent of audit procedures

Syllabus links

Risk assessment has already been covered in some detail in the Assurance syllabus. At this Professional level, the key issue is being able to carry out risk assessment, that is, identify and assess, not merely understand the components of risk and be able to identify them.

Examination context

Risk assessment is a very important area for your exam.

1 Business risk

> **Section overview**
>
> - There are three general categories of business risk:
>   - Financial risk
>   - Operational risk
>   - Compliance risk

Business risk was introduced in your Assurance studies.

Definition

Business risk: Is the risk inherent to the company in its operations. It includes risks at all levels of the business. ISA (UK) 315 defines business risk as a "risk resulting from significant conditions, events, circumstances, actions or inactions that could adversely affect an entity's ability to achieve its objectives and execute its strategies, or from the setting of inappropriate objectives and strategies." There are three general categories of business risk:

- **Financial risks** are the risks arising from the financial activities or financial consequences of an operation, for example, cash flow issues or overtrading.

- **Operational risks** are the risks arising with regard to operations, for example, the risk that a major supplier will be lost and the company will be unable to operate.

- **Compliance risk** is the risk that arises from non-compliance with laws and regulations that surround the business, for example a restaurant failing to comply with food hygiene regulations might face fines, enforced closure, legal action from customers and so on.

Directors are required to manage business risks. The Turnbull Report sets out recommendations for business in how to manage those risks.

Business risk management is an area in which assurance can be required. Why? Because the risk that the company accepts has a direct impact on the risk of the investment that anyone purchasing shares in a company (a minority share or a company takeover) or loaning money to a company is making.

However, it is not simply shareholders and lenders that will want assurance in this area. Management might want assurance services to provide an indication of how well they are performing in controlling the risks to the company, to ensure it continues in business, but also as evidence that it is operating efficiently and cost-effectively. Criteria for assurance services could be the Turnbull guidelines, or management's own written policy on risk. Management may employ an internal audit department to (among other things) monitor internal controls or may seek external assistance.

Auditors are interested in business risk because issues which pose threats to the business may in some cases also be a risk of the financial statements being misstated (which is a component of audit risk). For example, if a particular division of a business was threatened with closure, the valuation of all the assets associated with that division would be affected. In more general terms, if an economic downturn puts pressure on a company to meet the expectations of providers of finance, management might be tempted to manipulate the financial statements.

2 Audit risk

Section overview

- There are three components of audit risk:
    - Inherent risk
    - Control risk
    - Detection risk

You have already covered audit risk (the risk of giving an inappropriate opinion in relation to the financial statements) in detail.

Remember that it has three components:

- Inherent risk
- Control risk
- Detection risk

2.1 Inherent risk

Definition

Inherent risk: Is the susceptibility of an assertion to misstatement that could be material, individually or when aggregated with other misstatements, assuming that there were no related internal controls.

In other words, how likely is it that the account balance or transaction will be wrong? And how likely is it that, as a result, the financial statements will be misstated by a material amount? Inherent risk can be analysed on a number of levels which are covered in turn below.

2.1.1 At industry or sector level

Different industries have different levels of inherent risk.

Worked example: Industry level risk

In recent years the banking and financial services sector has been characterised as a high risk sector.

- In 2007 the UK experienced a run on the bank Northern Rock, before the Bank of England stepped in with a rescue loan of approximately £25 billion.

- In the US in 2008 poor liquidity, caused in part by 'sub-prime' mortgage lending, led to the collapse of investment bank Lehman Brothers. The bank was driven to manipulate its statement of financial position in order to mask high levels of borrowing.

- Another investment bank, Goldman Sachs, came under scrutiny for making vast profits from the economic crisis by 'betting' on the collapse of the US housing market.

Governments have been criticised for applying a 'light touch' to regulation in the financial sector and may have to consider imposing tighter controls over this sector in the future.

Remember that the inherent risk attached to different sectors changes over time – for example the so-called dot com boom in the 1990s led to the internet-based sector being regarded as high risk.

2.1.2 At entity level

At entity level there will also be different levels of inherent risk.

Worked example: Entity level risk

For two similar clients A and B, if one of the companies was:

- A takeover target
- Up to its overdraft limit
- Had a major supplier or customer in difficulties

It would clearly be more inherently risky than the other.

Again you should remember that the picture does not remain static.

2.1.3 At balance level

Different balances can also carry different inherent risks.

Worked example: Balance level risk

The inventory at a jewellers, for example might be considered higher risk than the same company's non-current assets, consisting of shopfittings, office equipment and, hopefully, some rather impressive safes and security equipment.

Remember that the inventory itself will still be inherently risky, even though the company may have well thought-out security arrangements. The impact of these falls into the category of 'control risk' which we will revisit in a moment.

2.2 Control risk

Definition

Control risk: Is the risk that a misstatement that could occur in an assertion and that could be material, individually or when aggregated with other misstatements, will not be prevented or detected and corrected on a timely basis by the entity's internal control.

So the key questions are:

- What is management doing to stop things going wrong?
- If measures have been taken, are they effective?

Control risk will be lower where effective control measures are taken. However there will always be control risk due to the limitations of internal controls:

- Cost > benefit
- Routine/non-routine transactions
- Human error
- Management override
- Circumvention by collusion
- Changes in procedures

2.3 Detection risk

Judgements about inherent risk and control risk, depend on the assurance provider's understanding of the client's business and the systems and controls set up by the client's management.

The third component of audit risk – detection risk – depends on matters which are under the assurance provider's control.

Definition

Detection risk: Is the risk that an auditor's procedures will not detect a misstatement that exists in an assertion that could be material, individually or when aggregated with other misstatements.

It is up to the auditor to organise the way the engagement is handled, so that the risk of material misstatement is reduced to acceptable levels.

This will include:

- Ensuring the audit team (including the engagement partner) has the necessary mix and depth of experience and skills

- Devising an audit plan which tackles the audit risks

The audit approach (which we shall look at in Chapter 10) is the way in which the auditor assembles sufficient audit evidence to build up a satisfactory level of audit confidence, and which can come from tests of controls, analytical procedures and tests of details.

Because the auditor cannot check every transaction, audit work is carried out on a test basis. The auditor will select a sample.

The possibility that the opinions you form, perfectly validly, from the results of your sample, are different from those you would have formed if you had been able to examine the whole population is called **sampling risk.**

Non-sampling risk is the possibility of coming to the wrong conclusion about the financial statements for any other reason, for example:

- Lack of understanding of the nature of your client's business
- Use of invalid sampling techniques
- Failure to investigate a particular class of assets, liabilities or transactions

3 Assessing the risks of material misstatement

Section overview

- The best way to learn the skill of identifying and assessing risk of misstatement is to practice doing it in exam questions.

Try the interactive questions that follow.

Interactive question 1: Assessing the risks of material misstatement

Your firm has recently been appointed auditor of Trendy Products Ltd, a wholesaler of clothing and fashion accessories geared to the younger market. You are responsible for planning the audit, and have obtained the following background information.

The company imports most of its goods from manufacturers in the Far East. The suppliers issue invoices in dollars, payable within 30 days. The finance director uses a mixture of forward exchange contracts and spot purchases of dollars to pay these suppliers.

Most of the company's customers are small retailers. However, the company has increased its sales by 50% in the last quarter due to a new contract to supply a large retailer. In order to secure this new business, credit terms had to be relaxed from the standard 30 days to 60 days for this customer.

As a result of this expansion the company is finding it difficult to stay within its overdraft limit and is currently negotiating with the bank to increase the facility.

The company recently upgraded its PC-based modular purchases, sales and nominal ledger systems to an integrated system. The accounting package was supplied by a software company which had recently commenced trading.

The software supplier assisted the company with the changeover from the old system to the new. As a result management decided that there was no need to involve the previous auditor or to have a parallel run.

Mrs Evans is solely responsible for the input of data, but due to the changeover she is several weeks behind with her work. She hopes to be up-to-date by the time of the audit as she intends to work overtime to clear the backlog.

The company has introduced an incentive scheme under which the directors are entitled to a bonus on achieving a certain level of profit. The bonus will be paid 30 days after the audited accounts are available.

Requirements

Identify the factors that impact on audit risk in respect of the above matters, and state what effect these would have on audit procedures.

You should set out your answer in a two column format using the headings 'Risk factor' and 'Effect on audit procedures'.

See **Answer** at the end of this chapter.

4 Significant risks

Section overview
- Significant risks are referred to in ISA (UK) 315
- Significant risks are items that are unusual or one-offs

ISA (UK) 315 refers to what it calls significant risks.

Definition

A **significant risk**: Is a risk of material misstatement that, in the auditor's judgement, requires special audit consideration.

These are usually items that are unusual or one-offs.

Worked example: Significant risks

- Property purchases and sales
- Acquisition and disposal of businesses
- Decision to factor receivables
- Potential sale of the business
- Diversification into new sectors

Of course, remember that what is unusual for one company is not necessarily unusual for another. Hence, we are reminded of the importance of knowledge of the particular business being audited.

5 Documentation

Section overview

- ISAs (UK) 315 and 330 contain a number of requirements regarding documentation

You know about the need for auditors to document their audit work from your Assurance studies. ISAs (UK) 315 and 330 contain a number of requirements about documentation, and we shall briefly run through those here.

The following matters should be documented:

- The discussion among the audit team concerning the susceptibility of the financial statements to material misstatements, including any significant decisions reached

- Key elements of the understanding gained of the entity including the elements of the entity and its control specified in the ISA (UK) as mandatory, the sources of the information gained and the risk assessment procedures carried out

- The identified and assessed risks of material misstatement

- Significant risks identified and related controls evaluated

- The overall responses to address the risks of material misstatement

- Nature, extent and timing of further audit procedures linked to the assessed risks at the assertion level

- If the auditors have relied on evidence about the effectiveness of controls from previous audits, conclusions about how this is appropriate

Summary and Self-test

Summary

Self-test

Answer the following questions.

1   As part of the audit planning for a client the auditor has evaluated the components of audit risk, namely, control risk, detection risk and inherent risk.

    His tests of controls reveal deficiencies in the operation of the system of internal control, and he is now reassessing the risks to the audit.

    Since control risk has increased, describe the effect of this on the other components of risk.

2   What is the meaning and implication of high inherent risk?

3   What is the meaning and implication of high detection risk?

4   If an auditor decides that an acceptable level of audit risk is 5%, what does this mean?

5   Auditors should plan and perform their audit procedures recognising that fraud and error may materially affect the financial statements.

    Give four examples of indicators in a business that the risk of fraud and error may be high.

6   Earthmovers Ltd is a civil engineering company that provides a pipe-laying service to the energy, water and telecommunications industries. It uses much heavy plant and machinery, and is subject to the strict provisions of health and safety at work regulations.

    Identify the risks to which breaches of these regulations could expose the company, and the implications for the audit in the event of such breaches.

Exam-style questions

7   **Shades Ltd**

    You are planning the audit of Shades Ltd for the year ending 30 June 20X9. The principal activities of the company are the manufacture and distribution of a range of window blind systems and of the component parts for window blinds. Approximately 50% of revenue is generated from overseas customers.

    During your preparation for the planning meeting with the finance director, the following matters have been highlighted as significant.

(i)   Operating results

The company has had a successful year to date with revenue, gross and operating margins up on the previous year.

	10 months to 30 April 20X9 £'000	10 months to 30 April 20X8 £'000	Year to 30 June 20X8 £'000
Revenue	22,656	19,597	22,557
Cost of sales	13,367	12,472	14,313
Gross profit	9,289	7,125	8,244
Operating expenses	4,531	4,115	4,732
Operating profit	4,758	3,010	3,512
Gross profit margin	41%	36%	37%
Operating profit margin	21%	15%	16%

Inventories at 30 April 20X9 were £4.3 million compared with £3.6 million at 30 April 20X8 and £3.4 million at 30 June 20X8.

(ii)   New computer system

During the year the company replaced its accounting software with a fully integrated standard package modified by the supplier to the company's requirements.

(iii) Incentive scheme

During the year the company introduced an incentive scheme under which the executive directors are entitled to a bonus based on pre-tax profits. The bonus will be paid thirty days after the audited accounts are available.

Requirement

In respect of the above, identify and explain the potential audit risks and indicate the matters you would discuss with the finance director at your planning meeting.

(20 marks)

Now, go back to the Learning outcomes in the Introduction. If you are satisfied you have achieved this outcome, please tick it off.

Technical reference

Answers to Interactive questions

Answer to Interactive question 1

Risk factor	Effect on audit procedures
• This is a new audit appointment. New appointment increases detection risk due to lack of cumulative/prior knowledge from previous audits.	• Accounting systems and internal controls need to be ascertained. • Current period audit work should have regard to the opening balances and comparatives. ISA (UK) 510 and ISA (UK) 710 will assist the auditor.
• Trendy Products Ltd operates in the fashion industry. The nature of the industry contributes to high inherent risk, as clothes and accessories do not stay in fashion and year end allowances to reduce inventory to NRV may be inadequate.	• Evaluate inventory count instructions for procedure to identify obsolete items. • Review post year-end order book to establish adequacy of allowances to reduce inventory to NRV.
• Most purchases are imported and paid for in dollars. Inherent risk is increased by exposure to dollar fluctuations.	• Any gains and losses on dollar transactions/year-end balances should be taken to the statement of profit or loss and monetary items should be translated at the year-end rate.
• Economic dependence on a principal customer. Pressure from the new customer may increase inherent risk.	• Having expanded to accommodate this customer, ensure the going concern assumption remains appropriate if the new contract is terminated.
• The company is currently renegotiating its overdraft. Deterioration of cash flows increases going concern risk, which will be made worse if the overdraft is withdrawn.	• The auditor should review management assessment of going concern. • The effect on liquidity ratios, debtor days etc should be calculated and actions to remedy the cash flow problems discussed with directors.

• The bank may seek to place reliance on the audited accounts before negotiations are finalised.
 	
This increases risk as management have a motive to manipulate the accounts.
	• Particular attention should be given to:
	  – Bank overdraft/creditor cut-off
	  – Most likely areas of misstatement and significant areas where judgement is involved, eg, provisions
	  – Impact of potential audit adjustments on key ratios
	
	• If a satisfactory outcome to the negotiations is not reached before the audit is completed, a qualification is likely.

Risk factor	Effect on audit procedures
• The software company being used has only recently commenced trading. Inherent risk may be increased by the inexperience of the software company.	• The level of audit testing of the new system is likely to be higher than for an accounting package with a good track record.
• There is a potential risk that data transfer was inaccurate or incomplete. If any significant problems with the changeover are encountered then, in the absence of a parallel run, proper accounting records may not have been kept.	• The lack of proper accounting records may need referring to in the auditor's report.
• There is a backlog of data input. Human error is more likely if overtime working is excessive, therefore inherent risk is increased.	• Cut-off should be carefully reviewed as errors are more likely if data processing is not up-to-date at the year end.
• The introduction of the incentive scheme may cause management to overstate the profit.	• Extended checks and/or increased sample sizes to look for potential understatement of liabilities and expenses, and overstatement of assets and income.

Audit risks	Matters to discuss
Gross profit increase • Gross profit may be overstated as a result of items in transit to overseas customers being included in both year end inventories and revenue purchases being understated.	• The reasons for the increase this period. • Procedures used to ensure that transactions just before or after the year end are recorded in the correct accounting period. • How adequate provision is made for purchases, particularly those invoiced post year end.
Operating profit increase • Operating expenses may be understated due to recording being incomplete and the client failing to fully accrue for such expenses.	• The procedures for ensuring the completeness of recording expenditure. • The methods used for identifying and making adequate provision for accruals.
Increasing inventory values • The company may have difficulty in selling certain lines of inventory if items are made to customer specification and then orders cancelled. Such lines may be overvalued in the financial statements.	• The proportion of lines of inventory made specifically to order. • The adaptability of such lines in the event of order cancellations. • The anticipated future revenue from sales of the type of blinds. • The level of advanced orders received.
Change in accounting system • Misstatements may increase as a result of information being lost or incorrectly transferred from the old to new systems.	• The procedures used to ensure that all accounting information was correctly transferred from old to new systems. • The type of changeover which was used eg, parallel running, stepped changeover direct changeover.
New computer system • Modifications to the new computer software may reduce its reliability. This, together with the relative unfamiliarity of client staff with the new system, will increase the risk of errors arising.	• The extent and nature of any problems being experienced with the new system. • The extent of training and system support given to staff operating the new system. • The criteria used to choose the new system and the reason for the change.

CHAPTER 9

Audit risks	Matters to discuss
Bonus scheme • The scheme provides an incentive for directors to overstate income and understate expenditure.	• The nature of any conditions attached to the bonus. • The effect on profits since the introduction of the scheme. • The anticipated level of bonus payable this period.
Disclosure • The audited accounts may fail to properly disclose such bonuses within directors' emoluments. • Similarly, failure to properly include such bonuses may result in current liabilities being understated.	• The proposed treatment and disclosure of the directors' bonuses within the financial statements. • Whether the directors are aware of the auditors' legal duty to make good any disclosure lapses in this area in the auditor's report.

CHAPTER 10

Audit approach

Introduction

Examination context

TOPIC LIST

Summary and Self-test

Technical reference

Answers to Interactive questions

Answers to Self-test

Introduction

Learning outcomes

2   Planning engagements

Students will be able to plan assurance engagements in accordance with the terms of the engagements and appropriate standards

- Assess the impact of risk and materiality on the engagement plan, including the nature, timing and extent of assurance procedures, for a given organisation ☐

- Determine an approach appropriate for an engagement for a specified organisation which addresses: ☐

    - possible reliance on controls (including those within IT systems)

    - using the work of internal audit

    - using the work of other experts

    - using the work of another auditor

    - probable extent of tests of controls and of substantive procedures, including analytical procedures and data analytics

    - the nature and extent of client-generated information, including reliability of clients' reports and underlying system-generated data including the use of client-generated information in data analytics routines

    - the probable number, timing, staffing and location of assurance visits

Syllabus links

This area was introduced, in connection with evidence, in Assurance.

Examination context

In the exam, you could be asked to identify risks and then justify an approach towards those risks.

1 Responding to the risk assessment

Section overview

- The auditor must formulate an approach to assessed risks of material misstatement
- Overall responses include issues such as emphasising to the team the importance of professional scepticism, allocating more staff, using experts or providing more supervision
- The auditor must also determine further audit procedures to address the risks of material misstatement
- There are three sources of audit confidence: tests of controls, tests of details and analytical procedures
- Remember, some substantive procedures (that is, tests of details and/or analytical procedures) must be carried out

The main requirement of ISA (UK) 330 *The Auditor's Responses to Assessed Risks* is that in order to reduce audit risk to an acceptably low level, the auditor should determine overall responses to assessed risks at the financial statement level, and should design and perform further audit procedures to respond to assessed risks at the assertion level.

In other words, having assessed the risks of material misstatements in the financial statements, the auditor has to **plan the work** that will be carried out **to ensure** that **he can draw a conclusion** about whether the financial statements give a true and fair view, that is, that any material misstatements have been identified and amended if necessary.

1.1 Overall responses

Overall responses to risks of material misstatement will be changes to the general audit strategy or re-affirmations to staff of the general audit strategy. For example:

- Emphasising to audit staff the need to maintain professional scepticism
- Assigning additional or more experienced staff to the audit team
- Using experts, the work of internal auditors or other auditors
- Providing more supervision on the audit
- Incorporating more unpredictability into the audit procedures

The evaluation of the control environment that will have taken place as part of the assessment of the client's internal control systems will help the auditor determine whether they are going to take a substantive approach (focusing mainly on substantive procedures) or a combined approach (tests of controls and substantive procedures).

1.2 Responses to the risks of material misstatement at the assertion level

The ISA (UK) says that "the auditor shall design and perform further audit procedures whose **nature**, **timing** and **extent** are based on and are responsive to the assessed risks of material misstatement at the assertion level". Nature refers to the purpose and the type of test that is carried out. The extent of audit tests is determined by sampling, which we covered in our Assurance studies. The auditors must also have to consider the timing of tests – before the year end or after, or possibly, continuously throughout the year using CAATs.

1.3 Sources of audit confidence

To reduce the level of risk that the financial statements might be wrong, the auditors have to build up audit confidence based on sufficient appropriate audit evidence.

We have looked at the nature and sources of audit evidence in your Assurance studies. In summary, there are three sources of audit confidence.

Figure 10.1: Sources of audit confidence

You know what internal controls are from your Assurance studies.

To derive audit confidence from the client's controls, auditors have to ascertain them (by enquiry), document them and then test them to make sure that:

- They operate in the way they think they do (by walkthrough procedures); and
- They are effective (by tests of controls).

You covered the nature of controls and their strengths and weaknesses in your Assurance studies. We will revisit some key issues in section 2 of this chapter.

During the planning process the audit team decides on the use of these sources to give sufficient audit confidence and what the mix should be.

The audit plan will record the approach to be used as decided on by the audit team.

1.4 Additional guidance

ISA (UK) 501 *Audit Evidence – Specific Considerations for Selected Items* illustrates how the principles of ISA (UK) 500 *Audit Evidence* should be applied to certain items in the financial statements. Two areas that it covers are particularly relevant in this syllabus:

- Attendance at physical inventory counting
- Litigation and claims

You will have looked at the procedures normally performed at an inventory count in your studies for the Assurance paper.

Worked example: Audit of inventories

You could audit inventory by counting it all and working out what it is worth by exhaustive checking to invoices etc – **reliance on tests of details** (substantive approach).

Alternatively you could look at the client's systems for recording purchases and revenue, for checking goods into the warehouse, and for ensuring security of the warehouse site. Should you conclude that the systems are sound you may wish to place **reliance on controls.**

You could also look at the breakdown of inventory over the last few years, consider the normal inventory levels the client carries and their relationship to purchases and cost of sales, the basis for overhead and labour recovery, and you might think that, all in all the inventory figure looks about right – **reliance on analytical procedures.**

In practice you are likely to do a combination of all three. Auditing standards require you to carry out some substantive procedures (tests of details or analytical procedures) so **placing reliance solely on controls is not an option.** Carrying out some controls testing reduces the amount of substantive testing to be carried out but it does not eliminate the need for substantive tests. The precise mix changes depending on the nature of the client:

- For a small scale client at a single location it may be just as efficient to observe the inventory count and to carry out a number of test counts as it is to spend a great deal of time evaluating the system, or calculating ratios. You will be relying on controls such as the reliability of the inventory checkers to a limited extent, but you will also have a good deal of confidence about the final figure deriving from the substantive work you have done; ie, your own test counts

- For a large national building supplies company with a large number of depots, you are likely to rely to a greater extent on your assessment of controls and analytical review.

Interactive question 1: Reliance on controls

Requirement

List the factors that you would consider in deciding at the planning stage of the audit whether to seek to rely on internal controls as part of the audit.

See **Answer** at the end of this chapter.

2 Reliance on controls

Section overview

- The auditors carry out tests of controls when:
    - They are intending to rely on controls; or
    - They are unable to derive sufficient evidence from substantive procedures.

- In summary, ISA (UK) 330 says that if auditors want to rely on a control:
    - They have to test it
    - The have to obtain evidence that it is effective
    - They have to obtain evidence that it operated throughout the period under review
    - They have to flex their approach in accordance with the nature of the control and the risk it is seeking to mitigate

ISA (UK) 330 says auditors need to carry out tests of controls under two sets of circumstances:

- When they are intending to rely on controls to reduce audit risk; or
- When they are unable to derive sufficient evidence from substantive procedures.

The type of testing will depend on the nature of the control.

The client's procedures for authorising expenditure, for example could take many forms:

- There could be an approval box in a grid rubber stamped on invoices – auditors would check that the stamp had been applied and the box signed or initialled on a sample of invoices

- Expenditure over a certain level may need to be approved by the board, or by a committee – auditors would check the minutes of the relevant meetings

- The client may operate a budgetary control system, where managers have responsibility for particular projects, and where the board, or a committee will periodically review actual performance against budget

Procedures here may be more difficult to devise.

- The auditors could review the minutes of the relevant meetings
- The auditors could select a sample of projects and make actual/budget comparisons and then follow up to see what the client did in response to any overruns
- The auditors could attend the relevant meetings and observe how they are conducted – but would need to be careful about whether the auditors' presence at the meeting will affect the way the meeting is conducted

In respect of IT controls the following questions are relevant.

- How do these operate?
- Is the auditor justified in assuming that they function properly?
- If a client uses a recognised accounting package such as QuickBooks or Sage Line 50, is the auditor justified in assuming that, for example VAT will be calculated correctly and that control accounts will be updated properly?

It may be necessary to use Computer Assisted Audit Techniques (CAATs) to prove these assumptions. We considered testing controls in Assurance.

Auditors will need to determine whether controls are manual or automated, and to adapt their approach accordingly. Manual controls, such as the physical counting of inventory, can be verified by auditor presence during the counting. An automated continuous inventory checking system, on the other hand, will need testing of the computer program that produces the information output.

It should be noted that not all entities will have systems of internal control in place, and in such circumstances only a fully substantive audit approach is possible.

Interactive question 2: Reliance on internal controls

Requirement

In the course of planning an audit several internal controls in the company's systems have been identified. List the conditions that each control must satisfy if it is to be relied upon in reducing the extent of substantive procedures to be performed.

See **Answer** at the end of this chapter.

Interactive question 3: Bix plc

You are the senior auditor in charge of the audit of Bix plc, a manufacturing company. You have been talking with the payroll supervisor who has commented on the strength of the company's payroll internal control system. She has assumed that this internal control system guarantees the completeness, accuracy and validity of the payroll accounting records.

Requirements

(a) State whether you agree with the supervisor's assumption that an internal control system can guarantee the completeness, accuracy and validity of the records, supporting your answer by using examples from a payroll system.

(b) The supervisor has also asked you to explain some internal control terminology which she does not understand.

Explain the meaning of the following terms, using payroll examples different from those you have given above.

(i) Segregation of duties

(ii) Approval and control of documents

See **Answer** at the end of this chapter.

3 Substantive approach

Section overview

- Substantive procedures constitute tests of details and/or analytical procedures
- Auditors always carry out a number of substantive procedures
- The number of substantive procedures carried out will depend on the level of risk, the amount of reliance on controls and the results of controls testing

As you know, substantive procedures fall into two categories: analytical procedures and tests of details.

The auditor must always carry out substantive procedures on material items.

ISA (UK) 330 says "irrespective of the assessed risk of material misstatement, the auditor shall design and perform substantive procedures for each material class of transactions, account balance and disclosure".

In addition, the auditor **must** carry out the following substantive procedures:

- Agreeing the financial statements to the underlying accounting records
- Examining material journal entries
- Examining other adjustments made in preparing the financial statements

The auditor must determine when it is appropriate to use which type of substantive procedure.

Analytical procedures tend to be appropriate for large volumes of predictable transactions (for example, wages and salaries). **Other procedures (tests of details)** may be appropriate to gain information about account balances (for example, inventories or trade receivables), particularly verifying the assertions of existence and valuation. Substantive procedures were covered in detail in your studies for Assurance where you studied the principles of audit evidence outlined in ISA (UK) 500 *Audit Evidence* as well as specific procedures such as those described in ISA (UK) 505 *External Confirmations*.

Tests of details rather than analytical procedures are likely to be more appropriate with regard to matters which have been identified as **significant risks**, but the auditor must determine procedures that are specifically responsive to that risk, which may include analytical procedures. Significant risks are likely to be the most difficult to obtain sufficient appropriate evidence about.

How much substantive testing is carried out will depend on:

- whether the auditor wants to rely on controls in the first place (in which case substantive testing might be reduced)
- whether controls testing reveals that controls can be relied on (if they cannot, the auditors will have to increase substantive testing)

In the Assurance paper you studied ISA (UK) 530 *Audit Sampling* and saw how sample sizes are determined based on the assessment of audit risk. Improvements in technology and the use of audit data analytics can enable auditors to perform testing on 100% of a population, and can also be used to monitor transactions on a more frequent or even continuous basis.

3.1 Data analytics

The FRC's Thematic Review *The Use of Data Analytics in the Audit of Financial Statements* provides the following definition:

Definition

"**Data Analytics**, when used to obtain audit evidence in a financial statement audit, is the science and art of discovering and analysing patterns, deviations and inconsistencies, and extracting other useful information in the data underlying or related to the subject matter of an audit through analysis, modelling and visualisation for the purposes of planning and performing the audit."

(FRC, Thematic Review, January 2017)

Data analysis has been used in the business and other sectors for some time. It was originally developed by technology firms for the purposes of data mining and modelling, especially in banking and retail. More recently data analytics is being seen as a practical way for auditors to approach IT issues and the complex uses of data, especially in large organisations.

Auditors have been using computer-assisted audit techniques (CAATs) since the days when their audit clients started computerising their accounting systems. Such CAATs tended to be entity-specific and were therefore not widely used as a general audit tool. Standard tools were first developed in 2005 to enable auditors to test journal entries as part of their responsibilities in relation to fraud under ISA (UK) 240.

Data analytics is now also seen as a means of improving audit quality, from its use in the risk assessment process through to the testing of controls and substantive procedures including analytical procedures. The quality of audit information is also enhanced through the use of graphics and other means to visualise the results of audit procedures. In addition, audit procedures can be carried out on a continuous basis rather than being concentrated at the year end.

ISAs are based on the systems based approach to audit, which seeks to obtain audit evidence by placing reliance on internal controls rather than on carrying out extensive substantive testing. The emergence of the use of data analytics in audit engagements, especially by the larger firms, enables 100% checking to take place, thereby eliminating sampling risk.

An example of how data analytics can be used is in the analysis of journals to show, for example:

- Year on year comparisons
- The number of manual input vs system-generated journals
- Identifying who is raising journals and when
- Activity identifying potential fraud risk

The use of data analytics has the potential to transform the way in which audits are carried out for the better, but there are some negative impacts that need to be addressed:

- The cost of setting up the infrastructure can be prohibitive, especially for smaller firms
- The quality of the underlying data is crucial
- Staff need training in the new skills needed to manipulate data and to interpret the results
- Ensuring the security of client and audit data

You can read more in the ICAEW publication *Data analytics for external auditors*, which can be viewed on the ICAEW website.

3.1.1 Commonly performed data analytics routines

The ICAEW report lists the following routines that auditors can perform when carrying out risk analysis, transactions and controls testing, and analytical procedures, or to support judgements and to provide insights. Many routines can be carried out with little or no management involvement, which enhances the independence of the evidence or information obtained.

- Comparing the last time an item was bought with the last time it was sold, for cost/NRV purposes.

- Inventory ageing and how many days inventory is in stock by item.

- Receivables and payables ageing and the reduction in overdue debt over time by customer.

- Analyses of revenue trends split by product or region.

- Analyses of gross margins and revenues, highlighting items with negative margins.

- Matches of orders to cash and purchases to payments.

- 'Can do did do testing' of user codes to test whether segregation of duties is appropriate, and whether any inappropriate combinations of users have been involved in processing transactions.

- Detailed recalculations of depreciation on fixed assets by item, either using approximations (such as assuming sales and purchases are mid-month) or using the entire data set and exact dates.

- Analysis of capital expenditure v repairs and maintenance.

- Three-way matches between purchase/sales orders, goods received/despatched documentation and invoices.

The FRC's Thematic Review identified the use in the audit market of data analytics to:

- Analyse all transactions in a population, stratify that population and identify outliers for further examination

- Reperform calculations relevant to the financial statements

- Match transactions as they pass through a processing cycle

- Assist in segregation of duties testing

- Compare entity data to externally obtained data

- Manipulate data to assess the impact of different assumptions

(FRC, Thematic Review, January 2017)

The use of data analytics means that procedures can be performed much more quickly and also, more significantly, to a higher standard. The extent to which this activity contributes to improvements in audit quality is largely dependent on the skills and judgement applied to analysing and drawing conclusions from the results obtained.

3.1.2 Data analytics and audit quality

The FRC's Thematic Review noted that potential improvements in audit quality provide a key driver to audit firms when using data analytics. These improvements include:

- Deepening the auditor's understanding of the entity

- Facilitating the focus of audit testing on the areas of highest risk through stratification of large populations

- Aiding the exercise of professional scepticism

- Improving consistency and central oversight in group audits

- Enabling the auditor to perform tests on large or complex datasets where a manual approach would not be feasible

- Improving audit efficiency

- Identifying instances of fraud

- Enhancing communications with audit committees

(FRC, Thematic Review, January 2017)

Interactive question 4: Substantive testing

King Ltd is a new audit client of your firm. The finance director has attended a seminar on 'Understanding how your auditors work', and has come away convinced that you will be able to rely on the internal controls within the company to reduce the overall amount of work done.

Requirement

Identify the circumstances in which this approach may not be possible, leading you to undertake full substantive testing.

See **Answer** at the end of this chapter.

Interactive question 5: Hydra Ltd

Your firm acts as auditor to Hydra Ltd, which manufactures and bottles non-alcoholic drinks in the UK under licence from a Swiss company.

Hydra Ltd has two products only: 'Eau Vital', a sparkling cold drink made from fruit juices, herbal extracts and mineral water, and 'Glowvine', which is to be served hot, made from grape juices, herbs and spices.

Royalties are payable to the Swiss company, which is not related to Hydra Ltd, at the rate of 20p per bottle of Eau Vital or Glowvine sold. Royalties are included in cost of sales, and Hydra Ltd expects to make an average mark-up on total cost of 150% for Eau Vital and 120% for Glowvine.

To reflect environmental concerns the customer is charged a deposit of 10p, which is reimbursed on return of the bottle. This scheme was introduced during the year. The theme of concern for the environment is echoed in Hydra Ltd's advertising, which emphasises the natural ingredients.

The final audit is scheduled to commence in two weeks' time. You have recently received a copy of Hydra Ltd's management accounts, which reflect the position for the current year.

	20X6 £'000	20X5 £'000
Revenue	3,280	1,876
Gross profit	1,940	1,042
Profit from operations	1,345	807

Requirements

(a) Prepare a schedule that indicates the analytical procedures which would form part of your year end substantive procedures. Where relevant, suggest possible reasons for the changes between 20X6 and 20X5.

(b) Explain what impact the new scheme involving deposits on bottles will have on the audit of liabilities at the year end.

See **Answer** at the end of this chapter.

4 Use of the work of others

Section overview

- External auditors may make use of work internal audit have done when carrying out their own external audit procedures
- External auditors may make use of the work of an auditor's expert when carrying out audit procedures
- Auditors of a group have a duty to report on the truth and fairness of group accounts
- Auditors of a group have the right (CA 2006) to require from auditors of subsidiaries the information and explanations they need

4.1 Use of the work of internal audit

ISA (UK) 610 *Using the Work of Internal Auditors* states that as part of their planning procedures, auditors must determine whether or not they wish to use the work of the audit client's internal audit function. While the external auditor has sole responsibility for the opinion expressed, some internal audit work may be helpful to him in forming a decision.

As you learnt in your Assurance Study Manual, the scope and objectives of internal auditing can vary widely. Normally however, internal audit operates in one or more of the following broad areas.

- Review and monitoring internal control systems
- Examination of financial and operating information
- Review of operating activities, eg, economy, efficiency and effectiveness of operations
- Review of compliance with laws and regulations
- Risk management
- Governance

An effective internal audit function may reduce, modify or alter the timing of external audit procedures, but it can **never** eliminate them entirely. Even where the internal audit function is deemed ineffective, it may still be useful to be aware of the internal audit conclusions. The effectiveness of internal audit will have a great impact on how the external auditors assess the whole control system and the assessment of audit risk.

The ISA (UK) says that the external auditor shall determine 'whether the work of the internal audit function … can be used, and if so, in which areas and to what extent' and shall determine 'whether that work is adequate for purposes of the audit'.

4.1.1 Evaluating the internal audit function

The following table is a summary of the factors that the external auditors will take into account when making their assessment of internal audit.

Assessment of internal audit	
Objectivity	Consider the **status** of the function within the entity, who they **report** to, whether they have any **conflicting responsibilities** or **restrictions** placed on their function. Consider also to what extent management acts on internal audit **recommendations**
Competence	Consider whether internal auditors have adequate **resources, technical training and proficiency,** and whether internal auditors possess the **required knowledge** of financial reporting. They will also consider whether the internal auditors are **members of professional bodies**
Systematic and disciplined approach	Consider whether internal audit is **properly planned, supervised, reviewed** and **documented,** whether the function has appropriate **quality control procedures, audit manuals, work programmes** and **documentation**

If any one of the above factors is lacking, the external auditor shall **not** use the work of the internal audit function.

Interactive question 6: Using the work of internal audit

You are currently involved in planning the audit of Midget Ltd. At the beginning of the year that you are auditing, the company set up an internal audit department, and this is the first visit since you were aware of its existence. From your initial discussions with the managing director, you have established that Mr Gnome, the internal auditor, has undertaken a number of assignments across the company, and fed back to the board on his findings.

Requirements

What factors should you take into account when considering whether you can rely on the work undertaken by Mr Gnome and his staff?

See **Answer** at the end of this chapter.

4.1.2 Using the work of internal audit

The **objectives** of internal audit will differ from those of the external auditors. However, some of the **means** of achieving their respective objectives are often **similar**, and so some of the internal auditors' work may be used by the external auditors. External auditors may use internal auditors' work on the following areas:

- Testing of the operating effectiveness of controls
- Substantive procedures involving limited judgement
- Observations of inventory counts
- Tracing transactions through the information system relevant to financial reporting
- Testing of compliance with regulatory requirements
- In some circumstances, audits or reviews of the financial information of subsidiaries

4.1.3 Timing of liaison and co-ordination

All timing of internal audit work should be agreed as early as possible, and in particular how it co-ordinates with the external auditors' work. Liaison with the internal auditors should take place at regular intervals throughout the audit. Information on tests and conclusions should be passed both to and from internal auditors.

4.1.4 Determining the nature and extent of work of the internal audit function that can be used

The ISA (UK) states that, 'As a basis for determining the areas and the extent to which the work of the internal audit function can be used, the external auditor shall consider the nature and scope of the work that has been performed … and its relevance to the external auditor's overall audit strategy and audit plan.'

The evaluation here will consider whether:

- the work was properly planned, performed, supervised, reviewed and documented

- sufficient, appropriate evidence was obtained to enable the internal auditors to draw reasonable conclusions

- conclusions reached are appropriate and reports are consistent with the work performed

The nature, timing and extent of the testing of the specific work of internal auditing will depend upon the external auditor's judgement of the risk and materiality of the area concerned, the preliminary assessment of internal auditing and the evaluation of specific work by internal auditing. Such tests may include examination of items already examined by internal auditors, examination of other similar items and observation of internal auditing procedures.

If the external auditors decide that the internal audit work is not adequate, they should extend their own procedures in order to obtain appropriate evidence.

ISA (UK) 610 does not allow external auditors to use internal audit for 'direct assistance', which is a point of different between the UK and international IAASB ISAs. This means that in the UK, external auditors cannot use internal auditors to directly perform audit procedures (under the direction, supervision and review of the external auditor). This work should instead by done by the external auditors themselves.

Interactive question 7: Extensions plc

Extensions plc is a retailer of fashion accessories. It has revenue of £54 million and 150 shops throughout the United Kingdom. It also has six regional warehouses from which the shops are supplied with goods.

The company has an internal audit department which is based at the company's head office in London. Internal auditors make regular visits to the shops and warehouses.

This is the first year that your firm has acted as auditor for Extensions plc. The partner in charge of the audit has expressed his opinion that the internal audit department might be able to assist the external audit team in carrying out its work.

Requirements

(a) State, with reasons, the information that you would require to make an assessment of the likely effectiveness and the relevance of the internal audit function

(b) Describe four typical procedures that might be carried out by the internal auditors during their visits to the shops and warehouses, and on which you might wish to rely

(c) Assuming that you intend to rely on the work of the internal audit department of Extensions plc, describe briefly the effect this will have on your audit of the company's financial statements.

See **Answer** at the end of this chapter.

4.1.5 Monitoring of internal audit by the audit committee

Where the work of the internal audit function is monitored by the entity's audit committee, the external auditor may wish to review any performance indicators used by the audit committee as part of their monitoring role. Performance indicators for assessing the work of internal audit might include:

- Progress against annual and long-term plans of work to be completed
- Recommendations accepted as a percentage of recommendations made
- Recommendations implemented within a specified time period as a percentage of recommendations accepted
- Total time taken for an audit assignment compared to planned/budgeted time
- Number of reports produced within target dates
- Feedback from users via satisfaction surveys

4.2 Using the work of an expert

Definitions

Expert: Is a person or firm possessing special skill, knowledge and experience in a particular field other than accounting and auditing.

Auditor's expert: Is an individual or organisation possessing expertise in a field other than accounting or auditing, whose work in that field is used by the auditor to assist the auditor in obtaining sufficient appropriate audit evidence. An auditor's expert may be either an auditor's internal expert (who is a partner or staff, including temporary staff, of the auditor's firm or a network firm), or an auditor's external expert (ISA (UK) 620).

Management's expert: Is an individual or organisation possessing expertise in a field other than accounting or auditing, whose work in that field is used by the entity to assist the entity in preparing the financial statements (ISA (UK) 500).

Professional audit staff are highly trained and educated, but their experience and training is limited to accountancy and audit matters. In certain situations it will therefore be necessary to employ someone else with different expert knowledge.

Auditors have **sole responsibility** for their opinion, but may use the work of an expert. An expert may be engaged by:

- A client (management's expert) to provide **specialist advice** on a particular matter which affects the financial statements

- The auditors (auditor's expert) in order to obtain **sufficient audit evidence** regarding certain financial statement assertions

ISA (UK) 620 *Using the Work of an Auditor's Expert* defines an auditor's expert as someone who has expertise in a field other than accounting or auditing including expertise in such matters as:

- **Valuations of complex financial instruments and certain types of assets**, eg, land and buildings, plant and machinery

- **Actuarial calculations of insurance or employee benefit liabilities**

- **Estimation of oil and gas reserves**

- **Valuation of environmental liabilities**

- **Interpretations of contracts, laws and regulations**

- **Analysis of complex or unusual tax compliance issues**

Auditors may also use experts when designing procedures and evaluating the results of procedures performed using data analytics.

The ISA (UK) states that the auditor 'has sole responsibility for the audit opinion expressed, and that responsibility is not reduced by the auditor's use of the work of an auditor's expert'.

4.2.1 Determining the need to use the work of an auditor's expert

Considerations when deciding whether to use an auditor's expert may include:

- Whether management has used a management's expert in preparing the financial statements

- The nature and significance of the matter, including its complexity

- The risks of material misstatement in the matter

- The expected nature of procedures to respond to identified risks, including: the auditor's knowledge of and experience with the work of experts in relation to such matters; and

- The availability of alternative sources of audit evidence

When management has used a management's expert in preparing the financial statements, the auditor's decision on whether to use an auditor's expert may also be influenced by such factors as:

- The nature, scope and objectives of the management's expert's work

- Whether the management's expert is employed by the entity, or is a party engaged by it to provide relevant services

- The extent to which management can exercise control or influence over the work of the management's expert

- The management's expert's competence and capabilities

- Whether the management's expert is subject to technical performance standards or other professional or industry requirements

- Any controls within the entity over the management's expert's work

4.2.2 Competence, capabilities and objectivity of the auditor's expert

Experts used by the auditor must have the necessary competence (nature and level of expertise) capabilities (the time, resources and physical ability to exercise that competence) and objectivity (lack of bias, conflict of interest or the influence of others) for the auditor's purposes. In the case of external experts, the auditor must consider whether any interests or relationships are a potential threat to that expert's objectivity.

Information regarding the above qualities may come from a variety of sources, including:

- Personal experience with previous work of that expert

- Discussions with that expert

- Discussions with other auditors or others who are familiar with that expert's work

- Knowledge of that expert's qualifications, membership of a professional body or industry association, license to practice, or other forms of external recognition

- Published papers or books written by that expert

- The auditor's firm's quality control policies and procedures

The auditor will take into account whether the expert's work is subject to technical performance standards, other professional or industry requirements, ethical standards and other standards of professional bodies, or legislative requirements.

4.2.3 Agreement with the auditor's expert

The nature, scope and objectives of the auditor's expert's work will vary from one assignment to another and these must therefore be agreed between the auditor and the expert, whether the expert is internal or external.

The following circumstances indicate the need for the agreement to be in writing:

- The auditor's expert will have access to sensitive or confidential entity information

- The respective roles or responsibilities of the auditor and the auditor's expert are different from those normally expected

- Multi-jurisdictional legal or regulatory requirements apply

- The matter to which the auditor's expert's work relates is highly complex

- The auditor has not previously used work performed by that expert

- The greater the extent of the auditor's expert's work, and its significance in the context of the audit

The agreement between the auditor and the auditor's external expert may take the form of an engagement letter (as you have seen in your Assurance studies) although this is not the only form that the agreement may take. Where an engagement letter is used ISA (UK) 620 recommends that the following are included:

- Nature, scope and objectives of the auditor's external expert's work
- The respective roles and responsibilities of the auditor and the auditor's external expert
- Communications and reporting
- Confidentiality

4.2.4 Evaluating the adequacy of the auditor's expert's work

Auditors should assess whether the work of the expert is adequate for the auditor's purposes. In order to evaluate the adequacy the auditor may carry specific procedures such as:

- Inquiries of the auditor's expert

- Reviewing the auditor's expert's working papers and reports

- Corroborative procedures such as observing the expert's work and confirmation with third parties

- Discussion with another expert with relevant expertise

- Discussing the auditor's expert's report with management

4.2.5 Using the work of a management's expert

If information to be used as audit evidence has been prepared using the work of a management's expert, the auditor shall:

- Evaluate the competence, capabilities and objectivity or that expert
- Obtain an understanding of the work of that expert
- Evaluate the appropriateness of that expert's work as audit evidence for the relevant assertion

Worked example: Valuation of a commercial building

An expert valuation of a commercial building could be compared to the value of other, similar commercial buildings in estate agents' windows or on the web.

The auditors do **not** have the expertise to judge the assumptions and methods used; these are the responsibility of the expert. However, the auditors should seek to obtain an understanding of these assumptions etc, to consider their reasonableness based on other audit evidence, knowledge of the business and so on.

This may involve discussion with both the client and the expert. Additional procedures (including use of another expert) may be necessary.

4.3 Other auditors (in a group situation)

When an audit firm audits a company that is a parent in a group of companies, they will be responsible for carrying out the audit on that parent company's individual financial statements and also the audit on that parent's group financial statements. The group financial statements are known as consolidated financial statements, defined by IFRS 10 as 'financial statements of a group in which the assets, liabilities, equity, income, expenses and cash flows of the parent and its subsidiaries are presented as those of a single economic entity.' In simple terms this means that the individual statements of each company in a group are combined (subject to adjustments for intra-group transactions) to produce one set of financial statements for the group as a whole.

In respect of the group financial statements, the audit firm may or may not be the auditor for other companies in that group whose financial statements are consolidated into the group financial statements.

ISA (UK) 600 *Special Considerations – Audits of Group Financial Statements (Including the Work of Component Auditors)* provides guidance to the auditor of a group where one or more of the components of that group are audited by other auditors.

Definitions

Component: Is an entity whose financial information is included in the group financial statements.

Component auditors: Are auditors who perform work on financial information related to a component of the group audit.

Group engagement team: Are the auditors with responsibility for performing work on the consolidation process, communicating with component auditors and reporting on the group financial statements.

4.3.1 Responsibility

The group engagement partner is responsible for the audit opinion for the group, and for conducting the audit in accordance with legal and regulatory requirements. The auditor's report on the group financial statements should not therefore contain a reference to component auditors unless such a reference is required by law.

4.3.2 Understanding the Component Auditor

If a group engagement team is planning to request work on the financial information of a component from a component auditor, the team shall obtain an understanding of the following:

- Whether the component auditor understands and will comply with **ethical requirements** and can demonstrate **independence**

- The component auditor's **professional competence**

- Whether the group engagement team will be able to be involved in the work of the component auditor to the extent necessary to obtain **sufficient appropriate audit evidence**

- Whether the component auditor operates in a regulatory environment that actively oversees auditors

If a component auditor does not meet the independence requirements that are relevant to the group audit the group engagement team will need to obtain sufficient appropriate audit evidence relating to the financial information of the component without using the audit work of the component auditor.

4.3.3 Responding to Assessed Risks

ISA (UK) 600 states that "the auditor is required to design and implement appropriate responses to address the assessed risks of material misstatement in the financial statements." It is up to the group engagement team to determine the nature of the work to be done and whether it should be done by the group engagement team or by component auditors.

Where reliance is to be placed on the effective operation of group-wide controls at component level, these controls shall be tested, by either the group engagement team or by the component auditor.

4.3.4 Communication with the Component Auditor

The group engagement team will need to communicate its requirements, such as work to be performed, to the component auditor. Communication includes the following:

- Detail of the work to be performed and the use to be made of that work

- The form and content of communication from the component auditor to the group engagement team

- Request for confirmation that the component auditor will cooperate with the group engagement team

- Ethical and independence requirements

- Materiality levels for the financial information of the component

- Significant risks of fraud and error relating to the group that are relevant to the component auditor

- A list of related parties and a request that the component auditor advises the group engagement team of any other related parties not on the list

The group engagement team will require the component auditor to communicate to them matters relevant to the conclusion on the group audit, including:

- Confirmation that the component auditor has complied with ethical, independence, and professional competence requirements

- Confirmation that the component auditor has complied with the group engagement team's requirements

- Financial information of the component audited by the component auditor

- Information on instances of non-compliance with laws or regulations

- A list of uncorrected misstatements

- Indicators of possible management bias

- Significant deficiencies in component internal control

- Significant matters communicated to those charged with governance including suspected fraud

- Any other matters relevant to the group audit

- Overall findings, conclusions or opinions

4.3.5 Evaluating the sufficiency and appropriateness of audit evidence obtained

The group engagement team is responsible for evaluating communication from the component auditor and discussing any significant matters arising. On the basis of this the group engagement team will decide whether other documentation of the component auditor will need to be reviewed.

Where the work of the component auditor is deemed to be insufficient, the group engagement team will determine what additional procedures need to be performed, and by whom.

The group engagement team needs to ensure that sufficient appropriate audit evidence has been obtained by both its own procedures and those of the component auditor.

Where is has not been possible to obtain sufficient appropriate audit evidence the group engagement partner needs to evaluate the effect on the group audit opinion.

Interactive question 8: Using the work of other auditors

You are the group auditor of Golden Holdings plc, a listed company, which has components in the UK and overseas, many of which are audited by other firms. All components are involved in the manufacture or distribution of metal goods and have the same accounting period as Golden Holdings plc.

Requirement

Outline why you would wish to review the work of the auditors of components not audited by your firm and detail the work you would carry out in that review.

See **Answer** at the end of this chapter.

5 Audit of accounting estimates

Section overview

- Financial statements contain many estimates
- These estimates are often made when there are uncertainties about the outcome of events and involve the use of judgement
- As a result the risk of material misstatements is higher where estimates are involved

5.1 The nature of estimates

Right from the start of your accounting studies you will be aware of some of the main types of estimates. Examples include:

- Allowances for receivables
- Allowances to reduce inventories to net realisable value
- Useful lives for depreciation of non-current assets
- Warranty provisions
- Provisions for losses on lawsuits

The risk of misstatement in these areas is obvious. If management intended to overstate profits, for example, they are much more likely to attempt to reduce the amount of the allowance for receivables than, say, to omit the last week's worth of supplier invoices received in the financial year.

5.2 The audit approach

ISA (UK) 540 *Auditing Accounting Estimates, Including Fair Value Accounting Estimates, and Related Disclosures* emphasises the basic requirement to obtain **sufficient appropriate audit evidence.** The standard goes on to require the auditor to obtain an understanding of the following:

- Financial reporting framework applicable to accounting estimates

- How management identifies transactions, events and conditions that give rise to accounting estimates

- How management makes the accounting estimates and on what data they are based. This includes consideration of:

    - Method used in making the accounting estimate;

    - Relevant controls;

    - Whether management has used an expert;

- The assumptions underlying the accounting estimates;

- Whether there has been or ought to have been a change from the prior period in the methods and, if so, why; and

- Whether and, if so, how management has assessed the effect of estimation uncertainty.

5.3 Evaluation of results

The auditor must assess the reasonableness of estimates in the light of:

- The auditor's understanding of the entity and its environment
- Whether the estimates are consistent with other evidence obtained during the audit

Interactive question 9: Estimated allowances

Requirement

Explain how the auditor would approach the audit of an allowance for receivables.

See **Answer** at the end of this chapter.

6 Practical issues

Section overview

- The audit strategy will also address practical issues such as audit timing, staffing and location

6.1 The audit team

As part of the audit planning process, the right team will need to be selected:

This will depend on matching the need for:

- Experience
- Specialist knowledge
- Ensuring that work is done at the right level

with the risks associated with the audit.

As discussed in Chapter 5, for every engagement there will be an engagement partner who takes overall responsibility for the engagement and who has specific responsibility for:

- Ensuring the firm and the team's competence

- Ensuring the firm and the team's objectivity

- Approving the audit strategy

- Communicating his or her knowledge of the client to the audit team

- Ensuring that staff are briefed and supervised appropriately

- Ensuring appropriate reviews are carried out of staff's work

- Reviewing the financial statements, the key areas and any working papers not otherwise reviewed

There should normally be at least one other person involved on the audit to review the work done.

Beyond this the precise make-up of the team will depend on the scale of the engagement and the different roles can be filled by people with different levels of experience within the firm.

However, most engagements will have a 'senior' or 'in charge' responsible for the day-to-day running of the audit and supervising assistants.

There may well be a 'manager' or 'supervisor' who has more responsibilities for the administration, planning and review of the engagement and would be expected to do less of the detailed testing work than the senior.

Finally there are the assistants who, depending on their experience will take on the execution of the more detailed audit tasks.

The audit strategy should make clear who is responsible for which aspects of the audit, and should strike the difficult balance between:

- Ensuring each member of the team has sufficient experience for the job in hand
- Setting new challenges so that experience can be gained, and
- Cost

6.2 Budgets and deadlines

Audit firms, like any business, are in business to make a profit. The pursuit of profit must not take precedence over professional and quality considerations, nevertheless the audit plan should make perfectly clear:

- When the deadline is
- How much the budget is

6.3 Interim and final audits

Typically much of the systems assessment work and tests of details on the statement of profit or loss will be carried out at the interim stage, with greater focus on the statement of financial position at a final audit.

However, think about a number of factors here:

- What about the statement of profit or loss for the last couple of months of the year?

- If the auditors are relying on controls, were they effective in the period between the interim audit and the year end?

- If the auditors have tested inventory, or receivables at the interim stage, are they happy with the 'roll forward' to the year end?

6.4 Location

As hinted at above, the location that the audit work takes place at will depend on the nature of the client and the risk assessment. Some clients will only have one location, in which case the audit will take place at that location. Other clients may have several locations, and the auditors will have to make judgements about which locations are more risky than others and need the auditor to visit them. It may be necessary to attend all locations that a client has at some stage during the audit.

6.5 Nature of evidence

It will be important to address the practical issue of what sources of evidence the audit firm expects to obtain during the audit. You learnt about the quality of audit evidence in your Assurance Study Manual. Information generated by the client is never as good quality as information generated by the auditor or from third parties. The audit strategy should set out where information should be sought from third parties (such as in respect of receivables or confirmation of a loan).

Summary and Self-test

Summary

Self-test

Answer the following questions.

1 The three sources of audit confidence are:

(i) ....

(ii) ....

(iii) ....

2 It is appropriate to rely solely on controls testing in relation to the existence of inventory.

☐ True

☐ False

3 The auditor must always carry out substantive procedures.

☐ True

☐ False

4 Which of the following will external auditors consider in their assessment of whether to use the work of internal audit?

☐ To whom the internal audit department reports

☐ The technical training of the staff in the department

☐ The fact that the fee will fall if much use can be made of internal audit work

☐ Whether internal audit work is properly documented

5 External auditors will not rely on the work of an expert who works for the entity.

☐ True

☐ False

6 Group engagement teams may refer to the work of component auditors in their report on the group financial statements.

☐ True

☐ False

7 Group engagement teams will not be able to form an opinion on group financial statements if:

A The component auditors are not from the same firm

B They have knowledge of the whole group

C The component auditors do not carry out all the procedures as specified by the group engagement team

D The portion of the financial statements they do not audit is material

8 The minimum ideal number of staff used in an audit is:

A One

B Two

C Three

D Four

Exam-style question

9 **Gasoleum Ltd**

Your firm is the auditor of Gasoleum Ltd which operates 15 petrol stations in and around London. You are the senior in charge of the audit for the year ending 31 July 20X7 and are engaged on the audit planning.

Most of the company's sites are long-established and, as well as supplying fuel, oil, air and water, have a car wash and a shop.

Over the last few years, due to the intense price competition in petrol retailing, the shops have been expanded into mini-markets with a wide range of motor accessories, food, drinks and household products. They also now sell National Lottery tickets.

Point-of-sale PCs are installed in all the petrol stations, linked on-line via a network to the computer at head office. Sales and inventory data are input direct from the PCs.

The company has an internal auditor, whose principal function is to monitor continuously and test the operation of internal controls throughout the organisation. The internal auditor is also responsible for co-ordinating the year end inventory count.

Requirements

Prepare notes for a planning meeting with the audit partner which:

(a) Identify, from the situation outlined above, circumstances particular to Gasoleum Ltd that should be taken into account when planning the audit, explaining clearly why these matters should be taken into account. **(6 marks)**

(b) Describe the extent to which the work performed by the internal auditor may affect your planning, and the factors that could limit the use you may wish to make of his work. **(6 marks)**

(12 marks)

Now, go back to the Learning outcomes in the Introduction. If you are satisfied that you have achieved these outcomes, please tick them off.

Technical reference

Answers to Interactive questions

Answer to Interactive question 1

The factors are:

- The approach that has been taken in previous years

- Whether a substantive approach would be more effective

- The results of walk-through tests on the systems (that is, do the systems operate as the auditor has been lead to believe, if so, it may be possible to rely on internal controls)

- The results of preliminary evaluations of the effectiveness of the controls

- Improvements made to the system of control (perhaps as a result of a management letter in prior years)

Answer to Interactive question 2

The conditions are as follows:

- Whether the controls have operated throughout the year

- Whether the control has been evidenced and tested

- Whether reliance on the control assists audit objectives, that is, whether it is relevant to the validity of a financial statement assertion, such as that revenue is complete

- Whether it is cost-effective to test controls

- Whether the results of tests of controls are satisfactory

Answer to Interactive question 3

(a) **Supervisor's assumptions**

Objectives and limitations

Due to inherent limitations (including human error/misunderstanding, collusion and override), an internal control system can only provide reasonable confidence that internal control objectives (including completeness, accuracy and validity) are met.

(i) **Completeness**

To ensure that all workers who should be paid are included on the payroll

- Payroll expense could be reconciled to production output records

- Management could review exception reports of employees having personnel records but not included on the payroll

However,

Cost/benefit

The expense of setting up computerised personnel records may outweigh the benefit to the company. (Risk is of over payment as employees entitled to pay are likely to bring non-payment to management's attention promptly!)

Changes in conditions

A reduction in the ratio of production to support staff may limit the usefulness of production output records as a basis of comparison.

(ii) **Accuracy**

To prevent errors in payroll deductions:

- Calculations of PAYE, NICs etc can be checked prior to processing

- Non-statutory deductions (eg, pension contributions, union subscriptions) should require prior authorisation in writing

However,

Human error/misunderstanding

Errors in deductions may not be detected, due to fatigue, distraction, misjudgement or misinterpretation.

Non-routine transactions

Systematic checking procedures may be directed at routine deductions (eg, PAYE) rather than non-routine transactions (eg, give as you earn, maintenance payments).

(iii) **Validity**

To ensure that employees are only paid for work done:

- Hours worked per time sheets (or clock cards) can be approved by a departmental manager (or supervisor)

- The duties of payroll preparation and payment should be segregated

However,

Abuse or override

Authorisation could be given for a new employee to be added to the payroll without the proper checks being carried out by the authoriser.

Collusion

The person responsible for paying wages could collude with the person responsible for accounting for wages to perpetrate and conceal a theft of wages.

(b) **Internal control terminology**

(i) **Segregation of duties**

Meaning

Segregation of duties is a factor reflected in the control environment (the overall attitude, awareness and actions of management regarding internal controls in the entity).

If one person has responsibility for the recording and processing of a complete transaction, he may also have the power to falsify the records or to misappropriate money or assets without being discovered.

Separation of these responsibilities will reduce the risk of intentional or unintentional errors occurring.

The functions that should normally be separated include authorisation, execution, custody and recording.

Examples

- Calculations of PAYE and NIC deductions should be reviewed and authorised by the payroll supervisor who is not actually involved in performing the calculations.

- Unclaimed wages should be kept by someone (eg, the cashier) other than the person responsible for recording payroll entries, otherwise there could be a temptation to falsify the figures and pocket some of the wages.

(ii) **Approval and control of documents**

Meaning

Approval and control of documents is a specific control procedure (aimed at preventing or detecting and correcting errors).

Approval is concerned with ensuring that transactions are properly authorised prior to execution.

Control of documents is aimed at ensuring that all, and only valid transactions, are promptly recorded.

Examples

- Overtime pay should be approved by a manager or director prior to payroll preparation, to ensure that employees are paid at authorised rates.

- Clock cards should be batched and control totals established (eg, number of cards, total hours worked, hash total of employee number) prior to submission to payroll department, to prevent (or detect for early investigation) any omissions (or unauthorised insertions).

- The numerical sequence of forms for new joiners should be checked periodically to detect omissions (or unauthorised insertions).

Answer to Interactive question 4

Full substantive testing will be used when:

- The auditor's initial assessment is that controls are not strong
- There is a lack of evidence that controls are in operation
- The controls are tested and results show that the controls are not strong
- It is not cost-effective to test controls

Answer to Interactive question 5

(a)

Analytical procedures	Possible reasons for change
• Analyse revenue per product type by month.	A difference in the rate of increase would indicate a switch from one product to the other. Seasonal variations are expected as Glowvine is largely a winter product and Eau Vital a summer product.
• Analyse gross profit per product type by month.	GP margin has increased from 55.5% to 59.1%. The higher margin indicates a move from Glowvine to Eau Vital (possibly due to a mild winter in 20X5/X6).
• Analyse cost of goods sold per product type by month.	Cost of goods sold only increased by 60.6%, while revenue increased by almost 75%. Again, a possible reason could be the switch from one product to the other. It does seem a disproportionately small increase, especially as royalties are included in cost of goods sold and remain constant per bottle sold, regardless of product. However, recycling of glass bottle returns could account for the slower rate of increase.

Analytical procedures	Possible reasons for change
• Analyse distribution and administrative costs into:	These have increased by 153%, contributing to the fall in net profit margin from 43% to 41%. The increase in these costs could have been caused by:
– Administrative cost (especially deposit scheme)	• Implementation of the deposit scheme (unlikely to account for the whole increase as not operational for the whole year)
– Advertising costs	• Increased advertising costs to promote the deposit scheme and 'environment friendly' nature of the products (this could also have contributed to the increase in revenue)
– Transport costs	• Increased transport costs in proportion to the 75% increase in revenue
– Labour costs	• Increased labour costs, again in proportion to the rise in revenue
• Analysis of nature, valuation and consistency of treatment of closing inventories. Compare with inventories held at end of previous years. The disproportionately smaller increase in cost of goods sold could be caused by an error in the counting or valuation of closing inventories, causing them to be overstated and thus cost of goods sold reduced.	The disproportionately smaller increase in cost of goods sold could be caused by an error in the counting or valuation of closing inventories, causing them to be overstated and thus cost of goods sold reduced.

(b) **Impact of deposit scheme on audit of liabilities**

Liabilities at the 20X6 year end will have increased, as this is the first year in which the scheme has been implemented. This should be evident in analytical procedures on sundry payables.

The amount may be material as the number of bottles sold and not returned per annum could be high.

It is necessary to ascertain and evaluate the client's procedure for recording:

(i)   The number of bottles (or cases) sold
(ii) The number of bottles returned
(iii) The number outstanding

As this is the first year of the scheme there will be no opening liability to provide added assurance.

Consideration should be given to the length of time the client intends to keep the provision in place. It may be that, each year, the previous year's provision can be written back.

Because of the uncertainty in calculating the liability required and the fact that the final figure may rest on an estimate of the number of bottles likely to be returned, the auditor's main concern will be that liabilities are not understated.

The auditor therefore needs to be satisfied that returns are recorded with reasonable accuracy.

Records of returns will be received from retailers (mainly supermarkets and off-licences) and the auditor will need to be satisfied that the client can reasonably rely on these records. Since the retailers will be requesting a refund of money paid by them with the returns, there is a risk that the number of returns may be overstated.

In summary, the principal impact on the audit of liabilities will be:

(i) An additional year end liability in 20X6
(ii) Uncertainty in the calculation of the liability, and therefore
(iii) The risk that this liability may be understated

Answer to Interactive question 6

- The objectivity of the department, including its freedom from conflicting responsibilities and the level of management it reports to. In this case, you know that Mr Gnome reports directly to the board of directors, so the department has an important status in the company. You would also consider whether there is any limitation on the assignments carried out, and to what extent recommendations are acted upon by management.

- The competence of the people carrying out the work. In this case it would be necessary to inquire about the competence of Mr Gnome; for example, is he a qualified accountant? It would also be necessary to identify the other members of the internal audit team (if there are any) and assess their competence as well.

- The application of a systematic and disciplined approach. The external auditors should review the work carried out by the internal auditors to check that it was documented in the first place, and to assess whether it was planned and whether there is evidence of its being supervised and reviewed.

- Communication with external audit. You would need to enquire what arrangements have been put in place to enable internal audit to communicate freely and effectively with external audit.

Answer to Interactive question 7

(a)

Information	Reasons

• The organisational status and reporting responsibilities of the internal auditor and any constraints and restrictions thereon.	• The degree of objectivity is increased when internal audit:
	  – Is free to plan and carry out its work and communicate fully with the external auditor
	  – Has access to the highest level of management.

• Areas of responsibility assigned by management to internal audit, such as review of:
  – Accounting systems and internal controls
  – Implementation of corporate plans
	• Not all areas in which internal audit may operate will be relevant to the external auditor.
	
	(Relevant)
	
	(Not relevant)

Information	Reasons
• Routine tasks carried out by internal audit staff such as authorisation of petty cash reimbursements.	• In these respects staff are not functioning as internal audit (simply as an internal control).

• Internal auditor's formal terms of reference.	• Internal auditor's role will be most relevant where it:
	
	  – Has a bearing on the financial statements
	
	  – Involves a specialization

• Internal audit documentation such as an audit manual and audit plans.	• It is more likely that due professional care is being exercised where the work of internal audit is properly planned, controlled, recorded and reviewed.
• Professional membership and practical experience (including computer auditing skills) of internal audit staff.	• Unless internal audit is technically competent it is inappropriate to place reliance on it.
• Internal audit reports generated and feedback thereon.	• How the company responds to internal audit findings may be regarded as a measure of the department's effectiveness.
• Number of staff, computer facilities and any other resources available to internal audit.	• The effectiveness of internal audit (and hence the reliance placed thereon) will be limited if the department is under-resourced.

(b) Typical procedures (**four** only)

(i) **Inspection of tangible non-current assets**

Assets seen at the warehouses (eg, delivery vehicle fleet) should be noted and subsequently agreed to the fixed asset register maintained at head office (HO). Assets recorded in the register (eg, shop fixtures and fittings) should be selected for inspection prior to visits to ensure their existence.

(ii) **Attendance at inventory counts**

Periodic counts (eg, monthly) should be attended:

– On a rotational basis
– At warehouses and larger shops

to ensure adherence to the company's procedures. Test counts should be made to confirm the accuracy and completeness of the inventory counts.

(iii) **Cash**

Cash counts should be carried out on cash register takings (and petty cash floats) whenever shops (and warehouses) are visited on a 'surprise' basis.

(iv) **Goods despatch**

Internal control procedures should be observed to be in operation, for example, to ensure that all despatches are documented and destined for the company's retail outlets.

(v) **Employee verification**

Payroll procedures are likely to be carried out at HO, warehouses and shops informing HO on a weekly basis of hours worked by employees, illness and holiday etc. However, new employees, especially in the shops (and probably also in the warehouses) will be recruited locally and their details notified to HO.

Internal audit will be able to select a sample of employees from HO records and ensure on their visits to shops and warehouses that these represent bona fide employees.

(c) **Effect on audit**

(i) **Systems documentation**

The accuracy of systems documentation which has been prepared by internal audit need only be confirmed using 'walk-through tests'. This saves time (if the systems documentation is correct) since only copies will be required for the audit file.

(ii) **Tests of controls**

The level of independent testing (ie, by the external auditor) can be reduced where controls have been satisfactorily tested by internal audit, especially if error rates are found to be similar. In particular, attendance at stocktaking at the year end may be limited to those locations with the highest stockholdings.

(iii) **Substantive procedures**

Internal audit's evidence (eg, concerning the existence of tangible non-current assets) will reduce sample sizes for year end verification work. Substantive procedures may also be reduced where the internal audit checks reconciliations (eg, of suppliers' statements to ledger balances, receivables and payables control accounts and bank reconciliations).

Answer to Interactive question 8

Reasons for reviewing the work of other auditors

The main consideration which concerns the audit of all group accounts is that the parent company's auditors are responsible to the members of that company for the audit opinion on the whole of the group financial statements.

It may be stated (in the notes to the financial statements) that the financial statements of certain components have been audited by other firms, but this does not absolve the parent company auditors from any of their responsibilities.

The auditors of a parent company have to report to its members on the truth and fairness of the view given by the financial statements of the company and its components dealt with in the group financial statements. The auditors should have powers to obtain such information and explanations as they reasonably require from the components and their auditors, or from the parent company in the case of overseas components, in order that they can discharge their responsibilities as parent company auditors.

The auditing standard ISA (UK) 600 clarifies how the group engagement team can carry out a review of the audits of components in order to satisfy themselves that, with the inclusion of figures not audited by themselves, the group financial statements give a true and fair view.

The scope, standard and independence of the work carried out by the auditors of components (the component auditors) are the most important matters which need to be examined by the group engagement team before relying on financial statements not audited by them. The group engagement team need to be satisfied that all material areas of the financial statements of components have been audited satisfactorily and in a manner compatible with that of the group engagement team's requirements.

Work to be carried out by group engagement team in reviewing the component auditors' work

(i)   Before commencing the audit the group engagement team needs to provide instructions to the component auditor in the form of an engagement letter which should include the following matters relating to planning the audit work:

- Confirmation that the component auditor will cooperate with the group engagement team

- Timetable for completing the audit

- Dates of planned visits

- Key contacts

- Work to be performed by the component auditor

- Ethical requirements

- Component materiality levels

- Details of related parties

- Work to be performed on intra-group transactions

- Guidance on statutory reporting responsibilities

- Specific instructions for a subsequent events review where required

(ii) Carry out a detailed review of the component auditors' working papers on each component whose results materially affect the view given by the group financial statements. This review will enable the group engagement team to ascertain whether (inter alia):

- An up-to-date permanent file exists with details of the nature of the component's business, its staff organisation, its accounting records, previous year's financial statements and copies of important legal documents.

- The systems examination has been properly completed, documented and reported on to management after discussion.

- Tests of controls and substantive procedures have been properly and appropriately carried out, and audit programmes properly completed and signed.

- All other working papers are comprehensive and explicit.

- The overall review of the financial statements has been adequately carried out, and adequate use of analytical procedures has been undertaken throughout the audit.

- The financial statements agree in all respects with the accounting records and comply with all relevant legal requirements and accounting standards.

- Minutes of board and general meetings have been scrutinised and important matters noted.

- The audit work has been carried out in accordance with approved auditing standards.

- The financial statements agree in all respects with the accounting records and comply with all relevant legal and professional requirements.

- The audit work has been properly reviewed within the firm of auditors and any laid down quality control procedures adhered to.

- Any points requiring discussion with the parent company's management have been noted and brought to the group engagement team's' attention (including any matters which might warrant a qualification in the auditor's report on the component company's financial statements).

- Adequate audit evidence has been obtained to form a basis for the audit opinion on both the components' financial statements and those of the group.

If the group engagement team are not satisfied as a result of the above review, they should arrange for further audit work to be carried out either by the component auditors on their behalf, or jointly with them. The component auditors are fully responsible for their own work; any additional tests are those required for the purpose of the audit of the group financial statements.

Answer to Interactive question 9

Audit approach

- Review the requirements of the appropriate financial reporting framework for allowances for receivables.

- Discuss with management how the allowance has been calculated.

- Obtain a breakdown of the allowance, agree balances to the receivables ledger and reperform calculations.

- Compare actual receivables written off in prior periods with previous estimates.

- Ascertain who is responsible for reviewing and approving the allowance.

- Obtain an aged listing of receivables as at the reporting date and identify overdue amounts and review correspondence relating to these accounts and arrive at an independent estimate of the allowance required.

- Compare this with management's estimate.

- Review cash received from customers after the reporting date up to the date of the auditor's report to identify whether any receivables balances that appeared to be doubtful have subsequently been settled.

Answers to Self-test

1   (i)   Tests of controls
    (ii)   Analytical procedures
    (iii) Tests of details

2   False

3   True

4   To whom they report
    Their technical training
    Whether internal audit work is properly documented

5   False

6   False

7   C

8   B (one to carry out the work and another to review it)

Exam-style question

9   **Notes for a planning meeting**

    (a)

Circumstance	Why taken into account
• Multiple business locations.	• Increases inherent risk (eg, if the organisational structure is loose and difficult to manage).
• Intense price competition.	• May lead to uneconomic price discounting, possibly threatening viability of business.
• Recent expansion of outlets into minimarkets.	• Increases complexity of business and may lead to loss of management control.
• Perishable nature and limited shelf-life of food and drinks inventories.	• Increase risk of overstatement of inventory values.
• Large volume of cash transactions.	• Increases risk of incomplete income recording.
• Nature of the business (garage environment).	• Increases risk of loss of inventories and cash due to theft or staff pilferage. • May limit effectiveness of physical security controls (eg, over access to terminals).
• Recent introduction of sales of National Lottery tickets.	• Increases inherent risk (eg, the risk of loss to Gasoleum Ltd if incorrect amounts are paid out on winning tickets).
• Direct input via PCs at branches.	• Increases risk of misstatement, as batch controls will not be feasible and scope for other input controls may be limited.
• Small number of staff at each location (eg, one or two).	• Limits scope for segregation of duties within branches and therefore increases control risk.

Circumstance	Why taken into account
• Branch-based nature of business.	• Limits effectiveness of management control over activities of individual branches thereby increasing control risk.
• Use of part-time staff and high staff turnover.	• May inhibit effectiveness of controls within branches.

(b) **Effect of work of internal auditor on audit planning**

(i) The internal auditor's identification and documentation of areas of weakness will give direction to areas requiring increased substantive procedures.

(ii) Work of the internal auditor may assist in selection of branches for audit visits, (eg, where control failures have occurred).

(iii) The internal auditor may attend year end inventory counts at one or more branches, potentially reducing the number of branches to be visited by us.

(iv) Work performed by the internal auditor may provide evidence to confirm operation of control procedures, on which we may seek to rely to reduce the extent of our own procedures.

(v) Documentation of systems and controls by the internal auditor, including changes due to the National Lottery, may reduce extent of our planning visits, as walk-through checks may be sufficient to confirm systems documentation.

CHAPTER 11

Audits of different types of entity

Introduction

Examination context

TOPIC LIST

Summary and Self-test

Technical reference

Answer to Interactive question

Answers to Self-test

Introduction

Learning outcomes

2   Planning engagements

Students will be able to plan assurance engagements in accordance with the terms of the engagements and appropriate standards.

- Discuss the differences between the audit of a non-specialised profit oriented entity and the audit of a given specialised profit oriented entity;

- Discuss the differences between the audit of a non-specialised profit oriented entity and the audit of a given not-for-profit entity;

- Specify and explain the steps necessary to plan, perform, conclude and report on the audit of the financial statements of a non-specialised profit oriented entity in accordance with the terms of the engagement including appropriate auditing standards;

Syllabus links

You have covered the key issues relating to planning non-specialised audits in this Study Manual. You covered obtaining evidence on non-specialised audits in greater detail in your Assurance studies.

Examination context

Complex auditing requirements relating to specialised entities are not examinable.

1 Non-specialised and specialised entities

Section overview

- The majority of audits relate to non-specialised profit orientated entities

- The standard audit features outlined in this manual and the Assurance manual apply to this type of entity

- Some entities are 'special' in some way, for example:

    - The entity is subject to extra regulations, such as banks or insurers, or charities (note that we shall look in particular at not-for-profit entities below)

    - The entity is subject to professional rules, such as solicitors

- Such entities may be subject to special auditing guidance, all of which is outside the scope of your syllabus

- It is important to note that many of these entities require a 'normal' statutory audit as well as any additional requirements upon them

- In which case, the auditors need to assess the particular risks associated with the specialised entities which will cause any differences in audit approach

Many audits undertaken in the UK relate to non-specialised profit-making entities (that is a 'normal' company operating for profit. For example, a manufacturing company, a service company, a retail company). The audit procedures outlined in this Study Manual so far and in your Assurance manual all relate to this type of entity, and the majority of questions in your paper are likely to be set in this context. However, some entities are 'special' in some way, for example, they are subject to extra laws and regulations (for example, banks or insurers) or they are subject to particular professional rules, such as solicitors. Such entities may or may not require a statutory audit. As always the auditor must be aware of the particular risks associated with the entity in order to plan and conduct the audit.

Specialised entities are often subject to particular requirements that pose additional factors for auditors. For example, under their professional rules, solicitors require a 'solicitors' accounts rules audit'. Some specialised entities are subject to special accounting and auditing guidance, which adds detail to the audit, in addition to the normal statutory audit that is being carried out. Such specialised guidance is beyond the scope of your syllabus. You should simply be aware that audits of such specialised entities will have special requirements in addition to normal audit requirements that makes auditing them more complex.

2 Not-for-profit entities

Section overview

- There are various types of organisations which do not exist for the purpose of maximising shareholder wealth, which may require an audit

- The audit risks associated with not-for-profit organisations may well be different from other entities

- Cash may be significant in small not-for-profit charities and controls are likely to be limited. Income may well be a risk area, particularly where money is donated or raised informally

- Obtaining audit evidence may be a problem, particularly where small charities have informal arrangements and there might be limitations on the scope of the audit

- In all not-for-profit audits it will be necessary to ensure accounting policies used are appropriate

- The nature of the report will depend on statutory and entity requirements, but it should conform to ISA (UK) 700 criteria

- The public sector comprises a large number of varied not-for-profit organisations, and also private companies which are profit oriented, running (outsourced) public services

The key objective of most companies is to manage the shareholders' investments well. In a large majority of cases, 'manage the shareholders' investment' means 'create a profit', as this will create returns to the shareholders in the terms of dividends or growth in the capital value of the share. However, some companies and other entities do not operate for the purpose of making profit but have other objectives. Examples include charities and organisations in the public sector.

Many of these organisations are legislated for and the Acts which relate to them may specify how they are to report their results. Some of the organisations mentioned above may be companies (often companies limited by guarantee) and so are required to prepare financial statements and have them audited under companies legislation.

Where a statutory audit is required, the auditors will be required to produce the statutory audit opinion concerning the truth and fairness of financial statements.

Where a statutory audit is not required, it is possible that the organisation might have one anyway for the benefit of interested stakeholders, such as the public or people who give to a charity.

It is also possible that such entities will have special, additional requirements of an audit. These may be required by a Regulator, or by the constitution of the organisation. For example, a charity's constitution may require an audit of whether the charity is operating in accordance with its charitable purpose.

An audit of a not-for-profit organisation may vary from a 'for-profit audit' due to:

- Its objectives and the impact on operations and reporting
- The purpose an audit is required

When carrying out an audit of a not-for-profit organisation, it is vital that the auditor establishes:

- Whether a statutory audit is required
- If not, what the objectives of the engagement are
- What the engagement is to report on
- To whom the report should be addressed, and
- What form the report should take

2.1 Charities

Charities are regulated under the Charities Act 2016. This sets out what a charity is and outlines how they are regulated. The charities' regulator is the Charity Commission.

 Definition

Charity: An institution which:

- Is established for charitable purposes **only**; and

- Falls to be subject to the control of the High Court in the exercise of its jurisdiction with respect to charities.

Charities Act 2016 s1

The Charities Act 2016 recognises the following charitable purposes:

- Prevention or relief of poverty

- Advancement of one or more of the following:
    - Education
    - Religion
    - Health/saving lives
    - Citizenship/community development
    - Arts/culture/heritage/science
    - Amateur sport
    - Human rights/conflict resolution/promotion of religious or racial harmony/equality/diversity
    - Environmental protection/improvement
    - Animal welfare

- The relief of those in need by reason of youth, age, ill-health, disability, financial hardship or other disadvantage

- The promotion of the efficiency of the armed forces of the Crown, the police, fire and rescue or ambulance services.

The Charities Statements of Recommended Practice (SORP) is based on the Financial Reporting Standard (FRS) 102. The SORP was issued in July 2014, with further amendments in February 2016.

- For accounting periods beginning on/after 1 January 2016, the SORP (FRS 102) Update Bulletin 1 should be applied, which takes into account changes to FRS 102 and the Charities Act 2011 (Accounts and Audit) Order 2015.

- The older SORP, without the Update, is applied for charities whose accounting periods begin from 1 January 2015 (but from 1 January 2016, the Update applies – above).

Charities' accounts should comprise the following.

- A **statement of financial activities** (SOFA) that shows all resources made available to the charity and all expenditure incurred and reconciles all changes in its funds

- Where the charity is required to prepare accounts in accordance with the Companies Act, or similar legislation, or where the governing instrument so requires, a **summary income and expenditure account** (in addition to the SOFA) in certain circumstances

- A **balance sheet** that shows the assets, liabilities and funds of the charity. The balance sheet (or its notes) should also explain, in general terms, how the funds may, because of restrictions imposed by donors, be utilised

- A **statement of cash flows** is mandatory
- **Notes**

The accounts must include the following.

- Legacies are to be recognised only when they are probable rather than certain
- Disclosure of total employee benefits received by key management personnel
- Disclosure that no employees received pay of over £60,000 or disclose the number that were
- Separate disclosure of material rather than exceptional items, and of extraordinary items
- A list of institutional grants

The financial thresholds for determining whether charity accounts require auditing are fairly complex, but in general terms for years ending on or after 1 April 2009 unincorporated charities are exempt if gross income is less than £1 million **unless**:

- Gross assets are greater than £3.26 million; **and**
- Gross income is greater than £250K, 000.

All charities with a gross income of more than £25,000 are required to send a copy of their accounts to the Charity Commission.

Charities with a gross income of between £25,000 and £1 million are required to have an independent verification of their financial statements. Where gross income is more than £250,000 the independent examination must be by a member of an approved professional organisation (for example a qualified accountant).

A charity's governing document may contain specific provisions about audit requirements. In such cases the charity must follow the higher standard of scrutiny required by either the statutory framework or governing document.

The verification process is a less onerous form of scrutiny than an audit and correspondingly gives a lower level of assurance. The examiner is not required to give an opinion as to whether the accounts give a true and fair view. Instead he must report whether or not any matter has come to his attention indicating that:

- Proper accounting records have not been kept
- The accounts do not comply with such records
- The accounts fail to comply with relevant Regulations

In addition, if such matters have become apparent, the report should include details of:

- Material expenditure or actions contrary to the trusts of the charity
- Failure to provide information or explanations to which the examiner is entitled
- Evidence that the accounts prepared on an accruals basis are materially inconsistent with the trustees' annual report

In order to produce this report, the verifier should:

- Carry out procedures to be satisfied the charity qualifies for this independent verification
- Agree a timetable for the verification
- Obtain an understanding of the charity and its environment
- Record the examination procedures carried out and any matters important to support the statements made in the report
- Compare the accounts of the charity with the charity's accounting records in sufficient detail to be able to decide the accounts are in accordance with the records

- Review the accounting records
- Carry out analytical procedures to identify unusual items in the accounts
- Carry out detailed procedures as judged necessary
- Consider whether accounting policies are reasonable
- Enquire about subsequent events
- Consider if the Trustee's report is consistent with the accounts
- Review the evidence obtained

2.1.1 Planning

When planning the audit of a charity, the auditors should particularly consider the following:

- The **scope** of the audit
- Recent **recommendations** of the **Charity Commissioners** or the other regulatory bodies
- The **acceptability of accounting policies** adopted
- **Changes in circumstances** in the sector in which the charity operates
- **Past experience** of the effectiveness of the charity's accounting system
- **Key audit areas**
- The **amount of detail included** in the financial statements on which the auditors are required to report

In order to identify the key audit areas, the auditors will have to consider audit risk.

There are certain risks applicable to charities that might not necessarily be applicable to other companies. The auditors should consider the following:

Problem	Key factors
Inherent risk	<ul><li>The complexity and extent of regulation</li><li>The significance of donations and cash receipts</li><li>Difficulties of the charity in establishing ownership and timing of voluntary income where funds are raised by non-controlled bodies</li><li>Lack of predictable income or precisely identifiable relationship between expenditure and income</li><li>Uncertainty of future income</li><li>Restrictions imposed by the objectives and powers given by charities' governing documents</li><li>The importance of restricted funds (funds which the company is only allowed to put to a specific purpose)</li><li>The extent and nature of trading activities must be compatible with the entity's charitable status</li><li>The complexity of tax rules (whether Income, Capital, Value Added or local rates) relating to charities</li><li>The sensitivity of certain key statistics, such as the proportion of resources used in administration</li><li>The need to maintain adequate resources for future expenditure while avoiding the build up of reserves which could appear excessive</li></ul>

Problem	Key factors
Control risk	• The amount of time committed by trustees to the charity's affairs • The skills and qualifications of individual trustees • The frequency and regularity of trustee meetings • The form and content of trustee meetings • The independence of trustees from each other • The division of duties between trustees • The degree of involvement in, or supervision of, the charity's transactions on the part of individual trustees
Control environment	• A recognised plan of the charity's structure showing clearly the areas of responsibility and lines of authority and reporting • Segregation of duties • Supervision by trustees of activities of staff where segregation of duties is not practical • Competence, training and qualification of paid staff and any volunteers appropriate to the tasks they have to perform • Involvement of the trustees in the recruitment, appointment and supervision of senior executives • Access of trustees to independent professional advice where necessary • Budgetary controls in the form of estimates of income and expenditure for each financial year and comparison of actual results with the estimates on a regular basis • Communication of results of such reviews to the trustees on a regular basis

2.1.2 Internal controls

Small charities in particular will generally suffer from internal control weaknesses common to small enterprises, such as **lack of segregation of duties** and use of **unqualified staff**. Shortcomings may arise from the staff's lack of training and also, if they are volunteers, from their attitude, in that they may resent formal procedures.

The auditors will have to consider particularly carefully whether they will be able to obtain adequate assurance that the accounting records do reflect all the transactions of the enterprise and bear in mind whether there are any related statutory reporting requirements.

The following sorts of internal control might be typical of a number of charities.

Cash donations

Source	Examples of controls
Collecting boxes and tins	• Numerical control over boxes and tins • Satisfactory sealing of boxes and tins so that any opening prior to recording cash is apparent • Regular collection and recording of proceeds from collecting boxes • Dual control over counting and recording of proceeds
Postal receipts	• Unopened mail kept securely • Dual control over the opening of mail • Immediate recording of donations on opening of mail or receipt • Agreement of bank paying-in slips to record of receipts by an independent person

Other donations

Source	Examples of controls
Gift aid	• Regular checks and follow-up procedures to ensure due amounts are received • Regular checks to ensure all tax repayments have been obtained
Legacies	• Comprehensive correspondence files maintained in respect of each legacy • Regular reports and follow-up procedures undertaken in respect of outstanding legacies
Donations in kind	• In the case of charity shops, separation of recording, storage and sale of inventory

Other income

Source	Examples of controls
Fund-raising activities	• Records maintained for each fund-raising event • Other appropriate controls maintained over receipts • Controls maintained over expenses as for administrative expenses
Central and local government grants and loans	• Regular checks that all sources of income or funds are fully utilised and appropriate claims made • Ensuring income or funds are correctly applied

Use of resources

Resource	Examples of controls
Restricted funds	• Separate records maintained of relevant revenue, expenditure and assets • Terms controlling application of fund • Oversight of application of fund monies by independent personnel or trustees

Grants to beneficiaries	• Records maintained, as appropriate, of requests for material grants received and their treatment
	• Appropriate checks made on applications and applicants for grants, and that amounts paid are *intra vires*
	• Records maintained of all grant decisions, checking that proper authority exists, that adequate documentation is presented to decision-making meetings, and that any conflicts of interest are recorded
	• Control to ensure grants made are properly spent by the recipient for the specified purpose, for example requirements for returns with supporting documentation or auditors' reports concerning expenditure, or monitoring visits

Conversely, large charities might have very strong controls and the auditors may find that they are able to rely on them to a great extent. Remember, however, that while relying on controls might be acceptable in order to determine whether the financial statements give a true and fair view, it might not be acceptable to meet any special additional auditing requirements that the charity has.

2.1.3 Substantive procedures

When designing substantive procedures for charities the auditors should give special attention to the possibility of:

- **Understatement or incompleteness** of the **recording of all income** including gifts in kind, cash donations, and legacies

- **Overstatement of cash grants or expenses**

- **Misanalysis** or misuse in the application of funds (such as restricted funds which the charity might only be able to use for specific purposes)

- **Misstatement** or omission of **assets** including donated properties and investments

- The existence of **restricted or uncontrollable funds** in foreign or independent branches.

Completeness of income can be a particularly problematic area. Areas auditors may check:

- Loss of income through fraud
- Recognition of income from professional fund raisers
- Recognition of income from branches, associates or subsidiaries
- Income from informal fund-raising groups
- Income from grants

2.1.4 Overall review

The auditors must consider carefully whether the **accounting policies** adopted are **appropriate** to the activities, constitution and objectives of the charity, and are consistently applied, and whether the financial statements adequately disclose these policies and fairly present the state of affairs and the results for the accounting period.

In particular, the auditors should consider the basis of disclosing income from fund raising activities (for example net or gross), accounting for income and expenses (accruals or cash), the capitalising of expenditure on non-current assets, apportioning administrative expenditure, and recognising income from donations and legacies.

Charities without significant endowments or accumulated funds will often be dependent upon future income from voluntary sources. In these circumstances auditors may question whether a going concern basis of accounting is appropriate.

2.1.5 Reporting

On not-for-profit audits where a statutory auditor's report is required, the auditors should issue the standard auditor's report which we will consider in Chapter 13. They should also consider whether any additional statutory requirements fall on the auditor's report.

Where an association or charity is having an audit for the benefit of its members or trustees, the standard auditor's report may not be required or appropriate. The auditor should bear in mind the objectives of the audit and make suitable references in the auditor's report. However, the ISA (UK) 700 format will still be relevant. The auditor should ensure that he makes the following matters clear:

- The addressees of the report
- What the report relates to
- The scope of the engagement
- The respective responsibilities of auditors and management/trustees/directors
- The work done
- The opinion formed

The points made above are general points. Remember that not all clubs and charities will be the same. If you have a question in the exam relating to a charity, apply this general knowledge to the specifics given in the question and be **logical** when formulating your answer.

2.1.6 Glossary of terms

The following definitions refer to some of the terms used with respect to charities:

- Trustees: the people responsible for the overall control of the charity and for ensuring that it is properly managed.

- Endowments: these may be in the form of investments or property, the income from which can be spent by the charity.

- Restricted funds: funds which can be spent at the discretion of the trustees.

- Designated funds: funds which may be used for specific purposes only, which may be requested by the donor of the funds.

Worked example: Charity

Headington Hospice Co is a small, local charity which operates a small children's hospice and two charity shops which raise money for the ongoing work of the hospice. The hospice receives grants from the health authority, sponsorship from some local businesses, receives income from the charity shops which are entirely voluntarily operated and receives donations from individuals. It employs three nurses, a part-time hospice manager and an accountant donates his time to keep the books and produce the annual accounts. As the company's turnover falls below the exemption limit, it is not required to have an audit by law, but the terms of its constitution require that an audit of the accounts is required for the benefit of the trustees that gives an opinion as to whether the financial statements give a true and fair view and to whether the charity is meeting its objectives, as set out in the constitutional document.

The scope of this audit is therefore two-fold. The auditors are to report on the truth and fairness of the financial statement for the benefit of the trustees and also on whether the charity is meeting its objectives. The auditors should therefore establish what the objectives of the charity are, and consider whether the objectives are being met.

The auditors should consider whether any recommendations of the Charity Commissioners apply to Headington Hospice. It is unlikely that there have been any substantial changes in the sector in which it works.

In terms of audit approach, the auditor will need to devote attention to cash receipts and income, as the Hospice receives donations from the public and also receives cash income from the charity shops. The auditors will need to determine if there is a good control system in place and whether they feel that they can place reliance on it.

In terms of substantive procedures, in particular, it will be necessary to consider non-current assets, to determine whether the premises the hospice and charity shops should be included on the balance sheet of the charity. The auditor will also need to assess the nature of the grants received from the health authority to determine how they should be accounted for. These things should all be considered as part of the accounting policy review. The auditor should also be aware of issues such as depreciation during this review, as the hospice may own specialised medical equipment which makes such issues complex.

Another matter which the auditor must consider is the issue of going concern. This will include an assessment of the sponsorship deals which the charity has in place and any consideration of future sponsorship. The grant position must also be considered, as must the likelihood of future donations. The auditors should also consider matters such as personnel, for example, whether any existing arrangements with doctors' practices will continue in existence.

The issues relating to cash donations and grants will be particularly relevant.

Particular matters which might be an issue at Headington Hospice are:

- Completeness of cash income from various sources
- Accounting for the grants from the local authority

Interactive question: Links Famine Relief

You have recently been appointed to audit Links Famine Relief, a small registered charity which receives donations from individuals to provide food in worldwide famine areas.

The charity is run by a voluntary management committee, which has monthly meetings, and it employs the following full-time staff:

(a) A director, Mr Roberts, who suggests fund raising activities and payments for relief of famine, and implements the policies adopted by the management committee; and

(b) A secretary (and bookkeeper), Mrs Beech, who deals with correspondence and keeps the accounting records.

Links Famine Relief is required by its constitution to have an annual external audit of its financial statements.

You are planning the audit of income of the charity for the year ended 5 April 20X7 and are considering the controls which should be exercised over income.

The previous year's accounts, to 5 April 20X6 (which have been audited by another firm) show the following income.

	£	£
Gifts under non-taxing arrangements		15,335
Tax reclaimed on gifts under non-taxing arrangements		4,325
		19,660
Postal donations		63,452
Autumn Fair		2,671
Other income		
Legacies	7,538	
Bank deposit account interest	2,774	
		10,312
		96,095

Notes

1   Income from gifts under non-taxing arrangements is stated net. Each person who pays by gift aid has filled in a special tax form, which is kept by the secretary, Mrs Beech.

2   All gifts under non-taxing arrangements are paid by banker's order – they are credited directly to the charity's bank account from the donor's bank. Donors make their payments by gift aid either monthly or annually.

3   The tax reclaimed on these gifts is 28.2% (22/78) of the net value of the gifts, and relates to income received during the year – as the tax is received after the year-end, an appropriate amount recoverable is included in the balance sheet. The treasurer, who is a voluntary (unpaid) member of the management committee, completes the form for reclaiming the income tax, using the special tax forms (in Note 1 above) and checks to the full-time secretary's records that each donor has made the full payment in the year required by the arrangement.

4   Donations received through the post are dealt with by Mrs Beech. These donations are either cheques or cash (bank notes and coins). Mrs Beech prepares a daily list of donations received, which lists the cheques received and total cash (divided between the different denominations of bank note and coin). The total on this form is recorded in the cash book. She then prepares a paying-in slip and banks these donations daily. When there is a special fund-raising campaign, Mrs Beech receives help in dealing with these donations from voluntary members of the management committee.

5   The Autumn Fair takes place every year on a Saturday in October – members of the management committee and other supporters of the charity give items to sell (for example food, garden plants, clothing) – a charge is made for entrance to the fair and coffee and biscuits are available at a small charge. At the end of the fair, Mrs Beech collects the takings from each of the stalls, and she banks them the following Monday.

6   Legacies are received irregularly, and are usually sent directly to the director of the charity, who gives them to Mrs Beech for banking – they are stated separately on the daily bankings form (in (d) above).

7   Bank deposit account interest is paid gross of income tax by the bank, as the Links Famine Relief is a charity.

Requirement

List and briefly describe the work you would carry out on the audit of income of the charity, the controls you would expect to see in operation and the problems you may experience for the following sources of income, as detailed in the statement of profit or loss above.

(a)   Gifts under non-taxing arrangements
(b)   Tax reclaimed on gifts made under non-taxing arrangements
(c)   Donations received through the post
(d)   Autumn Fair

See **Answer** at the end of this chapter.

2.2   Public sector

The following provides a brief introduction to public sector auditing and some of the concepts used in the audit of public sector entities. You are only required to have knowledge of how audit of public sector entities differs from the audit of non-specialised entities. In depth knowledge of the working of the public sector, the operation of the NAO (National Audit Office) and Public Sector Audit Appointments Ltd and the content of PSIAS (Public Sector Internal Audit Standards) is not required.

The public sector comprises a great variety of organisations including central and local government. It also includes private companies which are profit orientated, running outsourced public services. Auditing by an independent external auditor is important, in order to provide external accountability to the community at large. For example, local authorities which provide many local services such as schools will be subject to an audit of their financial statements, as will the NHS Trust that runs local hospitals. Audit helps to ensure that:

- Public funds have been spent for proper, authorised purposes and legally within statutory powers.

- Organisations install and operate controls to limit the possibility of corrupt practice, fraud and poor administration.

The manner in which the auditors conduct their work is affected by auditing standards and other regulatory influences including:

- Specific statutory requirements
- Requirements of the sponsoring (or funding) department
- Contractual requirements contained in terms of engagement

Organisations in the public sector are often subject to a high degree of regulation. The nature of regulation affecting public sector bodies ranges from statutory to detailed administrative requirements.

In England, the National Audit Office is a public sector organisation specialising in public sector audit work. These or similar bodies cover Northern Ireland, Scotland and Wales.

2.2.1 Principles of audit in the public sector

The purpose of audit in the public sector is accountability. It helps ensure that public money is spent wisely and handled with integrity. Audit in the public sector is not just an exercise in checking what has happened in the past, but making recommendations for future good practice.

The Public Audit Forum (a representative of the major public audit bodies in the UK) sets out three key principles of audit in the public sector:

- **Independence** of public sector auditors from organisations being audited

- The wide **scope** of audit in the public sector (see below)

- The ability of public sector auditors to **make their results available** to the public and democratically appointed officials.

The wide scope of audit in the public sector is an important issue and one in which it differs from the statutory 'private' companies audit we have focused on thus far in your studies. A public sector audit covers not only the audit of financial statements, and internal control systems if required, but also covers the issues of regularity, propriety and value for money.

Regularity

In a public sector audit, auditors must ensure that the transactions carried out by the organisation are **in accordance with the legislation that governs those transactions**, or the regulations issued by Parliament or HM Treasury in relation to that organisation.

Propriety

This concept is linked to the expectations of the public or the authority which sets up the organisation being audited, that is, auditors must ensure that transactions and business are **being carried out in the way that they should be**, that is ethically, with integrity and according to any existing standards of conduct.

Value for money

Finally, in a public sector audit it is critical to ensure that that **best use is being made of resources** (money raised from the public through taxation) in providing the service. Public sector audits therefore include evaluations of the economy (spend less), efficiency (spend well) and effectiveness (spend wisely) of use of public resources.

2.2.2 The Public Accounts Committee

The Public Accounts Committee is an all-party committee appointed by the House of Commons to examine public expenditure to ensure that it achieves value for money. The Commons itself decides how public money is spent on an annual basis.

2.2.3 The National Audit Office

The head of the National Audit Office is the Comptroller and Auditor General (C&AG) who is responsible for auditing the accounts of all government departments (such as the Department for Work and Pensions) and non-departmental government agencies (such as HM Passport Office) and reporting the results to Parliament. In practice this responsibility is delegated to the National Audit Office (NAO).

The NAO ensures that the public sector is accountable. The C&AG can report to Parliament on the way that public money is spent by central government. Evidence from reports produced by the C&AG may be used by the Public Accounts Committee to make recommendations to Government. The C&AG is appointed by the Queen, on the advice of the prime minister, and is accountable to the Public Accounts Committee.

Accounting officers are normally the most senior officials in a public sector entity with a personal responsibility for the propriety and regularity of the public finances for which he or she is answerable; for the keeping of proper accounts; for prudent and economical administration; for the avoidance of waste and extravagance; and for the efficient and effective use of all the available resources (HM Treasury definition). Accounting officers may be called to give evidence before the Committee of Public Accounts on the basis of reports by the C&AG.

2.2.4 Public Sector Audit Appointments Ltd

This company is responsible for appointing auditors to local government, police and local NHS bodies.

2.2.5 Audit of government grants

Government grants, such as enterprise development schemes, are issued in response to certain criteria, such as a need to improve employment in disadvantaged areas. It is important that such grant schemes are audited to ensure that the criteria for the grants are being met, that the schemes operate well and whether the government department responsible for the grant is managing it and ensuring its effectiveness.

The NAO audits the regional grant scheme in England, whilst Public Sector Audit Appointments Ltd is for the time being responsible for the audit of housing benefit subsidy administered by local government.

2.2.6 International Standards on Auditing

The International Standards on Auditing (UK) apply to audit work undertaken in the public sector. Where applicable the standards contain 'Considerations Specific to Public Sector Entities' which highlight some of the different considerations that apply in the audit of entities in the public sector. Some examples are given below:

- ISA (UK) 315 *Identifying and Assessing the Risks of Material Misstatement through Understanding of the Entity and its Environment*

    For the audits of public sector entities, law, regulation or other authority may affect the entity's operations. Such elements are essential to consider when obtaining an understanding of the entity and its environment.

- ISA (UK) 520 *Analytical Procedures*

  The relationships between individual financial statement items traditionally considered in the audit of business entities may not always be relevant in the audit of governments or other non-business public sector entities: for example, in many public sector entities there may be little direct relationship between revenue and expenditure.

  In the public sector industry data or statistics for comparative purposes may not be available.

- ISA (UK) 570 *Going Concern*

  Going concern risks may arise, but are not limited to, situations where public sector entities operate on a for-profit basis, where government support may be reduced or withdrawn, or in the case of privatisation. Events or conditions that may cast significant doubt on an entity's ability to continue as a going concern in the public sector may include situations where the public sector entity lacks funding for its continued existence or when policy decisions are made that affect the services provided by the public sector entity.

Additional guidance for public sector auditors is provided by the FRC Statement of Recommended Practice PN 10, which was issued in order to "assist auditors in applying Auditing Standards of general application to particular circumstances".

Summary and Self-test

Summary

Self-test

Answer the following questions.

1   Which of the following might require a specialist audit and why?

   ☐ Care Share Ltd, a charity limited by guarantee

   ☐ Pytox plc, a listed parent of a group of manufacturing companies

   ☐ Loyds plc, a bank

   ☐ Allied Insurance Company plc, an insurer

   ☐ Linens Ltd, a retail company

2   Will an auditor's report for a charity have to conform to ISA (UK) 700 criteria?

3   What is NAO?

4   Help the Kids Ltd, a registered charity, has income of £150,000 and assets of £750,000. It is required to have an audit of its financial statements.

   ☐ True

   ☐ False

5   What four issues are likely to fall within the scope of a public audit?

   (i)   ....

   (ii) ....

   (iii) ....

   (iv) ....

Exam-style question

6   You have been appointed the auditor of Safe Haven which has a year end of 31 May. Safe Haven is a small registered charity based in a small town in Warshire. The organisation provides shelter for abandoned dogs and puppies with the aim of finding new homes for as many as possible.

   The charity is managed by a voluntary committee, including a Chairman (Alun Jenkins), a Treasurer (Gordon Brand) and a Secretary (Amanda Jones). Appointment is by annual election by the committee each year however Alun, Gordon and Amanda have held their posts for a number of years as other committee members feel unable to give the required time commitment.

   Safe Haven also employs a number of paid employees. The shelter is managed by John and Jane Sheldon, who are husband and wife. There is a kennel maid and a part time bookkeeper. In addition a number of unpaid volunteers help out at the shelter as and when they are needed depending on the number of animals at the centre at a particular point in time.

   The main sources of income are as follows:

   - **Charity shop**

     This is run by a full time manager, assisted by a team of volunteers. Members of the public make donations (primarily clothes and toys) which are then sold in the shop. All transactions are in cash. The shop does not accept cheques or credit cards. The transactions are recorded by the till, with completed till rolls being passed on to the bookkeeper.

- **Collections**

  Volunteers make house to house calls on a regular basis. In addition, on Saturday mornings volunteers make collections in three local town centres. All cash is counted by the volunteers, and returned to the bookkeeper with a receipt confirming the amount.

- **Dog Show**

  Each year on 1st June, a Peace Festival is held in the town. As part of this event Safe Haven organise a dog show. Any member of the public can enter their dog by completing an entry form which can be obtained from the shop.

  Tickets to see the show can be purchased up to two weeks in advance from the shop or can be purchased on the day at the Festival. In recent years the show has been a great success although two years ago it had to be cancelled due to bad weather.

  T-shirts can also be purchased from a stall manned by volunteers.

- **Sponsorship**

  Safe Haven is sponsored by a local pet supplies company. The company makes an annual donation and provides prizes for the winners of the dog show. In return for this their services are advertised in the event programme and their logo is printed on the T-shirts.

The main expenses are as follows:

- **Rent, rates, heat and light**

  Both the shelter and the shop are rented properties. These expenses are all paid by monthly direct debit.

- **Employee costs**

  John and Jane Sheldon and the shop manager are salaried. They are paid directly into their bank accounts on a monthly basis. The kennel maid and the bookkeeper are paid by the hour. They are paid by cheque on a weekly basis.

- **Vet bills**

  The local vet provides his time free but any medicines etc do need to be paid for. Payments are made by cheque on receipt of the invoice.

- **Printing costs**

  Leaflets are produced to support fund raising campaigns. The most significant element of this cost is the dog show programme which outlines the timetable of events. The programmes are printed and delivered to Safe Haven in May. The printer invoices at the time of delivery.

The accounts are maintained by the bookkeeper on a computerised spreadsheet. Occasionally, the treasurer may also assist with the preparation of accounting information at particularly busy times in the year, for example, immediately after the dog show.

Requirements

(a) List the factors specific to the audit of a charity which would affect inherent and control risk.

(b) As the auditor of Safe Haven discuss the key planning issues based on the above scenario.

C H A P T E R

11

ICAEW 2019   Audits of different types of entity 259

(c) Outline the audit work you would plan to perform in respect of the following expenses:

   (i)   Rent, rates, light and heat
   (ii) Employee costs
   (iii) Vet bills
   (iv) Printing costs   **(20 marks)**

Now, go back to the Learning outcomes in the Introduction. If you are satisfied you have achieved this outcome, please tick it off.

Technical reference

Answer to Interactive question

The audit consideration in relation to the various sources of income of the Links Famine Relief charity would be as follows:

(a) **Gifts made under non-taxing arrangements**

This type of income should not present any particular audit problem as the donations are made by banker's order direct to the charity's bank account and so it would be difficult for such income to be 'intercepted' and misappropriated.

Specific tests required would be as follows:

(i) Check a sample of receipts from the bank statements to the cash book to ensure that the income has been properly recorded.

(ii) Check a sample of the receipts to the special tax forms to ensure that the full amount due has been received.

Any discrepancies revealed by either of the above tests should be followed up with Mrs Beech.

(b) **Tax reclaimed on gifts made under non-taxing arrangements**

Once again this income should not pose any particular audit problems. The auditors should check the claim form submitted to the tax authorities.

(c) **Donations received through the post**

There is a serious problem here as the nature of this income is not predictable and also because of the lack of internal check with Mrs Beech being almost entirely responsible for the receipt of these monies, the recording of the income and the banking of the cash and cheques received. The auditors may ultimately have to express a qualified opinion relating to the uncertainty surrounding the completeness of income of this type.

Notwithstanding the above reservations, specific audit tests required would be as follows:

(i) Check the details on the daily listings of donations received to the cash book, bank statements and paying-in slips, ensuring that the details agree in all respects and that there is no evidence of any delay in the banking of this income.

(ii) Check the donations received by reference to any correspondence which may have been received with the cheques or cash.

(iii) Consider whether the level of income appears reasonable in comparison with previous years and in the light of any special appeals that the charity is known to have made during the course of the year.

(iv) Carry out, with permission of the management committee, surprise checks to vouch the completeness and accuracy of the procedures relating to this source of income.

(d) **Autumn Fair**

Once again there is a potential problem here because of the level of responsibility vested in one person, namely Mrs Beech.

Specific work required would be as follows:

(i) Attend the event to observe the proper application of laid down procedures and count the cash at the end of the day.

(ii) Check any records maintained by individual stallholders to the summary prepared by Mrs Beech.

(iii) Check the vouchers supporting any expenditure deducted from the proceeds in order to arrive at the net bankings.

(iv) Agree the summary prepared by Mrs Beech to the entry in the cash book and on the bank statement.

Answers to Self-test

1   •   Care Share Ltd might have additional Charity Commissioner requirements
     •   Loyds plc is likely to have additional banking requirements
     •   Allied Insurance Company plc is likely to have additional insurance requirements

2   Only if the charity requires a statutory audit.

3   The National Audit Office (NAO) is an independent body which scrutinises public spending on behalf of Parliament. It is responsible for auditing the accounts of central government departments and other public bodies.

4   False. Help the Kids Ltd would only be required to have an audit if its income was over £500,000, or if its income was over £250,000 and it had assets greater than £3.26m.

5   (i)   Audit of financial statements
    (ii)   Regularity
    (iii)   Propriety
    (iv)   Value for money

Exam-style question

6   (a)   The following factors would be relevant:

Inherent risk

(i)   The extent of regulation depending on the specific nature of the charity

(ii)   The significance of donations and cash receipts

(iii)   The extent of credit card and internet donations

(iv)   The valuation of gifts of assets

(v)   Lack of predictable income

(vi)   Lack of direct relationship between income and expenditure

(vii)   The sensitivity of issues including the proportion of resources used in admin and fund raising

Control risk

(i)   The time committed by trustees to the charity's affairs
(ii)   The skills and qualifications of the individual trustees
(iii)   The frequency, form and content of trustee meetings
(iv)   The division of duties between trustees
(v)   The supervision by the trustees of volunteers

(b)   Planning issues for Safe Haven would be as follows:

Completeness of income

Overall this risk is high due to the following factors: the majority of the income is generated in cash, there are numerous different sources of income, and a wide range of people have access to the asset itself due to the use of volunteers.

Looking at each source of income in turn the following points are relevant:

Charity shop

Whilst till receipts can be agreed to cash received this does not guarantee that all revenue has been put through the till. The main problem here is that it may be difficult to establish an expected relationship between 'revenue' and 'cost of sales'. Items sold are donated by the public so much will depend on how these items are valued by the charity.

Street collections

Reconciliations can be performed between cash collected and the receipts submitted by the volunteers to determine accurate recording. Completeness of income, however, will depend largely on the integrity of the volunteers and the overall controls put in place by the charity. In this instance risk is increased by the unpredictable nature of this source of income and the fact that the collection boxes are not sealed. Those responsible for collecting the cash are also responsible for opening the boxes and counting the cash before handing it over to the bookkeeper. This increases the risk of misappropriation.

Dog show tickets and T-shirts sales

Completeness of income in respect of these sources of revenue is still a concern due to the cash nature of these transactions but more reliable evidence should be available. Revenue generated from ticket sales can be reconciled to the number of tickets sold. This assumes that the charity exercises some control over the issue of tickets for example, tickets are numbered so that it is possible to determine the number sold.

For the T-shirt sales it should be possible to validate the income by comparing the number of items sold with the revenue generated. This depends on the charity adopting very simple inventory control.

Sponsorship

Completeness should not be an issue here as the amount involved is predetermined and is likely to be paid by cheque or by bank transfer.

Controls

In addition to the specific control issue mentioned above the assessment of the overall control environment will be essential at the planning stage of the audit. As there are concerns about the completeness of income the control environment will provide key evidence about the integrity of the revenue balance.

The auditor will need to consider the ability of the committee to run the organisation effectively. The information suggests that the three main committee members are responsible for the majority of the management so it will be important to determine their respective skills and whether they are able to devote sufficient time.

The ability of the bookkeeper will also need to be established in particular the possible lack of segregation of duties and the fact that the job is currently only done on a part time basis. It may be that records are not being maintained as they should be due to the limited number of hours being worked by that individual. This is emphasised by the fact that the Treasurer is sometimes required to help out.

Accounting Treatment

At the planning stage the accounting policies of the charity will need to be reviewed to ensure that they are appropriate and consistent. In particular the point at which income is recognised will need to be established together with any related costs. This is relevant to the income generated from the sale of tickets for the annual dog show. Tickets are available in the last two weeks in May, that is, the last two weeks before the year end and the main cost involved in the show, being the printing of the show programme is also incurred and invoiced in May. The show itself takes place in June.

In respect of the ticket sales made in May it could be argued that this income should not be recognised until the show takes place as it is only earned at this point. However, if the proceeds are non-returnable irrespective of whether the show takes place or not it could be argued that it represents a donation which can be recognised on receipt.

In respect of the programme costs the treatment is a little clearer. These should be provided for at the end of the year even though they relate to an activity which will take place after the year end. Per FRS 12 there is an obligation to pay for the programmes as a result of a past event that is, the printing company have produced and delivered the programmes.

Evidence

At the planning stage the overall strategy to adopt will need to be determined. In this case it is likely that a controls based approach will be adopted (as completeness of income is one of the key risks) supported by substantive testing, the extent of which will depend on the results of the tests of controls. The use of analytical review will be more limited due to the lack of predictive patterns in relation to many aspects of the organisation and the lack of relationships between account balances.

(c) The audit plan would include the following:

Rent, rates, light and heat

(i) Agree total rent/rates for the year to the lease/annual bill.

(ii) Check direct debit amounts in the cash book/bank statement.

(iii) Compare the cost of heat and light for this year and the previous year and follow up if there are any major differences.

(iv) Look at the date on the last utility bill to determine the need for any prepayment or accrual adjustment.

Employee costs

(i) For salaried staff check annual salary to personnel details/contract of employment.

(ii) For the bookkeeper and the kennel maid review the controls over the recording of hours worked and check the hourly rates applied to personnel details/contracts of employment.

(iii) Check a sample of standing data used to process the payroll.

(iv) Recalculate a sample of monthly calculations to ensure that deductions are being made correctly.

(v) Review controls over the weekly authorisation of pay checks and monthly bank transfers.

Vet bills

(i) Confirm with the vet that he has given his time for free.

(ii) Compare the total vet bill for this year and last year and calculate a 'cost per animal rescued' if possible.

(iii) Trace a sample of entries made in the cash book in respect of vet fees back to the original invoice to confirm that the cost is in respect of this.

(iv) Review invoices received after the year end to ensure that any necessary accruals have been recognised.

Printing costs

(i) Obtain the printers' invoice and check that a provision has been included in the accounts at the year end for an amount matching that on the invoice.

(ii) Confirm that the programmes have been received.

CHAPTER 12

Audit completion

Introduction

Examination context

TOPIC LIST

1   The completion phase

2   Audit opinion

3   Financial statement review

4   Other matters

Summary and Self-test

Technical reference

Answers to Interactive questions

Answers to Self-test

Introduction

Learning outcomes

3 Concluding and reporting on engagements

Students will be able to conclude and report on assurance engagements in accordance with the terms of the engagements and appropriate standards.

- Describe the nature and timing of specific procedures designed to identify subsequent events that may require adjustment or disclosure in relation to the matters being reported on

- Describe the nature and timing of specific procedures designed to identify the appropriateness of the going concern assumption, including compliance with relevant legal and regulatory requirements

- Evaluate quantitatively and qualitatively, the results and conclusions obtained from assurance procedures including analytical procedures and data analytics where appropriate

- Draw conclusions on the ability to report on an assurance engagement which are consistent with the results of the assurance work

- Judge when to refer reporting matters for specialist help

- Draw conclusions on the ability to report on an audit engagement, including the opinion for a statutory audit, which are consistent with the results of the audit work

Syllabus links

You will have considered the issue of going concern in Accounting.

Examination context

The reviews carried out at the end of the audit, such as going concern and subsequent events reviews are extremely important so could easily be examined in a short form or a long form question in the exam.

1 The completion phase

Section overview

- Although completion should in theory be simple if the audit has been well-planned and executed, there are a number of aspects to it which can make it complex

There are three phases to the audit:

- Planning
- Evidence gathering
- Completion

In the theory, the completion phase should be relatively smooth:

- If the work has been well planned
- If the staff have been well briefed and well trained
- If the staff execute the plan efficiently and to time

All the partner has to do is review the file, come to a decision about the final issues demanding professional judgement and sign off the accounts. However, there are lots of components to the completion phase.

The fact is that if the various procedures and other activities which make up the completion phase are not accomplished efficiently and to time, almost everything else is wasted. Budget overruns and under-recovery also tend to happen if closedown is not managed well.

This chapter talks in terms of audit, due to the auditing standards covered in it, but similar procedures might be carried out as part of a review.

2 Audit opinion

Section overview

- The partner needs to consider:
  - The financial statements
  - The work done to support the audit opinion

Remember the possible cost of getting the audit opinion wrong:

- If someone can demonstrate that the auditor owed them a duty of care and they suffered loss by relying on the financial statements, they could sue the auditor.

- As a member of the ICAEW the auditor could also face disciplinary proceedings, fines and penalties.

Making sure the appropriate opinion is given is therefore important.

There are two components of the completion phase:

- The financial statements themselves; and
- The work which has been done to support the opinion.

2.1 The financial statements

When considering the financial statements at the completion stage, the partner responsible for signing the auditor's report is interested in the answers to three questions:

- Do the financial statements comply with the provisions of the Companies Act 2006?
- Do the financial statements make sense?
- Has the auditor's report been drafted properly? (We will look at this in Chapter 13.)

We will consider the first two questions in the next section of this chapter.

2.2 The work done to support the opinion

Your review of the work done has four aspects to it:

- Whether the work done was in-line with the audit plan

- Whether the right work has been done (perhaps the plan needed to be flexed in the light of conditions actually encountered by the client)

- Whether enough work has been done

- The issues arising

3 Financial statement review

Section overview

- The important questions are:

  - Do the financial statements comply with the law and regulations (which will be tested using a disclosure checklist)?

  - Do the financial statements make sense (which will be tested by analytical procedures)?

3.1 Do the financial statements comply with the Companies Act 2006?

Determining this ought to be relatively simple – every firm should use a checklist to ensure that the financial statements comply with the disclosure requirements of the Companies Act and relevant accounting standards. Such checklists usually form a part of the 'audit packs' which firms use.

To some extent the job has been made easier by the widespread use of accounts production software, but software is only as good as the people writing it, installing it and using it.

For example:

- If directors' emoluments are not coded to the right account in the chart of accounts they will not be disclosed properly in the financial statements

- If the client has a material accounting policy which is not in the 'standard list' in the template on which the financial statements are based, it will not appear in the accounting policies note unless you add it

Checklisting the accounts, therefore is still a good idea.

As you know from your other studies, the nature of financial statements these days is incredibly complex. For UK companies be aware that:

- There are a large number of financial reporting standards – either UK or International – applicable to financial statements

- The Companies Act itself is a substantial document which determines the format to be used in financial statements and the disclosures to be made on the face of the primary statements and in the supporting notes

- The directors' report, and other information released with the financial statements, need to be consistent with the financial statements so the auditor must read that information and resolve any inconsistencies

3.2 Do the financial statements make sense?

We have considered the techniques required to carry out analytical procedures as part of the risk assessment process at the planning stage and as a substantive procedure.

Analytical procedures **must** also be used in the overall review at the end of the audit to assist the auditor when forming an overall conclusion as to whether the financial statements are consistent with the auditor's understanding of the entity.

The steps for carrying out analytical procedures at this stage of the audit are very similar to those used as part of the risk assessment process at the planning stage, but they happen in a rather different way.

- Interpretation
- Investigation
- Corroboration

3.2.1 Interpretation

The person carrying out the analytical procedures, reads through the financial statements and interprets them, considering the absolute figures themselves and relevant ratios.

3.2.2 Investigation

When analytical procedures are used as risk assessment procedures or as a substantive procedure, the aim is to identify potential problems. The problems are then investigated during fieldwork by making enquiries and gathering audit evidence.

At the completion stage the reviewer will expect to find the answers to the issues raised by the review on the audit file.

3.2.3 Corroboration

Should those answers not be on the file, further work will need to be done.

From a practical point of view it is worth remembering the following:

- For the smaller client the working papers supporting the final analytical procedures may well be simply an update of the work done at the planning stage

- For the larger client the review becomes a much more specific exercise

- The financial statements used for the analytical procedures need to incorporate any adjustments made as a result of the audit

- Any problems identified by the procedures, which indicate that the financial statements should to be amended, need to be actioned

4 Other matters

At the completion stage the reviewer has to consider the issues which have been raised by the audit and what the firm's response in the auditor's report should be.

At this stage the reviewer needs to consider:

- Is the impact of errors and misstatements uncovered during the audit likely to be material?
- Are there matters of principle where the auditor disagrees with the client?

The second of these questions can cause severe difficulties for the audit firm in exercising its professional judgement.

It is possible for there to be points of principle which although not material in themselves, in the current period, could lead to problems in the future, or lead to the reassessment of audit risk.

4.1 Errors discovered

ISA (UK) 450 *Evaluation of Misstatements Identified During the Audit* requires the auditor to accumulate misstatements identified during the audit unless those misstatements are trivial. The auditor must evaluate the effect of identified misstatements on the audit and evaluate the effect of uncorrected misstatements, if any, on the financial statements.

- Identified misstatements: the auditor will need to consider revising the overall plan if:

    - The misstatements identified indicate that other misstatements may exist, which when accumulated could be material; or

    - Accumulated misstatements approach the materiality level set for the audit.

    Where management has corrected misstatements detected, the auditor shall perform additional procedures to determine whether misstatements remain.

- Communication and correction of misstatements:

    - The auditor shall inform management of all misstatements and request that they be corrected

    - If management refuses the auditor shall ascertain the reason and take this into account in the overall evaluation

- Examining the effect of uncorrected misstatements:

    - Reassess materiality

    - Determine whether uncorrected misstatements are material, whether individually or in aggregate

    Materiality will depend on the nature of the misstatement and its impact on the financial statements. The auditor is required to inform those charged with governance and to request that corrections be made.

- Written representations:

  The auditor shall request confirmation from management that the effect of uncorrected misstatements is immaterial.

- Documentation – audit documentation shall include:

  - The amount below which misstatements are considered trivial
  - All misstatements accumulated
  - The auditor's conclusion regarding materiality of uncorrected misstatements

  Certain circumstances may cause the auditor to deem misstatements material even if they are below the materiality level. These circumstances include:

  - Compliance with regulatory requirements

  - Masking a change in trends or affecting ratios

  - Increasing management compensation

  - Affecting other information in documents included with the audited financial statements

Worked example: Enron

US company Enron devised a way of hiding debt by manipulating the detailed accounting rules for dealing with subsidiaries. This led to the non-disclosure of debt in excess of $20 billion. According to the Washington Post website, the initial transaction on which this technique was first used, was to artificially preserve the value of an investment of $300,000 which was immaterial in terms of the Enron audit, but the use of the technique led to misstatements which were very material indeed.

4.2 Opening balances

It may seem odd to consider opening balances at the completion stages of the audit, but the auditor needs to consider whether there is sufficient evidence to support their reliability. If the opening balances are misstated this will mean that the profits for the current year may also be misstated.

Normally where the audit engagement is continuing from previous years, this will not cause a problem, but for a new client there are questions of professional judgement about the reliability of the previous year's accounts, which in turn leads to questions about the quality of work of the previous auditors.

Where the engagement is an initial engagement (financial statements for prior period were not audited or audited by a predecessor auditor) the auditor will again have to consider the risks of unaudited figures from past periods being materially misstated.

ISA (UK) 510 *Initial Audit Engagements – Opening Balances* states that, in conducting an initial audit engagement, the objective of the auditor with respect to opening balances is to obtain sufficient appropriate audit evidence about whether:

(a) Opening balances contain misstatements that materially affect the current period's financial statements; and

(b) Appropriate accounting policies reflected in the opening balances have been consistently applied in the current period's financial statements, or changes thereto are appropriately accounted for and adequately presented and disclosed in accordance with the applicable financial reporting framework.

The auditor shall obtain sufficient appropriate audit evidence about whether the opening balances contain misstatements that materially affect the current period's financial statements by:

(a) Determining whether the prior period's closing balances have been correctly brought forward to the current period or, when appropriate, have been restated;

(b) Determining whether the opening balances reflect the application of appropriate accounting policies; and

(c) Performing one or more of the following:

(i) Whether the prior year financial statements were audited, reviewing the predecessor auditor's working papers to obtain evidence regarding the opening balances;

(ii) Evaluating whether audit procedures performed in the current period provide evidence relevant to the opening balances; or

(iii) Performing specific audit procedures to obtain evidence regarding the opening balances.

Such procedures may include:

- Checking receipts from opening receivables
- Verifying opening payables in the light of payments made during the current period
- Reconciling from an inventory figure which has been audited back to the opening position
- Obtaining confirmations from relevant third parties – lenders, valuers etc

The auditor will also need to consider the comparative figures in the financial statements. ISA (UK) 710 *Comparative Information – Corresponding Figures and Comparative Financial Statements* states that the objectives of the auditor with respect to comparative information are:

- To obtain sufficient appropriate audit evidence about whether the comparative information has been presented, in all material respects, in accordance with the requirements for comparative information in the applicable financial reporting framework; and

- To report in accordance with the auditor's reporting responsibilities.

Interactive question 1: Opening balances

Your firm has just been appointed auditors of Cross Ltd after the previous auditors were removed following a dispute with the directors. This dispute related to certain costs capitalised by the directors, which the auditors believed should have been written off. (Last year's auditor's report was qualified because of the disagreement.)

Requirement

State the procedures you would carry out regarding the opening balances.

See **Answer** at the end of this chapter.

4.3 Going concern

The problem

The going concern concept is fundamental to the way in which financial statements are prepared and has been so for a very long time indeed.

If you think about it carefully, you will see that it is probably a major contributor to the expectations gap which is considered in a number of places in this Study Manual.

Worked example: The way financial statements are prepared

Consider the deceptively simple example of a non-current asset such as a car. We all know that, as soon as you drive your brand new car away from the showroom it loses a disproportionate amount of its resale value and that this depreciation happens very rapidly in the early stages of the car's life, before flattening out after a couple of years or so. However, in financial statements, the depreciation charge and resultant reduction in the car's net book value is usually dealt with on a straight line basis, because, over time, it is probably truer and fairer to amortise the car's value evenly over its life – it is, after all, an asset which is 'used up' evenly over its life, whatever its resale value at any particular point in time. It is also administratively easier to calculate depreciation this way.

The reason why this treatment is acceptable is because the company has no intention of disposing of the asset at the reporting date, but will use it in the normal course of business until the appropriate time arrives for its disposal. There is, nevertheless, a very real and potentially material difference between the market value of a company's fleet of vehicles and their carrying value in the statement of financial position.

The argument used in the example also applies to a number of other assets. If the company's complete inventory had to be disposed of, or the receivables all collected in on the first day of the new year, it is highly probable that the amounts realised would be less than those shown in the statement of financial position. In addition, liabilities not reflected in the financial statements will crystallise, such as redundancy payments or lease penalty clauses.

It follows from this that, if the going concern concept is not an appropriate basis on which to prepare the financial statements, the implications will be very serious, as almost all of the normal assumptions made will be called into question.

4.3.1 Work to be done

The auditor's responsibility is to obtain sufficient appropriate audit evidence about the appropriateness of management's use of the going concern assumption. The risks of the client not being a going concern will need to be considered and planned for at the planning stage, and, at the completion stage, certain specific tasks will have to be carried out.

These will include:

- Consideration of all areas of the statement of financial position to see whether there are indications that the going concern concept may be inappropriate such as:

    - Significant receivables unable to pay
    - Lines of inventory and WIP where net realisable value may be less than cost
    - Material non-current assets which are no longer usable
    - Deferred development expenditure which is irrecoverable against relevant revenues
    - Investments (in subsidiaries or other companies) which have lost value

- Review of future plans for the business including financial forecasts and projections, to ensure that it is probable that the company will be able to continue to trade for at least the forthcoming year (that is, not less than 12 months from the reporting date). If the period to which those charged with governance have paid particular attention in assessing going concern is less than one year from the date of approval of the financial statements, and those charged with governance have not disclosed that fact, the auditor shall do so within the auditor's report. ISA (UK) 570 requires the period of assessment to be at least one year from the date of approval of the financial statements, which differs from the IAASB requirement for the period to be from the end of the reporting period.

- Review of the company's borrowing facilities and other sources of finance to ensure that they will be adequate for the forthcoming year and that conditions and covenants imposed by lenders will not be breached.

- Review of minutes and other information such as correspondence with legal advisers, for indications of potential going concern problems.

ISA (UK) 570 contains requirements for those entities that are required (and those that choose voluntarily) to report on how they have applied the UK Corporate Governance Code. These requirements can be summarised as follows.

The auditor shall read and consider the following in evaluating management's assessment of the entity's ability to continue as a going concern:

- Confirmation from the directors in the annual report that they have considered the principal risks facing the entity, in terms of its business model and its future performance, solvency and liquidity.

- Disclosures in the annual report of those risks and how they are being managed or mitigated.

- Directors' statement in the financial statements about the suitability of using the going concern basis of accounting, and any material uncertainties that could affect this suitability for a period of at least twelve months from the date of approval of the financial statements.

- Directors' explanation in the annual report of their assessment of the entity's prospects and the assumptions upon which this assessment is based.

Should the auditor have anything material to add to the above then this should be included in the auditor's report. Matters that the auditor may wish to add include:

- Information that indicates that that the annual report and accounts are not fair and balanced with respect to the principal risks facing the entity.

- Matters relating to the robustness of the directors' assessment of risks that the auditor has communicated to the audit committee but that are not appropriately address in the annual report.

A list of possible symptoms of going concern problems from ISA (UK) 570 *Going Concern* is reproduced in Chapter 7, section 5.

ISA (UK) 570 also says that the auditors have to discuss the going concern issue with the client's management, to test the assumptions they have made to ensure they are justified, to obtain written representations from management about the things they are intending to do in the future to ensure that the going concern basis is appropriate and to review that disclosures made in the financial statements relating to going concern are sufficient to give a true and fair view in the UK. If, in making their assessment, the directors have used a period of less than a year from the date of approval of the financial statements and have not disclosed that fact in the financial statements, the auditors should do so in the auditor's report.

4.3.2 The liquidation basis

If it becomes clear that the client cannot be considered to be a going concern, the financial statements will need to disclose this and the basis for preparing them will change to the liquidation or 'break-up' basis.

This means that values will have to be adjusted to the amounts expected to be realised. In practice this tends not to be a problem for the auditor, because by the time this stage is reached, the client may well have passed into the hands of the receiver or 'corporate recovery' expert.

Alternatively, when it is intended to wind-up a solvent client within the next 12 months on a voluntary basis, the values may not in the event be very different.

4.3.3 Implications for the auditor's report

Unfortunately, this is not the end of the story because, where there are doubts about a company's going concern status, the auditors and management are likely to reach different conclusions, and this has implications for the auditor's report.

If the going concern assumption is appropriate but a material uncertainty exists about the ability of an entity to continue as a going concern and the uncertainty is adequately disclosed in the financial statements, the auditor should express an unqualified opinion but modify the auditor's report by adding a 'material uncertainty related to going concern' section (see Chapter 13).

If the financial statements fail to give a true and fair view because it is inappropriate to use the going concern basis, the auditor should express an adverse opinion (see Chapter 13).

Interactive question 2: Gamston Burgers plc

You are the auditor of Gamston Burgers plc, whose principal activities are haulage and warehousing services and the repair of lorries.

During the current year the company has suffered a significant fall in revenue and gross profit, which has led to a trading loss. The company is also experiencing cash flow problems.

You have been informed by the managing director that the fall in revenue is due to:

- The loss, half way through the year, of a long-standing customer to a competitor
- A decline in trade in the lorry repair business

Due to the reduction in the repairs business the company has decided to close the workshop and sell the inventory of equipment and spares.

During the year the company replaced a number of vehicles, funding them by a combination of leasing and an increased overdraft facility. The facility is to be reviewed early next year after the audited accounts are available.

The draft accounts show a loss for the current year but the forecasts indicate a return to profitability in 20X6, as the managing director is optimistic about generating additional revenue from new contracts.

Requirements

(a) Explain why an auditor attaches so much importance to considering an entity's ability to continue as a going concern

(b) Describe the audit work you would undertake in order to ascertain whether Gamston Burgers plc is a going concern

(c) Explain the effect on your auditors' report on the financial statements of Gamston Burgers plc if you:

    (i)   Agree with the director's assertion

    (ii) Conclude that trading conditions will not improve

See **Answer** at the end of this chapter.

4.4 Subsequent events

If the auditor's report says that the financial statements give a true and fair view, but the company goes under shortly after the financial statements are published, someone is likely to question whether the auditors knew what they were talking about.

If it then emerges that there were significant receivables who failed to pay up, or material amounts of inventory which turned out not to be realisable, you might think that such questions were justified.

Clearly, therefore, a review of events after the reporting period is both a sensible thing to do and, according to ISA (UK) 560 *Subsequent Events*, compulsory.

ISA (UK) 560 recognises the two different types of subsequent event according to IAS 10:

- Those that provide evidence of conditions that existed at the date of the financial statements (adjusting events); and

- Those that provide evidence of conditions that arose after the date of the financial statements (non-adjusting events).

Examples of adjusting events (that should be reflected in the financial statements):

- Resolution of a court case
- Bankruptcy of a major customer
- Evidence of the NRV of inventories
- Discovery of fraud or errors

Examples of non-adjusting events (that are not reflected in the financial statements but should be disclosed in the notes if they are material):

- Destruction of a major asset by flood or fire
- Major share transactions
- Announcement of a plan to close part of a business
- Dividends proposed/declared after the end of the reporting period

Note: If a 'non-adjusting event' occurs after the reporting date that means that it is no longer appropriate to assume that the entity is a going concern then the financial statements should be restated.

ISA (UK) 560 also recognises three time periods and recommends the following responses:

Period	Audit response
Up to the date of the auditor's report	• Carry out audit procedures outlined in ISA (UK) 560 • Consider whether the appropriate amendments/disclosures have been made in the financial statements • Consider whether there is a need to amend the auditor's report
Between the date of the auditor's report and the date the financial statements are issued	No responsibility for further work in this period, but if the auditor becomes aware of material facts: • Discuss with management • Take appropriate action
After the financial statements are issued	No responsibility for further work in this period, but if the auditor becomes aware of material facts: • Discuss with management • Take appropriate action Where the relevant fact did not exist at the date of the auditor's report there are no statutory provisions for revising the financial statements: • Discuss with management whether to withdraw the financial statements • Take advice on possibility of withdrawing the auditor's report

4.4.1 Audit procedures up to the date of the auditors' report

Procedures testing subsequent events	

Enquiries of management	• Status of items involving **subjective judgement**/accounted for using preliminary data
	
	• Whether there are any new **commitments**, borrowings or guarantees
	
	• Whether there have been any:
	  – **Sales** or destruction of **assets**
	  – **Issues** of **shares/debentures** or changes in business structure
	  – **Developments** involving **risk areas, provisions** and **contingencies**
	  – **Unusual accounting adjustments**
	  – **Major events** (eg, going concern problems) affecting appropriateness of accounting policies for estimates

Other procedures	• **Review** management procedures for identifying subsequent events to ensure that such events are identified • **Read minutes** of general board/committee meetings and enquire about unusual items • **Review latest accounting records** and financial information and budgets and forecasts • **Obtain evidence** concerning any litigation or claims from the company's solicitors (only with client permission)

Interactive question 3: Subsequent events review

You are the auditor of Weekly Ltd, which derives half its revenue from sales to one large national company. During your audit you notice that the sales ledger balance of this customer has nearly doubled during the year, although sales to it have increased only marginally.

Requirement

Note down the main elements of your subsequent events review programme relating to this receivable balance.

See **Answer** at the end of this chapter.

4.5 Written representations

You learnt about the nature and purpose of written management representations in your studies for Assurance.

According to ISA (UK) 580 *Written Representations,* the auditor is required to obtain certain written representations from management as part of its audit evidence. These representations will usually be collated and finalised at the completion stage of the audit. The representation letter should be signed by the directors (or a directors' board minute of the representation obtained) before the auditors sign the auditor's report – if not, the auditors have not obtained all the evidence they required to sign the auditor's report in the first place.

Summary and Self-test

Summary

Self-test

Answer the following questions.

1   What three questions will the partner responsible for signing the auditor's report seek to answer at completion?

(i)   ....

(ii)   ....

(iii) ....

2   It is appropriate to use a checklist to determine whether the financial statements comply with the Companies Act.

☐ True

☐ False

3   Opening balances need only be checked in a new auditor situation.

☐ True

☐ False

4   List five financial indicators that a company has going concern problems.

(i)   ....

(ii)   ....

(iii) ....

(iv)   ....

(v)   ....

5   Is the auditor responsible for discovering relevant subsequent events after the auditor's report has been signed?

Exam-style questions

6   You have recently been appointed auditor of Supachill Ltd and are planning the audit for the year ending 31 December 20X5. You have obtained the following background information about the company.

The company prepares chilled foods and sells them to supermarkets under its own brand name and that of a national supermarket chain, with which it has a one year renewable contract. At present this contract represents 45% of revenue. The company is currently negotiating a substantial contract with another supermarket chain, but is reluctant to agree to the prices and 60 days' credit facility demanded.

On 1 January 20X5 the managing director, who was previously involved in property development, acquired all the shares in Supachill Ltd from Omega plc, a conglomerate, which was rationalising its operations.

Immediately following the acquisition Supachill Ltd had net assets of £2 million, after taking account of low interest loans of £5 million from Omega plc. These loans are secured on the freehold property of the company and are repayable in equal quarterly instalments over a five-year period until 31 December 20X9. Day-to-day working capital is funded by an overdraft facility of £1.5 million, secured by a fixed and floating charge on the other assets of the company. This facility is to be reviewed by the bank early in 20X6 after the audited accounts are available.

The original business plan envisaged the acquisition of an adjacent factory to enable the company to double its output, but this expansion has been postponed.

The managing director has explained that there will be a delay in preparing the draft accounts as the finance director has left and has yet to be replaced. The accountant is assisted in the day-to-day accounting function by temporary staff. There is a projected loss for the year but forecasts indicate a return to profitability in the next financial year.

Requirements

(a) From the situation outlined above, identify circumstances particular to Supachill Ltd that give you cause for concern. Explain why such factors give cause for concern.

(12 marks)

(b) Describe the procedures that you would undertake during the course of your audit in order to satisfy yourself on the status of Supachill Ltd as a going concern. **(6 marks)**

(18 marks)

7 Your client has lost a contract with its major customer. As a result the company is in financial difficulties. The bank is threatening to foreclose on its loan.

You are concerned that the company may not be a going concern, although, looking ahead nine months from the date of approval of the financial statements, the directors inform you that there is a good future for the business.

What steps would you take to enable you to assess whether the directors' assertions are reasonable?

What impact would the nine month period referred to above have on your auditor's report?

(3 marks)

Now, go back to the Learning outcomes in the Introduction. If you are satisfied you have achieved these outcomes, please tick them off.

Technical reference

C
H
A
P
T
E
R

12

Answers to Interactive questions

Answer to Interactive question 1

Regarding all opening balances:

- Check prior year closing balances have been correctly brought forward;

- Where appropriate, restated;

- Consider impact of current year work on opening balances (eg, irrecoverable debts write off in current year compared to opening allowance); or

- Review management's working papers, accounting and internal control systems for prior year.

For capitalised costs:

- Agree amounts capitalised to supporting documentation (to confirm amount).
- Discuss with previous auditors reason for the qualification.
- Decide whether opening balances need amendment.

Answer to Interactive question 2

(a) **Importance of going concern**

(i) 'Going concern' is an accounting concept. It is presumed to apply to any financial statements, unless contrary disclosure is given.

(ii) The amount at which assets and liabilities are included in the statement of financial position may be significantly different where the company is not a going concern. For example:

- Assets will be valued on a break-up basis
- Additional provisions (eg, for closure costs) may be required.

(iii) The classification of items will differ where financial statements reflect a break-up basis. For example, non-current assets/liabilities reclassified as current.

(iv) The risk of failure is a real threat to many businesses and the failure of the auditor to give any warning may result in litigation/adverse publicity.

(b) **Audit work regarding going concern**

To ascertain whether Gamston Burgers plc can meet its debts as they fall due:

(i) Obtain a written statement (management representation) from the managing director confirming his considered view that the company is a going concern.

(ii) Review management's profit and cash flow forecasts for the next financial year to ascertain, *inter alia*, the company's working capital requirements.

(iii) Confirm the appropriateness of relevant assumptions (eg, average trade receivables collection period) by comparison with ratios obtained from analytical procedures.

(iv) Request a statement of borrowing facilities to be included in the bank confirmation letter.

(v) Review the day-to-day utilisation of the bank overdraft facility and its proximity to the current limit.

(vi) Obtain a loan confirmation from the leasing company and confirm that all instalments to date have been met.

(vii) Discuss with the credit controller (or financial accountant) the current pressures under which the company is being placed by larger customers who may be seeking extended credit terms.

(viii) Undertake sensitivity analysis on client's forecasts to variable factors both within the managing director's control and outside it

(ix) Review the level of trade and other payables (including VAT and PAYE/NIC and whether any penalties are being incurred) after the reporting date and the extent to which they are financing short-term needs.

To ascertain whether Gamston Burgers plc can otherwise continue in business (ie, return to profitable trading):

(i) Obtain a copy of tenders submitted/correspondence to date concerning any new contracts currently being negotiated and monitor all subsequent developments.

(ii) Review drivers' logs, reports on warehouse utilisation etc and discuss with management how current spare capacity will be utilised by new contracts obtained.

(iii) Review the terms of the contract with the long-standing customer which was lost and the grounds on which it was lost to a competitor.

(iv) Verify reasonableness of estimates arising from closure of workshop (eg, concerning costs of external servicing of the transport vehicle fleet).

(v) Obtain written confirmation from the company's legal adviser as to whether or not there are any pending legal claims (eg, in respect of inventory losses from warehouses, late deliveries, damage to goods in transit etc).

(c) **Effect on auditor's report**

(i) **Agree with director's assertion**

If doubt surrounding the going concern status of the company is minimal, disclosure in the financial statements would not be required in order to give a true and fair view. The auditor's report would therefore be unqualified.

If the branch is so material that its inability to trade could affect the going concern status of the company (unlikely), the matter should be disclosed in the financial statements. If adequate disclosure is made in the financial statements, the auditor should express an unqualified opinion but modify his report by adding a paragraph headed 'Material Uncertainty Related to Going Concern' that:

- Highlights the existence of a material uncertainty relating to the event or condition that may cast significant doubt on the company's ability to continue as a going concern

- Draws attention to the note in the financial statements that discloses these matters.

(ii) **Disagree with director's assertion**

The form of auditor's report will depend upon the materiality of the branch and extent to which the uncertainty has been disclosed in the financial statements.

As the director appears confident about the future of this branch, it is unlikely that adequate (if any) disclosure has been made. The auditor's report would therefore be qualified on the grounds of material misstatement due to the inadequate disclosure of the uncertainty.

Answer to Interactive question 3

- Monitor post year end customer receipts (to confirm recoverability)

- Review of customer correspondence (to ascertain problem, eg, dispute)

- Calculation of trade receivables collection period, by month, after year end (to determine whether situation is deteriorating further)

- Consider likely effectiveness of any reservation of title clause/other security (to assess possible extent of recovery if customer liquidated)

- Review latest available audited accounts of customer (for indications of GC problems)

- Review level of post year end sales and orders (to determine whether situation is continuing unchecked).

Answers to Self-test

1   (i)   Do the financial statements comply with the provisions of the Companies Act 2006?
     (ii)   Do the financial statements make sense?
     (iii) Has the auditor's report been drafted properly?

2   True

3   False

4   Four from:

   (i)   Net liabilities or net current liability position

   (ii)   Necessary borrowing facilities have not been agreed

   (iii) Fixed-term borrowings approaching maturity without realistic prospects of renewal or repayment, or excessive reliance on short-term borrowings

   (iv)   Major debt repayment falling due where refinancing is necessary to the entity's continued existence

   (v)   Major restructuring of debt

   (vi)   Indications of withdrawal of financial support by creditors

   (vii) Negative operating cash flows indicated by historical or prospective financial statements

   (viii) Adverse key financial ratios

   (ix)   Substantial operating losses or significant deterioration in the value of assets used to generate cash flows

   (x)   Major losses or cash flow problems which have arisen since the reporting date

   (xi)   Arrears or discontinuance of dividends

   (xii) Inability to pay creditors on due dates

   (xiii) Inability to comply with terms of loan agreements

   (xiv) Reduction in normal terms of credit by suppliers

   (xv)   Change from credit to cash-on-delivery transactions with suppliers

   (xvi) Inability to obtain financing for essential new product development or other essential investments

   (xvii) Substantial sale of non-current assets not intended to be replaced

5   No – but he will have to take appropriate steps if made aware of them

6 (a)

Circumstance	Explanation
• The client's economic dependence on its principal customer (45% of revenue on a one year renewable contract).	• The going concern assumption may not be appropriate if, for any reason, this major contract is not renewed.
• Deterioration of cash flows, due to customers demanding/taking extended periods of credit (up to 60 days).	• The risk of irrecoverable and doubtful debts is increased, and year end receivables may be materially overstated if allowances are not adequate.
• Pressure from the potential customer's demands.	• Profit margins may be adversely affected, increasing doubts about the company's continuation as a going concern.
• Sale by conglomerate on favourable terms (low interest loans).	• Omega plc may not have been optimistic about Supachill Ltd's future prospects, which therefore raises going concern doubts.
• High gearing with repayments due in near future (£250,000 per quarter).	• Any breach in loan terms (eg, if instalments are not being met) may result in foreclosure. • Additional funding may be difficult to raise as security base is diminished.
• The postponement of plans for expansion (but it could be considered a mitigating factor).	• The adequacy of the working capital available, both the short and medium term must be assessed.
• The managing director's (MD) lack of knowledge of the nature of the business and the industry.	• The MD may lack the acumen to trade out of the loss-making situation, thereby increasing which it operates. Inherent risk.
• The loss of key staff (finance director).	• The reduction in supervision over the accounting functions may increase both inherent and control risk and result in: − More errors arising with the increase in the accountant's workload − Failure to detect and correct errors.
• The delay in preparing draft accounts may increase inherent risk if the audit deadline cannot be postponed.	• Increased pressure on the audit timetable to meet a possible bank deadline late in the year could result in a material misstatement being undetected by audit procedures.
• Only temporary accounts staff are available to assist accountant.	• The risk of errors arising is increased (eg, due to insufficient training/ supervision).

Circumstance	Explanation

• The bank's reliance on audited accounts, increasing management's motive to 'inflate' profit.	• Particular attention should be given to:
	
	  – The accuracy of bank overdraft/ payables cut-off
	
	  – The impact of potential adjustments on key ratios (eg, acid test ratio).

• The projected loss may cause the MD to bias the results. If, for example, the bank is already aware of (and accepts) the projection, the MD may ensure that the loss is met (eg, by over-providing against asset values). Alternatively, the reported loss may be understated by understating allowances.	• Attention should be given to all matters of judgement which materially affect the statement of profit or loss. In particular, the need for inventory and receivable allowances should be assessed (ie, tested for overstatement) as well as their adequacy (ie, tested for understatement).
• Lack of cumulative/prior knowledge from which assurance can be derived.	• Adequate planning is essential to audit efficiency to avoid over-auditing (due to increase in inherent risk) in the first year.
• The nature of the client's business.	• Chilled foods increase inherent risk as they are perishable and there may be understatement of year end allowances to reduce inventory to NRV.

(b) **Procedures**

To ensure that the company can meet its debts as they fall due

(i) Obtain a written statement from the managing director confirming his considered view that the company is a going concern.

(ii) Review management's profit and cash flow forecasts for the next financial year (and beyond, if available) to ascertain the company's working capital requirements.

(iii) Confirm the appropriateness of relevant assumptions, eg, average debt collection period, by comparison with ratios obtained through analytical procedures.

(iv) Request a statement of borrowing facilities to be included in the bank confirmation letter.

(v) Review the day-to-day utilisation of the bank overdraft facility and its proximity to the current limit.

(vi) Obtain confirmation of loan from Omega plc and that all quarterly instalments of loan repayment to date have been met.

(vii) Discuss with the credit controller (or financial accountant) the current pressures under which the company is being placed by larger customers seeking extended credit terms.

(viii) Review the MD's agreement with Omega plc for the purchase of Supachill Ltd to ascertain the circumstances under which interest rates or repayment terms could be varied.

(ix) Review the level of trade and other payables, including VAT and PAYE/NIC and whether any penalties are being incurred, and the extent to which they are financing short-term needs.

To ensure that the company can otherwise continue in business

(i) Obtain a copy of correspondence to date concerning the contract currently being negotiated, and monitor all subsequent developments.

(ii) Review production records and order books, and discuss with management how current spare capacity can accommodate substantial new contracts (as the expansion plans have been postponed).

(iii) Review the terms of the existing one-year renewable contract and correspondence with this customer, to ascertain whether there are any grounds for this contract not to be renewed.

(iv) Discuss with the MD any possible new sources of finance for the expansion.

(v) Obtain written confirmation from the company's legal advisor as to whether or not there are any pending legal claims (eg, in respect of food poisoning).

(vi) Discuss with the MD and/or the company's recruitment adviser the response to any advertisement for the position of finance director.

7 **Regarding ability to continue in business**

- Discuss with directors, eg:

    - Likelihood of alternative sales markets
    - Advertising/marketing strategy
    - Prospects of product diversification

- Scrutinise current year's order book

- Review tenders for new contracts

- Review published trading results for industry (expanding or in decline)

Regarding ability to meet debts as fall due

- Discuss with directors, eg:

    - Any intention to sell surplus assets
    - Impending negotiations for new sources of finance
    - Professional advice sought from bank
    - Confirm with bank/other lenders negotiations to date

Nine month period – effect in UK

- If period used for going concern assessment < 1 year from date of approval of financial statements

- And that fact not disclosed in financial statements

- Disclose in auditor's report

- But do not qualify auditor's report regarding this

ICAEW

CHAPTER 13

Reporting

Introduction

Examination context

TOPIC LIST

Summary and Self-test

Technical reference

Answers to Interactive questions

Answers to Self-test

Introduction

Learning outcomes

3 Concluding and reporting on engagements

Students will be able to conclude and report on assurance engagements in accordance with the terms of the engagements and appropriate standards.

- Draft suitable extracts for an assurance report (including any report to the management issued as part of the engagement) in relation to a specified organisation on the basis of given information, including in the extracts (where appropriate) statements of facts, their potential effects, and recommendations for action relevant to the needs and nature of the organisation being reported upon;

- Advise on reports to be issued to those responsible for governance in accordance with International Standards on Auditing, legislation, regulation and codes of corporate governance;

- Explain the elements (both explicit and implicit) of the auditor's report issued in accordance with the International Standards on Auditing and statutory requirements and recommend the nature of an audit opinion to be given in such a report; and

- Draft suitable extracts for an audit report (including any report to the management issued as part of the engagement) in relation to a specified organisation on the basis of given information, including in the extracts (where appropriate) statements of facts, their potential effects, and recommendations for action relevant to the needs and nature of the organisation being reported upon.

Syllabus links

The basic unmodified auditor's report was introduced in Assurance.

Examination context

This is an important area for the exam. Auditor's reports feature regularly in exam papers.

1 Communication with those charged with governance

Section overview

- Auditors are required to report privately to those charged with governance on various matters arising from the audit

- Relevant matters include:

    - Auditor's responsibilities in relation to the audit of financial statements
    - Planned scope and timing of the audit
    - Significant findings from the audit
    - Auditor independence

- Matters may be communicated orally or in writing

- They should be recorded in audit working papers

Various auditing standards require auditors to report certain audit matters arising to those charged with governance. This report will be 'private' and just for the attention of those charged with governance, as opposed to the auditor's report, which is a published document.

The requirements in relation to this private reporting are found in the main in ISA (UK) 260 *Communication with those Charged with Governance* which deals with the auditor's responsibility to communicate with those charged with governance in an audit of financial statements.

ISA (UK) 265 *Communicating Deficiencies in Internal Control to Those Charged with Governance and Management* specifically requires the auditor to communicate any significant deficiencies in internal control encountered during the course of their audit work. Whether a deficiency is significant is a matter of professional judgement for the auditor. Matters to consider will include the likelihood of material misstatements and potential losses or fraud.

1.1 Appropriate persons

Definition

Those charged with governance: Is the term used to describe the role of persons entrusted with the supervision, control and direction of the entity. Those charged with governance ordinarily are accountable for ensuring that the entity achieves its objectives, financial reporting and reporting to interested parties. Those charged with governance include management only when it performs such functions.

In the UK, those charged with governance include the directors (executive and non-executive) of a company and the members of an audit committee where one exists. For other types of entity, those charged with governance usually include equivalent persons such as the partners, proprietors, committee of management or trustees.

The auditors may communicate with the whole board, the supervisory board or the audit committee depending on the governance structure of the organisation. The auditor should ensure that those charged with governance are provided with a copy of the audit engagement letter on a timely basis.

To avoid misunderstandings, the engagement letter should explain that auditors will only **communicate matters** that come to their attention as a **result** of the **performance** of the audit. It should state that the auditors are **not required** to **design procedures** for the purpose of expressing an opinion on the effectiveness of the entity's internal control.

The letter may also:

- **Describe** the **form** which any **communications** on governance matters will take

- **Identify** the **appropriate persons** with whom such communications will be made

- **Identify** any **specific matters** of **governance** interest which it has agreed are to be communicated

1.2 Matters to be communicated

The scope of ISA (UK) 260 is limited to matters that come to the auditors' attention as a result of the audit; the auditors are not required to design procedures to identify matters of governance interest.

Such matters would include:

- The auditor's responsibilities in relation to the financial statement audit
- Planned scope and timing of the audit
- Significant findings from the audit
- Auditor independence (in the case of listed entities)

Under significant findings the standard lists the following:

- Written representations the auditor is requesting

- The auditor's views about significant qualitative aspects of the entity's accounting practices, including accounting policies, accounting estimates and financial statement disclosures

- Significant difficulties, if any, encountered during the audit

- Significant matters, if any, arising from the audit that were discussed with management

- Other matters, if any, arising from the audit that, in the auditor's professional judgement, are significant to the oversight of the financial reporting process.

Where the audited entity is listed, auditors shall:

- Confirm that the engagement team have complied with ethical requirements relating to independence

- Declare all relationships between the firm and the entity that may have a bearing on independence, including details of fees for non-audit services

- Detail the related safeguards that have been applied to eliminate identified threats to independence or reduce them to an acceptable level

For entities that report on how they have applied the UK Corporate Governance Code, the auditor should also report to the audit committee any information that the auditor deems relevant with respect to fulfilling its responsibilities under the Code.

1.2.1 Communicating deficiencies in internal control

ISA (UK) 265 does not require auditors to perform specific tests on internal control, over and above their normal audit work, but it does require them to report on deficiencies encountered during the course of that work. The specific requirements are the following:

- The auditor shall determine whether deficiencies in internal control have been identified

- Where deficiencies have been identified the auditor shall determine whether those deficiencies are significant

- Significant deficiencies shall be communicated in writing to those charged with governance

- Significant deficiencies shall be communicated in writing to management

- Other deficiencies shall be communicated to management if the auditor considers them important enough to warrant management attention
- Written communication shall include a description of the deficiencies and their potential effects, and sufficient information to understand the context of the communication

The written communication shall include sufficient information to enable those charged with governance and management to understand the context, in particular:

- The purpose of the audit was for the auditor to express an opinion on the financial statements
- The audit included consideration of internal control relevant to the preparation of financial statements in order to design audit procedures, not in order to express an opinion on those controls
- The matters being reported are limited to those deficiencies that the auditor has identified during the audit that merit being reported to those charged with governance

The standard gives examples of matters that the auditor may consider in determining whether deficiencies are significant. These examples include:

- The likelihood of the deficiencies leading to material misstatements
- The susceptibility to loss or fraud
- The financial statement amounts
- The volume of activity
- The importance of the controls to the financial reporting process

1.3 How?

Matters may be communicated orally or in writing, but they should be recorded in the audit working papers, however discussed. Certain matters must, however, be communicated in writing, for example significant deficiencies in internal controls. Auditors should make clear that the audit is not designed to identify all relevant matters connected with governance and they should have regard to local laws and regulations, and local guidance on confidentiality when communicating with management.

1.4 Attributes for effective communication to those charged with governance

The communication should have the following attributes:

- **Timing**: it should be sufficiently prompt to enable those charged with governance to take appropriate action, for example, items relating to the financial statements should be reported before the financial statements are approved.

- **Extent, form and frequency**: should be appropriate. What is appropriate will depend on the size of the entity and the way in which those charged with governance operate.

- **Expectations**: it should fulfil the expectations of the auditors and those charged with governance, and therefore, the nature of the communication should be agreed early in the audit process, for example, in the letter of engagement, so that misunderstandings are minimised.

- **Management comments**: should be included where they are relevant and will aid the understanding of those charged with governance.

- **Previous year's points**: should be repeated if no action has been taken and the auditors believe that they are still relevant. If there are no new points to be made, the auditors should make that point.

- **Disclaimer**: should be included so that third parties do not seek to rely on the information given within the report.

Effective communication is a two way process between auditors and those charged with governance. Communication received from the client should be documented and responded to appropriately.

Interactive question 1: Mouse and Ratty Ltd

You are currently undertaking an assurance engagement for Mouse and Ratty Ltd, a large firm of PR consultants in Leeds.

During the course of the work you have found a number of issues on which you need to report. These can be summarised as follows:

(1) You have found a total of £18,000 of unauthorised expenditure on IT equipment. Any IT expenditure in excess of £150 has to be authorised by a director.

(2) The IT expenditure for the year is 65% in excess of budget. There does not appear to have been an investment project which was not budgeted for. There seems to be little reason for the rise.

(3) Large sums for travelling expenses are not being authorised when in excess of nightly limits set. Four executives spent a total of £25,000 in excess of nightly limits throughout the year.

(4) When examining work in progress, it became clear that there were sums which have been there for more than six months without being billed. These total £56,000. There appears to be no explanation for this.

(5) When overtime forms are submitted, any amounts of more than three hours per month need to be authorised. This is rarely done. The company paid out £180,000 in unauthorised overtime.

(6) There are no controls over non-chargeable time. The proportion of non-chargeable time for individual executives varies from 5% to 34%.

Requirements

Identify:

(a) The internal control deficiencies arising from the above
(b) The risks to which each identified deficiency exposes the company
(c) Actions that the company should take to mitigate those risks

See **Answer** at the end of this chapter.

2 Unmodified auditor's reports

Section overview

- The report per ISA (UK) 700 contains a number of standard elements
- UK auditors also report by exception on a number of legal matters
- Some UK auditors include a 'Bannerman' paragraph in the auditor's report to ensure that the extent of their liability in respect of the report is understood
- With regard to listed companies, the auditor's report will also refer to the review of the corporate governance statement required by the UK Corporate Governance Code

The following sections will look at the types of auditor's reports that auditors may issue. ISA (UK) 700 *Forming an Opinion and Reporting on Financial Statements* and FRC Bulletin (October 2016) *Compendium of Illustrative Auditor's Reports on United Kingdom Private Sector Financial*

Statements for periods commencing on or after 17 June 2016 set out standardised auditor's reports for auditors to use. This has the benefit of providing a degree of consistency between auditor's reports on financial statements and enhances their understandability.

In all cases an opinion on the financial statements will need to be included. The opinion may be:

- An unmodified **opinion**: the auditor is satisfied that the evidence obtained is sufficient and appropriate and supports the view presented in the financial statements prepared by the company's management.

- A modified **opinion**: the auditor is either not satisfied with the sufficiency or appropriateness of the evidence that has been obtained, compared with what could reasonably be expected, or has issues with the content of the financial statements.

In some cases the auditor may need to add additional paragraphs in the auditor's report that would only be included under certain circumstances; these do not, however, indicate that there is anything wrong with the financial statements or the audit evidence obtained. These circumstances will be discussed in detail in section 4.

When the auditor makes amendments to a standard auditor's report (be it due to modifying the audit opinion or adding additional paragraphs) this is referred to as a modified **auditor's report**.

The opinions open to the auditor are therefore to issue:

(1) An unmodified auditor's report

(2) A modified auditor's report with an unmodified audit opinion

(3) A modified auditor's report with a modified audit opinion, which can be a qualified opinion (except for), an adverse opinion or disclaimer of opinion

2.1 Auditing standards and the auditor's report

A number of auditing standards deal with the auditor's report. In June 2016 the FRC issued a new suite of ISAs that are now largely in line with the equivalent IAASB standards, with additional clauses that are specific to the UK.

- ISA (UK) 700 *Forming an Opinion and Reporting on Financial Statements* deals with the content and format of the auditor's report. Key changes to this relate to the positioning of the opinion section before the basis for opinion section, enhanced auditor reporting on going concern, a statement about the auditor's independence and fulfilment of ethical responsibilities, and enhanced description of auditor's responsibilities.

- ISA (UK) 700 provides illustrations of auditor's reports in the Appendix, noting that these have not been tailored for the UK. For this it directs the reader to the current version of the FRC's *Compendium of Illustrative Auditor's Reports*. The current version was issued in October 2016.

- ISA (UK) 701 *Communicating Key Audit Matters in the Independent Auditor's Report*. This is a new standard that requires the auditor to communicate those matters that are viewed by the auditor as most significant, together with an explanation of how those matters were addressed during the course of the audit. The standard also requires a greater audit focus on going concern and how this is disclosed, and more transparency about the work of the auditor. The aim of the standard is to improve the quality of the auditor's report and of financial reporting in general. It applies primarily to listed entities.

The key requirements of ISA (UK) 701 are summarised below:

- Key audit matters (KAMs) are selected from those matters communicated with those charged with governance, taking into account significant risks, auditor judgements, and events or transactions

- A description of each KAM is provided

- KAMs are not a substitute for a modified opinion as required by ISA (UK) 705

- An explanation of how the concept of materiality was applied in planning and performing the audit is provided in the overview of the scope of the audit with specific reference to KAMs

FRC Bulletin (October 2016) on auditor's reports is included in your open book for this examination.

2.2 The main components of an auditor's report as required by ISA (UK) 700

Figure 13.1: Overview: unmodified report

2.2.1 Title

The report needs an appropriate title to distinguish it from the other material included with the financial statements and to try to reduce the 'expectations gap'.

In order to do this the title will include the words '**Independent Auditor**' to stress that, whilst the financial statements are management's responsibility, the auditor's report is the responsibility of the auditor alone. Using the term 'Independent Auditor' also serves to distinguish the auditor's report from any other report issued to shareholders.

The title usually also refers to the people to whom the report is addressed.

2.2.2 Addressee

Because in carrying out their audit work the auditors have to deal with management and work closely with the client's management team, it may be forgotten that their report is not directed towards management. The Companies Act requires the auditor's report to be addressed to the members or shareholders of a company because the audit is carried out on their behalf.

Remember the fundamental structure of an assurance engagement:

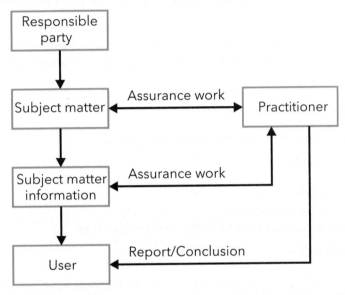

Figure 13.2: Assurance engagement

It is important to remember that the report will be addressed to the user in the tripartite relationship which exists in any assurance engagement, which for an audit in the UK means the company's shareholders.

Whilst the auditor's report does not represent a direct commentary on the performance of management over the period, it does state whether or not the account which management gives of its own performance is true and fair.

Understanding this relationship is important to all the parties involved, and clearly setting out the addressee of the report should also contribute to a reduction in the expectations gap.

2.2.3 Opinion paragraph

Identifying the statements

Identifying the statements covered by the auditor's report has traditionally been done by referring to the relevant page numbers. However, as well as leaving scope for silly errors if the number of pages changes whilst the financial statements are being finalised, to refer to page numbers has become irrelevant if the financial statements are published as web pages, which is permitted under UK law. Best practice, therefore is to refer to the statements by name.

The opinion itself

In the UK the auditors will normally express their opinion by reference to the 'true and fair view'. Whilst this term is at the heart of the audit, 'true' and 'fair' are not defined in law or audit guidance. However, for practical purposes the following definitions are generally accepted.

- **True**: Information is factual and conforms with reality, not false. In addition the information conforms with required standards and law. The accounts have been correctly extracted from the books and records.

- **Fair**: Information is free from discrimination and bias in compliance with expected standards and rules. The accounts should reflect the commercial substance of the company's underlying transactions.

ISA (UK) 700 requires the opinion paragraph to state clearly that the financial statements 'give a true and fair view'.

The financial reporting framework

All financial statements are prepared in accordance with a **financial reporting framework**. This may be in accordance with International Reporting Standards, or the standards used in other jurisdictions.

In the UK the Companies Act 2006 embraces 'applicable accounting standards' and the framework reference is usually '**have been prepared in accordance with the requirements of the Companies Act 2006**'.

2.2.4 Basis for opinion

This provides important context for the auditor's opinion.

It should therefore identify:

- That ISAs have been followed
- That the auditor is independent
- The ethical framework under which the auditor operates

2.2.5 Key audit matters (KAMs)

These are matters that the auditor considers to be of most significance during the audit. A brief description of each KAM should follow.

2.2.6 Application of materiality

This is an explanation of how the auditor applied the concept of materiality in planning and performing the audit.

2.2.7 Respective responsibilities of directors and auditors

In the UK there is usually a statement of directors' responsibilities towards the financial statements, included either in the directors' report or as a separate statement. A cross reference is therefore made in UK auditor's reports.

There is also a statement of the auditors' responsibilities, emphasising that the auditor reports on the truth and fairness of the financial statements.

2.2.8 Other responsibilities

In some jurisdictions the auditor reports on other matters as required by relevant legislation – in the Republic of Ireland, for example, the auditor's report includes a statement about the maintenance of the company's capital. In the UK, the auditor is required to express an opinion as to whether the information in the directors' report is consistent with the financial statements. The auditor is also required to report on whether the strategic report is consistent with the financial statements. All companies apart from small companies are required to produce a strategic report. UK auditors are also required to identify the matters that are required by the Companies Act 2006 to be reported on by exception.

2.2.9 Name and signature of engagement partner

This may seem obvious, but it is all to do with emphasising who has responsibility for what.

Companies Act 2006 requires that where the auditor is a firm, the report must be signed by the 'senior statutory auditor' in his own name, for and on behalf of the auditor. Prior to this, reports were signed in the name of the firm. In most cases the senior statutory auditor will be the engagement partner.

The Act also gives an exemption from the requirements to name the auditor, arising from circumstances such as the protests in 2003 by animal rights extremists against Deloitte and Touche, then the auditors of Huntingdon Life Services Group plc.

The auditor's name and, where the auditor is a firm, the name of the person who signed the report as senior statutory auditor, may be omitted from:

(a) Published copies of the report; and

(b) The copy of the report delivered to the registrar of companies.

If the following conditions are met:

(a) There are reasonable grounds that statement of the name would create or be likely to create a serious risk that the auditor or senior statutory auditor, or any other person, would be subject to violence or intimidation; and

(b) The company has given notice of the resolution to the Secretary of State, stating the:

(i) Name and registered number of the company;

(ii) Financial year of the company to which the report relates; and

(iii) Name of the auditor and (where the auditor is a firm) the name of the person who signed the report as senior statutory auditor.

2.2.10 Address

Again this is to ensure that there is no doubt who is responsible for the report.

ISA (UK) 700 requires the report to name the location in the jurisdiction where the auditor practises.

2.2.11 Date

The date of the report should be the date when the auditor has obtained sufficient appropriate evidence to support the opinion.

It should not be earlier than the date when management approves the financial statements.

Worked example: UK auditor's report

An example of a complete UK auditor's report is given below. It is taken from Appendix 6 of FRC Bulletin (2016) and is appropriate for a listed company using IFRS and applying the UK Corporate Governance Code.

Independent auditor's report to the members of [XYZ Plc]

Opinion

We have audited the financial statements of [XYZ Plc] (the 'parent company') and its subsidiaries (the 'group') for the year ended [date] which comprise [*specify the titles of the primary statements*] and notes to the financial statements, including a summary of significant accounting policies. The financial reporting framework that has been applied in their preparation is applicable law and International Financial Reporting Standards (IFRSs) as adopted by the European Union.

In our opinion the financial statements:

- give a true and fair view of the state of the group's and of the parent company's affairs as at [date] and of the group's and the parent company's [profit/loss] for the year then ended;

- have been properly prepared in accordance with [IFRSs as adopted by the European Union]; and

- have been prepared in accordance with the requirements of the Companies Act 2006 and, as regards the group financial statements, Article 4 of the IAS Regulation.

Separate opinion in relation to IFRSs as issued by the IASB

As explained in note [X] to the group financial statements, the group in addition to complying with its legal obligation to apply IFRSs as adopted by the European Union, has also applied IFRSs as issued by the International Accounting Standards Board (IASB).

In our opinion the group financial statements give a true and fair view of the consolidated financial position of the group as at [date] and of its consolidated financial performance and its consolidated cash flows for the year then ended in accordance with IFRSs as issued by the IASB.

Basis for opinion

We conducted our audit in accordance with International Standards on Auditing (UK) (ISAs (UK)) and applicable law. Our responsibilities under those standards are further described in the Auditor's responsibilities for the audit of the financial statements section of our report. We are independent of the group in accordance with the ethical requirements that are relevant to our audit of the financial statements in the UK, including the FRC's Ethical Standard as applied to listed public interest entities, and we have fulfilled our other ethical responsibilities in accordance with these requirements. We believe that the audit evidence we have obtained is sufficient and appropriate to provide a basis for our opinion.

Conclusions relating to principal risks, going concern and viability statement

We have nothing to report in respect of the following information in the annual report, in relation to which the ISAs (UK) require us to report to you whether we have anything material to add or draw attention to:

- the disclosures in the annual report [set out on page ...] that describe the principal risks and explain how they are being managed or mitigated;

- the directors' confirmation [set out on page ...] in the annual report that they have carried out a robust assessment of the principal risks facing the group, including those that would threaten its business model, future performance, solvency or liquidity;

- the directors' statement [set out on page ...] in the financial statements about whether the directors considered it appropriate to adopt the going concern basis of accounting in preparing the financial statements and the directors' identification of any material uncertainties to the group and the parent company's ability to continue to do so over a period of at least 12 months from the date of approval of the financial statements;

- whether the directors' statement relating to going concern required under the Listing Rules in accordance with Listing Rule 9.8.6R(3) is materially inconsistent with our knowledge obtained in the audit; or

- the directors' explanation [set out on page ...] in the annual report as to how they have assessed the prospects of the group, over what period they have done so and why they consider that period to be appropriate, and their statement as to whether they have a reasonable expectation that the group will be able to continue in operation and meet its liabilities as they fall due over the period of their assessment, including any related disclosures drawing attention to any necessary qualifications or assumptions.

Key audit matters

Key audit matters are those matters that, in our professional judgment, were of most significance in our audit of the financial statements of the current period and include the most significant assessed risks of material misstatement (whether or not due to fraud) that we identified. These matters included those which had the greatest effect on: the overall audit strategy, the allocation of resources in the audit; and directing the efforts of the engagement team. These matters were addressed in the context of our audit of the financial statements as a whole, and in forming the context of materiality in planning and performing the audit, our opinion thereon, and we do not provide a separate opinion on these matters.

[*Description of each key audit matter in accordance with ISA (UK) 701.*]

Our application of materiality

[*Explanation of how the auditor applied the concept of materiality in planning and performing the group and parent company audit. This is required to include the threshold used by the auditor as being materiality for the group and parent company financial statements as a whole but may include other relevant disclosures.*]

An overview of the scope of our audit

[*Overview of the scope of the group and parent company audit, including an explanation of how the scope addressed each key audit matter and was influenced by the auditor's application of materiality.*]

[*Explanation as to what extent the audit was considered capable of detecting irregularities, including fraud.*]

Other information

The other information comprises the information included in the annual report [set out on pages …][including [*specify the titles of the other information*][set out on pages …], other than the financial statements and our auditor's report thereon. The directors are responsible for the other information. Our opinion on the financial statements does not cover the other information and, except to the extent otherwise explicitly stated in our report, we do not express any form of assurance conclusion thereon. In connection with our audit of the financial statements, our responsibility is to read the other information and, in doing so, consider whether the other information is materially inconsistent with the financial statements or our knowledge obtained in the audit or otherwise appears to be materially misstated. If we identify such material inconsistencies or apparent material misstatements, we are required to determine whether there is a material misstatement in the financial statements or a material misstatement of the other information. If, based on the work we have performed, we conclude that there is a material misstatement of the other information, we are required to report that fact. We have nothing to report in this regard.

In this context, we also have nothing to report in regard to our responsibility to specifically address the following items in the other information and to report as uncorrected material misstatements of the other information where we conclude that those items meet the following conditions:

- **Fair, balanced and understandable [set out on page …]** – [the statement given/the explanation as to why the annual report does not include a statement] by the directors that they consider the annual report and financial statements taken as a whole is fair, balanced and understandable and provides the information necessary for shareholders to assess the group's performance, business model and strategy, is materially inconsistent with our knowledge obtained in the audit; or

- **Audit committee reporting [set out on page …]** – [the section describing the work of the audit committee does not appropriately address matters communicated by us to the audit committee/ the explanation as to why the annual report does not include a section describing the work of the audit committee is materially inconsistent with our knowledge obtained in the audit]; or

- **Directors' statement of compliance with the UK Corporate Governance Code [set out on page ...]** – the parts of the directors' statement required under the Listing Rules relating to the company's compliance with the UK Corporate Governance Code containing provisions specified for review by the auditor in accordance with Listing Rule 9.8.10R(2) do not properly disclose a departure from a relevant provision of the UK Corporate Governance Code.

Opinions on other matters prescribed by the Companies Act 2006

In our opinion, the part of the directors' remuneration report to be audited has been properly prepared in accordance with the Companies Act 2006.

In our opinion, based on the work undertaken in the course of the audit:

- the information given in the strategic report and the directors' report for the financial year for which the financial statements are prepared is consistent with the financial statements and those reports have been prepared in accordance with applicable legal requirements;

- the information about internal control and risk management systems in relation to financial reporting processes and about share capital structures, given in compliance with rules 7.2.5 and 7.2.6 in the Disclosure Rules and Transparency Rules sourcebook made by the Financial Conduct Authority (the FCA Rules), is consistent with the financial statements and has been prepared in accordance with applicable legal requirements; and

- information about the company's corporate governance code and practices and about its administrative, management and supervisory bodies and their committees complies with rules 7.2.2, 7.2.3 and 7.2.7 of the FCA Rules.

Matters on which we are required to report by exception

In the light of the knowledge and understanding of the group and the parent company and its environment obtained in the course of the audit, we have not identified material misstatements in:

- the strategic report or the directors' report; or

- the information about internal control and risk management systems in relation to financial reporting processes and about share capital structures, given in compliance with rules 7.2.5 and 7.2.6 of the FCA Rules.

We have nothing to report in respect of the following matters in relation to which the Companies Act 2006 requires us to report to you if, in our opinion:

- adequate accounting records have not been kept by the parent company, or returns adequate for our audit have not been received from branches not visited by us;

- the parent company financial statements and the part of the directors' remuneration report to be audited are not in agreement with the accounting records and returns;

- certain disclosures of directors' remuneration specified by law are not made;

- we have not received all the information and explanations we require for our audit; or

- a corporate governance statement has not been prepared by the parent company.

Responsibilities of directors

As explained more fully in the directors' responsibilities statement [set out on page ...], the directors are responsible for the preparation of the financial statements and for being satisfied that they give a true and fair view, and for such internal control as the directors determine is necessary to enable the preparation of financial statements that are free from material misstatement, whether due to fraud or error.

In preparing the financial statements, the directors are responsible for assessing the group's and the parent company's ability to continue as a going concern, disclosing, as applicable, matters related to going concern and using the going concern basis of accounting unless the directors either intend to liquidate the group or the parent company or to cease operations, or have no realistic alternative but to do so.

Auditor's responsibilities for the audit of the financial statements

Our objectives are to obtain reasonable assurance about whether the financial statements as a whole are free from material misstatement, whether due to fraud or error, and to issue an auditor's report that includes our opinion. Reasonable assurance is a high level of assurance, but is not a guarantee that an audit conducted in accordance with ISAs (UK) will always detect a material misstatement when it exists. Misstatements can arise from fraud or error and are considered material if, individually or in the aggregate, they could reasonably be expected to influence the economic decisions of users taken on the basis of these financial statements. A further description of our responsibilities for the audit of the financial statements is included in appendix [X] of this auditor's report. This description, which is located at [*indicate page number of other specific reference to the location of the description*], forms part of our auditor's report.

Other matters which we are required to address

Following the recommendation of the audit committee, we were appointed by [*state by whom or which body the auditor was appointed*] on [*date*] to audit the financial statements for the year ending [*date*] and subsequent financial periods.

The period of total uninterrupted engagement is [X] years, covering the years ending [*date*] to [*date*].

The non-audit services prohibited by the FRC's Ethical Standard were not provided to the group or the parent company and we remain independent of the group and the parent company in conducting our audit.

[*Indicate any services, in addition to the audit, which were provided by the firm to the group that have not been disclosed in the financial statements or elsewhere in the annual report.*]

Our audit opinion is consistent with the additional report to the audit committee.

[Signature]	*Address*
John Smith (Senior statutory auditor)	*Date*
For and on behalf of ABC LLP, Statutory Auditor	

2.2.12 Bannerman

Following a Scottish legal case when it was found that the Royal Bank of Scotland was entitled to rely on the published financial statements of a company for the purposes of lending the company money, many UK auditors have introduced an extra paragraph into their auditor's reports. Many previous legal cases on the subject had restricted the auditors' legal duty of care to the members of the company only, but the Bannerman decision (named after the auditors in the case, Bannerman Johnstone Maclay) called this into question. The wording of the paragraph is designed to restrict the auditor's duty of care.

The wording of a 'Bannerman' paragraph is as follows:

"This report is made solely to the company's members, as a body, in accordance with Chapter 3 of Part 16 of the Companies Act 2006. Our audit work has been undertaken so that we might state to the company's members those matters we are required to state to them in an auditor's report and for no other purpose. To the fullest extent permitted by law, we do not accept or assume responsibility to anyone other than the company and the company's members as a body, for our audit work, for this report, or for the opinions we have formed."

The FRC does not include such a paragraph in their standard report example.

2.2.13 UK Corporate Governance Code

Under the Companies Act 2006 publicly traded companies are required to include a Corporate Governance Statement in their annual report. If this is not included, the auditor must report by exception. Under the Listing Rules the auditor must also report on compliance with the specific provisions of the UK Corporate Governance Code (see example auditor's report above). The following is an example of this part of the auditor's report, taken from FRC Bulletin (2016) Appendix 7.

Directors' statement of compliance with the UK Corporate Governance Code

'The parts of the directors' statement required under the Listing Rules relating to the company's compliance with the UK Corporate Governance Code containing provisions specified for review by the auditor in accordance with Listing Rule 9.8.10R(2) do not properly disclose a departure from a relevant provision of the UK Corporate Governance Code.'

Where there is compliance with the Code, the auditor's report will state the following:

Corporate Governance Statements

Under the Listing Rules we are also required to review part of the Corporate Governance Statement relating to the company's compliance with certain provisions of the UK Corporate Governance Code. We have nothing to report arising from our review.

2.2.14 Real auditor's reports

Familiarity with real auditor's reports will help you with reporting questions in the exam so you should try to read as many real-life examples as possible. These are readily available on the websites of UK corporations; see for example www.centrica.com and www.bp.com.

2.3 ISA (UK) 720 *The Auditor's Responsibilities Relating to Other Information*

The audited financial statements are likely to be published in the annual report, which may also include other information. This is defined in the standard as financial and non-financial information, other than the audited financial statements, that is included in the entity's annual reports. Examples of other information would include:

- Management report, management commentary, or operating and financial review or similar reports by those charged with governance (for example, a directors' report)
- Chairman's statement
- Corporate governance statement
- Internal control and risk assessment reports

ISA (UK) 720 requires the auditor to read the other information. If it is materially inconsistent with the financial statements then this could indicate that there is a material misstatement in the financial statements themselves.

2.3.1 Strategic report and directors' report

UK auditors are also required to report on other information that the entity is required by law to produce and publish with the financial statements. This statutory other information includes:

- The directors' report
- The strategic report
- The separate corporate governance statement

According to ISA (UK) 720:

- The auditor shall read the information and assess whether it is consistent with the financial statements

- If the auditor identifies any inconsistencies between the information in the directors' report or strategic report, and the financial statements, the auditor shall seek to resolve them

- If the auditor is of the opinion that the information in the directors' report or strategic report is materially inconsistent with the financial statements (and has been unable to resolve the inconsistency), then the auditor shall state that opinion and describe the inconsistency in the auditor's report

- If an amendment is necessary to the financial statements (and management and those charged with governance refuse to make the amendment), then the auditor expresses a qualified or adverse opinion on the financial statements.

The purpose of the strategic report is to enable shareholders to assess how well the directors have performed in their duty to promote the success of the company.

The FRC's Bulletin (2016) *Compendium of Illustrative Auditor's Reports* states that the auditor has a specific responsibility to give an opinion on whether the strategic report and the directors' report are consistent with the financial statements, and also on whether those reports have been prepared in accordance with the applicable legal requirements (FRC, 2016: para. 23).

The FRC Bulletin (2016) prescribes the following forms of words to be included in the auditor's report in the various situations that the auditor might face.

Where only a directors' report is prepared	Where both a directors' report and a strategic report are prepared
Opinions on other matters prescribed by the Companies Act 2006	**Opinions on other matters prescribed by the Companies Act 2006**
In our opinion, based on the work undertaken in the course of the audit:	In our opinion, based on the work undertaken in the course of the audit:
• the information given in the directors' report for the financial year for which the financial statements are prepared is consistent with the financial statements; and	• the information given in the strategic report and the directors' report for the financial year for which the financial statements are prepared is consistent with the financial statements; and
• the directors' report has been prepared in accordance with applicable legal requirements.	• the strategic report and the directors' report have been prepared in accordance with applicable legal requirements.

FRC (2016): para. 24

Where a directors' report or strategic report is a legal requirement, then the auditor must also report on whether they have identified any misstatements in them (broadly speaking, all companies which are not small must prepare both a directors' and a strategic report):

Where only a directors' report is prepared	Where both a directors' report and a strategic report are prepared
Matters on which we are required to report by exception	**Matters on which we are required to report by exception**
In the light of the knowledge and understanding of the company and its environment obtained in the course of the audit, we have not identified material misstatements in the directors' report.	In the light of the knowledge and understanding of the company and its environment obtained in the course of the audit, we have not identified material misstatements in the strategic report or the directors' report.

FRC (2016): para. 25

Worked example: auditor's report extracts

This example is taken from the FRC Bulletin (2016), and features a small company which was exempt from preparing a strategic report.

Opinions on other matters prescribed by the Companies Act 2006

In our opinion, based on the work undertaken in the course of the audit:

- the information given in the directors' report for the financial year for which the financial statements are prepared is consistent with the financial statements; and

- the directors' report has been prepared in accordance with applicable legal requirements.

Matters on which we are required to report by exception

In the light of the knowledge and understanding of the company and its environment obtained in the course of the audit, we have not identified material misstatements in the directors' report.

We have nothing to report in respect of the following matters in relation to which the Companies Act 2006 requires us to report to you if, in our opinion:

- adequate accounting records have not been kept, or returns adequate for our audit have not been received from branches not visited by us;

- the financial statements are not in agreement with the accounting records and returns;

- certain disclosures of directors' remuneration specified by law are not made;

- we have not received all the information and explanations we require for our audit; or

- the directors were not entitled to prepare the financial statements in accordance with the small companies regime and take advantage of the small companies' exemptions in preparing the directors' report and from the requirement to prepare a strategic report.

3 Modified auditor's reports

Section overview

- The wording of an auditor's report may need to be **'modified'** in certain circumstances:
    - Where the auditor wishes to highlight an issue but where the audit opinion is **not** affected – an emphasis of matter paragraph (ie, modification to the **report)**
    - Where there is an impact on the audit opinion (ie, modification to the **opinion**)

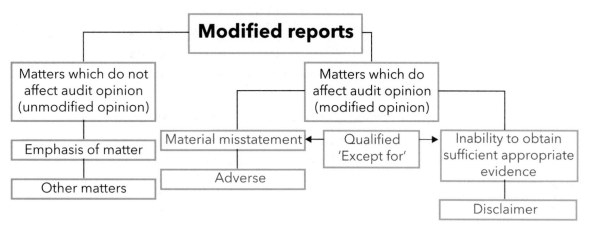

Figure 13.3: Overview: modified reports

Modifications to the auditor's report are covered in two ISAs (UK):

- ISA (UK) 705 *Modifications to the Opinion in the Independent Auditor's report.* Key points relate to the positioning of the 'Basis for Qualified/Adverse/Disclaimer of Opinion' section after the opinion section, and the omission of the 'Key Audit Matters' section when disclaiming an opinion, unless this is required by law or regulation.

- ISA (UK) 706 *Emphasis of Matter Paragraphs and Other Matter Paragraphs in the Independent Auditor's Report.* Revisions relate to Key Audit Matters (as required by ISA (UK) 701) in particular the Emphasis of Matter paragraph should not be used as a substitute for a description of a Key Audit Matter, and also the positioning of the Emphasis of Matter and Other Matter paragraphs.

In this section we shall be using the term 'modified report'. The ISAs that deal with auditor's reports do not use this term, but it is useful for distinguishing those reports that contain an emphasis of matter paragraph or another matter paragraph.

There are separate ISAs for matters in auditor's reports that **do not** modify the opinion (ISA (UK) 706) and those that do (ISA (UK) 705). For your examination you need to be able to follow the logic of figure 13.3 above and consider the impact of scenarios given in a question on the form of the auditor's report and the type of audit opinion.

The type of modified opinion expressed will depend on the circumstances and the effect of any actual or potential misstatements on the financial statements. Misstatements that are material but not pervasive will lead to an 'except for' qualified opinion, whereas if the misstatements are deemed to be pervasive the opinion will be adverse or will be disclaimed. The term 'pervasive' is defined in ISA (UK) 705 as something that affects the financial statements as a whole or a substantial part of them, and which is fundamental to the users' understanding of the financial statements. This is discussed further in section 4.2.

3.1 Emphasis of matter paragraphs and other matter paragraphs

The auditor should add an **'emphasis of matter' paragraph** to the auditor's report where the auditor considers it necessary to draw users' attention to a matter or matters **presented or disclosed in the financial statements** that are of such importance that they are fundamental to users' understanding of the financial statements.

The auditor should add an **'other matters' paragraph** to the auditor's report where the auditor considers it necessary to draw users' attention to any matter or matters other than those presented or disclosed in the financial statements that are relevant to users' understanding of the audit, the auditor's responsibilities or the auditor's report.

According to ISA (UK) 706 *Emphasis of Matter Paragraphs and Other Matter Paragraphs in the Independent Auditor's Report* the emphasis of matter paragraph should be included immediately after the opinion on the financial statements paragraph and shall:

- Use the heading 'Emphasis of Matter'

- Include a clear reference to the matter being emphasized and to where relevant disclosures can be found in the financial statements

- Indicate that the auditor's opinion is not modified in respect of the issue dealt with

Similarly, an 'other matter paragraph' should be included immediately after the opinion of the financial statements paragraph and any Emphasis of Matter paragraph or elsewhere in the auditor's report if the content of the Other Matters paragraph is relevant to the Other Reporting Responsibilities section.

If the auditor expects to include and Emphasis of Matter or Other Matter paragraph in the auditor's report, the auditor shall communicate with those charged with governance regarding this expectation and the proposed wording of the paragraph.

ISA (UK) 705 in paragraph A5 gives the following examples of circumstances where an Emphasis of Matter paragraph could be included:

- An uncertainty relating to the future outcome of exceptional litigation or regulatory action

- A significant subsequent event that occurs between the date of the financial statements and the date of the auditor's report

- Early application of a new accounting standard that has a material effect on the financial statements

- A major catastrophe that has had a significant effect on the entity's financial position.

The standard makes it clear that an Emphasis of Matter paragraph is not a substitute for a modified opinion or for reporting a material uncertainty relating to going concern.

Examples of where an auditor's report could include an 'other matter' paragraph are:

- Where the prior period financial statements were audited by another auditor
- Where the prior period financial statements were not audited

Worked example: Modified report – unmodified opinion – emphasis of matter

A firm being audited is awaiting the outcome of a lawsuit and as a result it is not possible to quantify the effect this will have on the financial statements.

The details are as follows:

- The UK non-public company in question prepares UK GAAP financial statements.

- A lawsuit alleges that the company has infringed certain patent rights and claims royalties and punitive damages. The company has filed a counter action, and preliminary hearings and discovery proceedings on both actions are in progress.

- The ultimate outcome of the matter cannot presently be determined, and no provision for any liability that may result has been made in the financial statements.

- The company makes relevant disclosures in the financial statements.

Requirement

Set out the modification to the auditor's report that the auditor should make in this instance.

Solution

The auditor issues a modified auditor's **report**, ie, with an emphasis of matter paragraph describing the situation giving rise to the emphasis of matter and its possible effects on the financial statements, including that the effect on the financial statements of the resolution of the uncertainty cannot be quantified. The audit **opinion** itself is an **unmodified opinion**.

In our opinion the financial statements:

- Give a true and fair view of the state of the company's affairs as at .... and of its profit (loss) for the year then ended

- Have been properly prepared in accordance with United Kingdom Generally Accepted Accounting Practice

- Have been prepared in accordance with the requirements of the Companies Act 2006

Emphasis of matter - possible outcome of a lawsuit

In the forming of our opinion on the financial statements, which is not qualified, we have considered the adequacy of the disclosures made in note x to the financial statements concerning the possible outcome of a lawsuit, alleging infringement of certain patent rights and claiming royalties and punitive damages, where the company is the defendant. The company has filed a counter action, and preliminary hearings and discovery proceedings on both actions are in progress. The ultimate outcome of the matter cannot presently be determined, and no provision for any liability that may result has been made in the financial statements.

Registered auditors   Address

Date

3.2 Modification of the audit opinion

Circumstances that have an impact on the audit opinion are discussed in ISA (UK) 705 *Modifications to the Opinion in the Independent Auditor's Report*.

The auditor shall modify the opinion when:

(a) The auditor concludes that the financial statements as a whole are not free from material misstatement, eg, where there is disagreement with management about:

  (i) Accounting policies;
  (ii) Accounting treatment; or
  (iii) Disclosure in the financial statements.

In these circumstances there are two possible outcomes:

  (i) The resulting misstatements are material, but not pervasive, to the financial statements – this will result in a 'qualified opinion' ('except for').

  (ii) The resulting misstatements are both material and pervasive to the financial statements such that the auditor concludes that the accounts do not give a true and fair view - an 'adverse opinion'.

(b) The auditor is unable to obtain sufficient appropriate audit evidence to conclude that the financial statements as a whole are free from material misstatements, eg, a limitation on the scope of the audit.

In these circumstances there are two possible outcomes:

(i) The possible effects of undetected misstatements, if any, could be material but not pervasive – this will result in a 'qualified opinion' ('except for').

(ii) The possible effects of undetected misstatements on the financial statements could be both material and pervasive, so serious that the auditor is unable to form an opinion on the financial statements – a 'disclaimer of opinion'.

Worked example: Qualified 'except for' opinion – material misstatement

An auditor is in disagreement with management regarding an accounting treatment. The details are as follows.

- The UK non-public traded company prepares UK GAAP financial statements.

- Included in the receivables shown on the statement of financial position is an amount of £Y which is the subject of litigation and against which no allowance has been made. The auditor considers that a full allowance of £Y should have been made.

Requirement

Set out the opinion on the financial statements that the auditor should make in this instance.

Solution

Modified opinion on financial statements arising from material misstatement in relation to accounting treatment

Included in the receivables shown on the statement of financial position is an amount of £Y due from a company which has ceased trading. XYZ Limited has no security for this debt. In our opinion the company is unlikely to receive any payment and a full allowance of £Y should have been made. Accordingly, receivables should be reduced by £Y, deferred tax liability should be reduced by £X and profit for the year and retained earnings should be reduced by £Z.

Except for the financial effect of not making the allowance referred to in the preceding paragraph, in our opinion the financial statements:

- Give a true and fair view of the state of the company's affairs as at… and of its profit (loss) for the year then ended

- Have been properly prepared in accordance with United Kingdom Generally Accepted Accounting Practice

- Have been prepared in accordance with the requirements of the Companies Act 2006

Registered auditor   Address

Date

Worked example: Qualified 'except for' opinion – inability to obtain sufficient appropriate audit evidence

An auditor was unable to observe an inventory count because they were not engaged by the company at the time the count took place. The details are as follows:

- The UK non-public traded company prepares UK GAAP financial statements (and therefore uses UK terminology).

- The evidence available to the auditor was limited because they did not observe the counting of the physical inventory as at 31 December 20X1, since that date was prior to the time the auditor was initially engaged as auditor for the company. Owing to the nature of the company's records, the auditor was unable to satisfy themselves as to inventory quantities by other audit procedures.

Requirement

Set out the audit opinion on financial statements that the auditor should make in this instance.

Solution

- The inability to obtain sufficient appropriate evidence causes the auditor to issue a modified opinion – except for any adjustments that might have been found necessary had they been able to obtain sufficient evidence concerning inventory.

- The limitation of scope was determined by the auditor not to be so material and pervasive as to require a disclaimer of opinion.

Modified opinion on financial statements arising from inability to obtain sufficient appropriate audit evidence

With respect to inventory having a carrying amount of £X the audit evidence available to us was limited because we did not observe the counting of the physical inventory as at 31 December 20X1, since that date was prior to our appointment as auditor of the company. Owing to the nature of the company's records, we were unable to obtain sufficient appropriate audit evidence regarding the inventory quantities by using other audit procedures.

Except for the financial effects of such adjustments, if any, as might have been determined to be necessary had we been able to satisfy ourselves as to inventory quantities, in our opinion the financial statements:

- Give a true and fair view of the state of the company's affairs as at 31 December 20X1 and of its profit (loss) for the year then ended

- Have been properly prepared in accordance with United Kingdom Generally Accepted Accounting Practice

- Have been prepared in accordance with the requirements of the Companies Act 2006

Matters on which we are required to report by exception

In respect solely of the limitation on our work relating to inventory, described above:

- We have not obtained all the information and explanations that we considered necessary for the purpose of the audit

- We were unable to determine whether adequate accounting records had been kept

We have nothing to report in respect of the following matters where the Companies Act 2006 required us to report to you if, in our opinion:

- Returns adequate for our audit have not been received from branches not visited by us;
- The financial statements are not in agreement with the accounting records and returns; or
- Certain disclosures of directors' remuneration specified by law are not made.

Registered auditors   Address

Date

Worked example: Disclaimer of opinion

An auditor was unable to observe all physical inventory and confirm trade receivables during an audit. The details are as follows.

- The UK non-public company prepares UK GAAP financial statements.

- The evidence available to the auditor was limited because the auditor was not able to observe all physical inventory and confirm trade receivables due to limitations placed on the scope of the auditor's work by the directors of the company.

Requirement

Set out the opinion that the auditor should make in this instance.

Solution

The auditor has been unable to form a view on the financial statements and issues a modified opinion disclaiming the view given by the financial statements.

Disclaimer of Opinion

We were engaged to audit the financial statements of ABC Company which comprise the statement of financial position as at December 31, 20X1, and the statement of comprehensive income, statement of changes in equity and statement of cash flows for the year then ended, and notes to the financial statements, including a summary of significant accounting policies.

We do not express an opinion on the accompanying financial statements of the Company. Because of the significance of the matter described in the *Basis for Disclaimer of Opinion* section of our report, we have not been able to obtain sufficient appropriate audit evidence to provide a basis for an audit opinion on these financial statements.

Basis for disclaimer of opinion

The audit evidence available to us was limited because we were unable to observe the counting of physical inventory having a carrying amount of £X and send confirmation letters to trade receivables having a carrying amount of £Y due to limitations placed on the scope of our work by the directors of the company. As a result of this we have been unable to obtain sufficient appropriate audit evidence concerning both inventory and trade receivables.

Because of the possible effect of the limitation in evidence available to us, we do not express an opinion as to whether the financial statements:

- Give a true and fair view of the state of the company's affairs at .... and of its profit (loss) for the year then ended

- Have been properly prepared in accordance with United Kingdom Generally Accepted Accounting Practice

- Have been prepared in accordance with the requirements of the Companies Act 2006.

Matters on which we are required to report by exception

In respect solely of the limitation of our work referred to above:

- We have not obtained all the information and explanations that we considered necessary for the purpose of our audit

- We were unable to determine whether adequate accounting records have been kept.

We have nothing to report in respect of the following matters where the Companies Act 2006 requires us to report to you if, in our opinion:

- Returns adequate for our audit have not been received from branches not visited by us;
- The financial statements are not in agreement with the accounting records and returns; or
- Certain disclosures of directors' remuneration specified by law are not made.

Registered auditors   Address

Date

Worked example: Adverse opinion

A company being audited has made no provision for losses expected to arise on certain long-term contracts. The details are as follows.

- The UK non-publicly traded company prepares UK GAAP financial statements.

- No provision has been made for losses expected to arise on certain long-term contracts currently in progress, as the directors consider that such losses should be off-set against amounts recoverable on other long-term contracts.

Requirement

Set out the opinion that the auditor should make in this instance.

Solution

- In the auditor's opinion, provision should be made for foreseeable losses on individual contracts as required by (specify accounting standards).

- The auditor issues an adverse opinion due to the failure to provide losses and quantifies the impact on the profit for the year, the contract work in progress and deferred tax liability at the year end.

Adverse opinion on financial statements

As more fully explained in note x to the financial statements no provision has been made for losses expected to arise on certain long-term contracts currently in progress, as the directors consider that such losses should be off-set against amounts recoverable on other long-term contracts. In our opinion, provision should be made for foreseeable losses on individual contracts as required by (specify accounting standards). If losses had been so recognised the effect would have been to reduce the carrying amount of contract work in progress by £X, the deferred tax liability by £Y and the profit for the year and retained earnings at 31 December 20X1 by £Z.

In view of the effect of the failure to provide for the losses referred to above, in our opinion the financial statements:

- Do not give a true and fair view of the state of the company's affairs as at 31 December 20X1 and of its profit (loss) for the year then ended

- Have not been properly prepared in accordance with United Kingdom Generally Accepted Accounting Practice

In all other respects, in our opinion the financial statements have been prepared in accordance with the requirements of the Companies Act 2006.

Registered auditors   Address

Date

3.3 Emphasis of matter or inability to obtain sufficient appropriate audit evidence?

An emphasis of matter paragraph is used when there is a degree of uncertainty surrounding the financial statements, for example where there is uncertainty regarding the outcome of a legal action, or where there are other significant uncertainties which have been disclosed in the financial statements. An inability to obtain sufficient appropriate audit evidence arises when evidence that can reasonably be expected to be available is not available, for example:

- Appointment after the year end may mean that the inventory check may not have been attended

- The values in the accounts of an overseas subsidiary subject to an oppressive or economically unstable regime may be difficult to ascertain with sufficient reliability

3.4 ISA (UK) 720 *The auditor's responsibilities relating to other information in documents containing audited financial statements*

3.4.1 Inconsistencies

ISA (UK) 720 also gives the auditor some limited responsibilities with regards to the other information, where there may be material inconsistencies when other information contradicts, or appears to be materially inconsistent with, information in the audited financial statements. This could cast doubt on the credibility of the auditor's report.

The auditor shall read the other information and take the following action if there are inconsistencies:

Amendment necessary to	Auditor response if uncorrected
Audited financial statements	• Qualified or adverse opinion.
The other information	• Describing the material inconsistency in the 'Other information' section of the auditor's report; or • Take other actions, eg, seek legal advice.

3.4.2 Material misstatements of the other information

A material misstatement of the other information exists when information, not related to matters appearing in the audited financial statements, is incorrectly stated or presented.

For example the auditor may believe that there are misstatements contained in some of the employment data within the annual report.

When the auditor considers that there is an apparent misstatement in the other information, he should request management to consult with a qualified third party, such as the entity's legal counsel and should consider the advice received.

If management refuses to correct the misstatement, the auditor should consider taking further action, such as notifying those charged with governance of the entity in writing or obtaining legal advice. The misstatement should be described in the 'Other information' section of the auditor's report.

3.5 Modified opinions - a summary

The available forms of **modification** to the **audit opinion** may be summarised by the following table:

	Auditor's Judgement about the Pervasiveness of the Effects or Possible Effects on the Financial Statements	
Nature of Matter Giving Rise to the Modification	Material but Not Pervasive	Material and Pervasive
Financial statements are materially misstated	Qualified opinion ('Except for')	Adverse opinion
Inability to obtain sufficient appropriate audit evidence	Qualified opinion ('Except for')	Disclaimer of opinion

Remember, that if an error or a lack of evidence is immaterial the audit opinion will not be modified at all.

Interactive question 2: Auditor's report

You are the auditor of Purity Ltd, a manufacturer of water filters for domestic use. The company headquarters are in Wapping but it also has 10 regional branches to organise the sales effort in each geographical area.

Head office issued instructions for all inventories to be counted at the year end. However, due to an administrative error, the new branch in Newcastle did not receive any instructions and no physical inventory count took place. The inventories were material, estimated at £50,000 and included in the financial statements. No alternative procedures could be applied.

Requirements

Answer the following questions.

(a) How will your auditor's opinion be modified?

(b) What additional statement(s), if any, will need to be made in the UK auditor's report?

See **Answer** at the end of this chapter.

Interactive question 3: Modified auditor's report

An auditor is considering possible modification of his auditor's report on the financial statements of three separate companies.

(1) Watkins Ltd is being sued by a customer for material damages. Legal opinion is divided as to the outcome of the case, and all relevant information has been included in the notes.

(2) Pope Ltd suffered a flood at its head office and a significant number of accounting records have been destroyed.

(3) Tilden Ltd has included an allowance for receivables of £100,000 in the financial statements. Obviously the allowance cannot be estimated with complete accuracy but the reporting partner believes it should be materially higher.

Requirement

Recommend, giving reasons, whether the opinion should be modified in each case.

See **Answer** at the end of this chapter.

4 Special considerations

Section overview

- Financial statements may be prepared using a different basis of accounting
- The auditor may be required to report on single financial statements

4.1 ISA (UK) 800 *Special Considerations – Audits of Financial Statements Prepared in Accordance with Special Purpose Frameworks*

This ISA (UK) aims to address special considerations that are relevant to complete sets of financial statements prepared in accordance with another basis of accounting (for example, other than IFRS or UK GAAP).

The aim of the ISA (UK) is to identify additional audit requirements relating to these areas.

Before undertaking a special purpose audit engagement, the auditor should ensure there is agreement with the client as to the exact nature of the engagement and the form and content of the report to be issued.

To avoid the possibility of the auditor's report being used for purposes for which it was not intended, the auditor may wish to indicate in the report the purpose for which it is prepared and any restrictions on its distribution and use.

4.2 ISA (UK) 805 *Special Considerations – Audits of Single Financial Statements and Specific Elements, Accounts or Items of a Financial Statement*

In certain circumstances, an auditor may be required to audit and report on a single financial statement, or a specific element, account or item of the financial statements. Guidance is provided in ISA (UK) 805.

Appendix 1 of ISA (UK) 805 includes the following examples:

- Accounts receivable, allowances for doubtful accounts receivable, inventory, the liability for accrued benefits of a private pension plan, the recorded value of identified intangible assets, or the liability for 'incurred but not reported' claims in an insurance portfolio, including related notes

- A schedule of externally managed assets and income of a private pension plan, including related notes

- A schedule of net tangible assets, including related notes

This ISA (UK) explains how other ISAs are applied in these circumstances. In particular, special considerations are required in relation to acceptance of the engagement, planning and performance and forming an opinion.

Summary and Self-test

Summary

Self-test

Answer the following questions.

1 A report to those charged with governance should be in writing.

   ☐ True

   ☐ False

2 Which of the following might be included in a report to those charged with governance?

   ☐ The audit approach

   ☐ Audit adjustments

   ☐ The audit opinion

   ☐ Material control deficiencies

3 What three opinions are stated in a UK unmodified auditor's report?

   (i) ....

   (ii) ....

   (iii) ....

4 What three things does the scope paragraph include?

   (i) ....

   (ii) ....

   (iii) ....

5 What is a 'Bannerman' paragraph?

6 In what two situations should an audit opinion be modified?

   (i) ....

   (ii) ....

Exam-style questions

7 You attempted parts (a) and some of (b) of this sample paper question in Chapter 7. Now try the rest of part (b) about the reporting implications.

Described below are situations which have arisen in three audit clients of your firm. The year end in each case is 31 March 20X6.

Jay plc (Jay)

The directors have included the following note to the financial statements for the year ended 31 March 20X6:

"Although the company has incurred significant trading losses and cash outflows during the last two years, the directors believe that the effects of internal restructuring and corporate disposals undertaken will bring about improved results as indicated in the detailed profit and cash flow forecasts for the period to the end of March 20X7. These forecasts indicate that the company will be able to trade within its agreed working capital facility for at least the next 12 months from the date of this report. Considerable progress has been made on the financial restructuring of the company.

On the basis of the above factors the directors consider it is appropriate that the financial statements are prepared on the going concern basis. Should the company fail to meet its forecasts, the going concern basis may prove to be inappropriate. In such circumstances adjustments are likely to have to be made to the net assets shown in these financial statements to reduce assets to their recoverable amounts, to reclassify non-current assets and payables due after more than one year to current assets and current liabilities and to provide for further liabilities that may arise."

Finch plc ('Finch')

Finch has included the results of Wren Ltd ('Wren'), a subsidiary, in the consolidated financial statements. Wren is audited by a different firm of auditors who have modified their opinion on Wren's financial statements for the year ended 31 March 20X6 because a fire at the company's premises destroyed the physical inventory count sheets which were the only record of the year end inventory. Wren has included inventory at its estimated cost of £500,000 in the financial statements for the year ended 31 March 20X6.

The consolidated pre-tax profit of Finch is £33.4 million and the pre-tax profit of Wren is £1.2 million for the year ended 31 March 20X6.

Sparrow Ltd ('Sparrow')

On 30 April 2006, the board of directors decided to undertake a restructuring programme which would commence in June 20X6. A provision of £1.8 million in respect of the restructuring costs has been included in the financial statements for the year ended 31 March 20X6.

The pre-tax profit of Sparrow for the year ended 31 March 20X6 is £7.2 million.

Requirements

(a) Discuss what is meant by the concepts of materiality and a true and fair view. **(6 marks)**

(b) Explain why there can be difficulties for auditors regarding materiality and true and fair in relation to the three cases above: Jay, Finch and Sparrow, and state how you might modify your auditor's report in each case. **(14 marks)**

(20 marks)

8 Described below are three situations which have arisen in three audits. The year end in each case is 31 March 20X8.

(i) Ash Ltd uses leased motor vehicles which have been accounted for as operating leases. However, you believe that these leases are finance leases and should have been capitalised at £51,000. The current treatment does not comply with accounting standards which require finance leases, where the user takes on the risks and rewards of ownership, to be included within non-current assets and capitalised. Profit for the year would then have been reduced by £4,000.

The pre-tax profits of Ash Ltd for the year ended 31 March 20X8 were £600,000, and total assets at 31 March 20X8 were £5.4 million.

(ii) A fire in the warehouse of Oak Ltd in April 20X8 destroyed the inventory sheets, which were the only record of the company's inventories at the year end. The company has included an estimated inventory figure of £780,000.

The pre-tax profits of Oak Ltd for the year ended 31 March 20X8 were £1.1 million and total assets at 31 March 20X8 were £6.5 million.

(iii) Elm Ltd has included a note in the financial statements explaining that 90% of its revenue is derived from a national retailer with whom it has a three-year renewable contract. This contract is due for renewal in September 20X8. However, the directors require the auditor's report on the financial statements to be signed on 31 May 20X8.

Requirements

(a) Critically evaluate the use of standardised auditor's reports. **(5 marks)**

(b) Discuss briefly each of the situations outlined above, referring to materiality considerations. For each situation describe the effect on the auditor's report. **(10 marks)**

(15 marks)

Now, go back to the Learning outcomes in the Introduction. If you are satisfied that you have achieved these outcomes, please tick them off.

Technical reference

1	**Communication with those charged with governance**	**ISA (UK) 260 and 265**
•	Relevant persons	ISA (UK) 260
•	Relevant matters	ISA (UK) 260
•	How?	ISA (UK) 260
2	**Unmodified auditor's reports**	**ISA (UK) 700** **FRC Bulletin (October 2016)**
3	**Modified auditor's reports**	**ISAs (UK) 705, 706 and 720** **FRC Bulletin (October 2016)**
4	**Special considerations**	**ISA (UK) 800** **ISA (UK) 805**

Answers to Interactive questions

Answer to Interactive question 1

(a) Deficiency	(b) Risks arising	(c) Action to mitigate
There has been a breakdown of controls over expenditure.	That IT expenditure is uncontrolled and investment is not always clearly for the benefit of the company.	Purchasing department to be warned that no IT expenditure should be incurred without authorisation; otherwise disciplinary action could result.
Excessive amounts are being spent on IT, adversely affecting profit.	IT expenditure is not planned properly, which means that investment may not be as beneficial as it should be.	IT expenditure must only be undertaken under the budget, unless authorised by two directors. Also, if additional investment is required the budget should be flexed.
Travelling expenses in some cases are excessive, with £25,000 being spent in excess of set limits.	Loss of profits due to excessive expenditure.	Travelling expenses should not be reimbursed when limits are exceeded, unless the prior consent of two directors has been received. The executives involved need to be informed of the problem.
Work-in-progress is not always being billed on a timely basis. This is to the extent that £56,000 has been held for more than six months.	Items involved are not being billed. This has an adverse effect on cash flow, and eventual recovery may be difficult.	Monthly billing meetings should be held at director level and within teams, where they should be told that any amounts more than two months' old must be billed.
The authorisation controls on overtime are not being exercised. This has resulted in the company paying £180,000 of excess overtime. Some may be genuine, but controls will reduce this amount.	Excessive costs, adversely affecting profits.	Overtime over one hour per week should be authorised prior to the work being undertaken, and should then be authorised once the timesheet is submitted.
There is no control over non-chargeable time. This leads to a variable amount of non-chargeable time by executives. This varies from 5% to 34%.	With some staff, an excessive amount of the time that they are spending at work is not being charged to clients, thus having an adverse effect on revenue, and hence profits.	Individual staff to be set targets for non-chargeable time, depending on their other responsibilities. Adherence to their targets must be monitored.

Answer to Interactive question 2

(a) 'Except for' limitation of scope because

    (i)   Matter is material but not so pervasive

    (ii)   Scope of the audit has been limited

(b) (i)   State all information and explanations not received

    (ii)   State proper accounting records have not been kept

Answer to Interactive question 3

Recommended opinion	Reasons
(i) Unmodified opinion but modified auditor's report by an emphasis of matter paragraph regarding the legal case if considered significant	• Significant uncertainty, properly disclosed, does not require a modification
(ii) Modified opinion – probably disclaimer	• Loss of records results in limitation of scope • 'Significant number' implies that auditors will probably be unable to form an opinion
(iii) Modified opinion – 'except for'	• Audit partner disagrees with size of allowance necessary • Problem limited to one area – unlikely to require adverse opinion

Answers to Self-test

1   True

2   Approach, adjustments, material control deficiencies. Although any expected modification to the audit opinion might be noted, the full audit opinion would not be given.

3   The financial statements:

   (i)   Give a true and fair view
   (ii)   Have been properly prepared in accordance with UK GAAP
   (iii) Have been prepared in accordance with CA 2006

4   (i)   A reference to appropriate accounting policies
   (ii)   A reasonable assurance statement
   (iii) A summary of the nature of audit work

5   A statement limiting the liability of the auditors to the company and its members.

6   (i)   The auditor has been unable to obtain sufficient appropriate audit evidence
   (ii)   The financial statements are materially misstated

Exam-style questions

7   **Report modifications**

   Part of (b) only – the remainder of the answer was given in Chapter 7.

   Jay

   If the financial statements are prepared on the going concern basis of accounting, and the auditor agrees with this, then an unmodified audit opinion will be issued but the auditor would include a paragraph headed 'Material Uncertainty Related to Going Concern' to bring this fact to the attention of the members.

   If the financial statements are prepared on the break-up basis, and the auditor agrees with this, then an unmodified audit opinion will be issued but the auditor would include an emphasis of matter paragraph to draw the fact that the company is not a going concern to the attention of the shareholders.

   If the auditor does not agree with the basis used to prepare the accounts, eg, going concern used when break-up is required, then the audit opinion will be modified, normally due to a material misstatement.

   Finch

   If not material by nature, the auditor's report on the consolidated financial statements will be unmodified. If material by nature then the audit opinion will be modified (except for) on the grounds of limitation on scope. This would require modifications to the basis of opinion section and the opinion section of the auditor's report. It would also require the auditor to report by exception on accounting records and the availability of information.

   Sparrow

   As the disagreement over the accounting treatment has a material impact on the financial statements, the audit opinion will be an 'except for' modification.

8 (a) **Use of standardised auditor's reports**

Advantages

(i)   The standard acts as a quality control mechanism, ie, all auditor's reports contain the same level of information for the shareholders.

(ii)   It enhances clarity and understanding as it is produced on a consistent basis. Shareholders know what the various forms of the auditor's report indicate and particularly with modified audit opinions can identify the problems immediately.

(iii) For the auditor it makes preparation easier. The auditor knows that he is satisfying his legal and professional responsibilities on the signing of this report.

Disadvantages

(i)   There is a danger that readers and users of accounts become over-familiar with the report and feel that as it is not tailored to their company it is not relevant to them.

(ii)   It could be seen as inflexible. There are certain situations where the auditor's report would provide a useful vehicle by which to pass on information to the shareholders but normally would not be used in this way, eg, problem of illegal loans to directors.

(iii) It does include a certain amount of technical jargon but does not allow for the auditor to explain or expand on these terms if he feels it would be of benefit to the user. This could be particularly relevant when dealing with smaller organisations.

Conclusion

While there are arguments for and against the use of standard auditor's reports on balance the advantages would seem to have more weight than the disadvantages.

(b) **Three situations**

(i)   **Ash Ltd**

The accounting treatment adopted by the company does not agree with the relevant accounting standard. This should be discussed with management who should be requested to comply with the accounting standard. If they refuse to do so this should be referred to in the report to management.

Materiality

The adjustment represents 0.67% of profit and 0.94% of total assets. Based on this information it does not appear to be material to the accounts in isolation. However, the impact on liabilities and net assets should also be considered.

Impact on auditor's report

As the adjustment is not material, even if the directors refuse to adopt accounting standard treatment the audit opinion would be unmodified, stating that the accounts give a true and fair view.

(ii)   **Oak Ltd**

The issue here is one of a limitation of scope. Due to the loss of the physical inventory count records the auditor will not be able to perform normal audit procedures in this area.

The auditor will need to establish the basis for the estimated figure, eg, book inventory records to determine whether it will provide a reasonable assessment of the year end balance.

Materiality

The inventory balance itself is clearly material to the accounts as it represents 70% of profit and 12% of total assets. However, in this instance the real issue is the extent to which the inventory balance quoted is incorrect. As the limitation in scope leads to uncertainty, it is not possible to quantify exactly the size of any adjustment. By its nature, however, inventory is a significant balance in the accounts and is therefore likely to be material.

Impact on auditor's report

Assuming that the limitation of scope is material but not so material or pervasive (as the problem is isolated to one balance in the accounts) the auditor's report would be affected as follows:

- It would refer to the fact that the audit work could not be performed fully in accordance with auditing standards.

- It would state that we planned our audit so as to obtain all information necessary but the reference to performance would be dropped.

- A description of the limitation would be given, ie, physical inventory records destroyed including an estimate of the effect.

- The opinion would be modified using the 'except for... might' opinion.

Note: In the UK the report would also refer to the implied opinions as proper accounting records have not been maintained and all information and explanations have not been received.

(iii) **Elm Ltd**

There is a significant uncertainty at the year end in respect of whether or not the company is a going concern. This is dependent upon the renewal of a contract which is significant to the viability of the company. The auditor needs to establish the likelihood of renewal. If the company is not a going concern the accounts should be prepared on a break-up basis.

Materiality

No information has been provided to quantify the adjustments necessary to prepare the accounts on a break-up basis but these are likely to be material.

Impact on auditor's report

Assuming the accounts are prepared on a going concern basis

- Provided that the auditor is satisfied that this treatment is appropriate and that disclosure of the situation is sufficient, an unmodified audit opinion will be issued. Reference to the significant uncertainty would be made by modifying the auditor's report using a section headed 'material uncertainty relating to going concern', together with a statement that the opinion itself is not modified.

- If the auditor disagrees with the treatment adopted (ie, if he feels that it is unlikely that the contract will be renewed) or the level of disclosure is inadequate, the opinion will be modified on the grounds of material misstatement.

- Normally the matter is of such significance that an adverse opinion is issued (ie, the accounts do not give a true and fair view).

If the accounts are prepared on a break-up basis

Provided the auditor agrees with this treatment and that the basis of preparation is fully disclosed, an unmodified audit opinion will be issued. The break-up basis of preparation may be referred to in an emphasis of matter paragraph.

In this instance the most likely outcome would be modified report with reference to the significant uncertainty but an unmodified audit opinion.

Note: One other disadvantage which could have been mentioned in part (a) is that the technical distinction between different types of modifications may not be appreciated by users.

ICAEW

CHAPTER 14

Other assurance engagements

Introduction

Examination context

TOPIC LIST

Introduction

Learning outcomes

2 Planning engagements

Students will be able to plan assurance engagements in accordance with the terms of the engagements and appropriate standards.

- Determine an approach appropriate for an engagement for a specified organisation which addresses:

    - the assurance of entities' published sustainability and corporate responsibility report

3 Concluding and reporting on engagements

Students will be able to conclude and report on assurance engagements in accordance with the terms of the engagements and appropriate standards.

- Draw conclusions on the ability to report on an assurance engagement which are consistent with the results of the assurance work;

- Draft suitable extracts for an assurance report (including any report to the management issued as part of the engagement) in relation to a specified organisation on the basis of given information, including in the extracts (where appropriate) statements of facts, their potential effects, and recommendations for action relevant to the needs and nature of the organisation being reported upon;

- Advise on reports to be issued to those responsible for governance in accordance with International Standards on Auditing, legislation, regulation and codes of corporate governance;

- Judge when to refer reporting matters for specialist help;

Syllabus links

Assurance reports were introduced in Assurance.

1 Other assurance engagements

Section overview

- Assurance services improve the quality of decision making for users of information
- Assurance engagements are classified in terms of their basic type, and the level of assurance provided
- Assurance engagements may give reasonable assurance or limited assurance

1.1 ISAE 3000 *Assurance Engagements Other than Audits or Reviews of Historical Financial Statements*

ISAE 3000 *Assurance Engagements Other than Audits or Reviews of Historical Financial Information*, which was revised in December 2013, provides guidance on other assurance engagements. As the title of the ISAE indicates, we are **not** discussing assurance engagements on 'historical financial information', such as reviews of financial statements. Examples of engagements that may fall within the scope of ISAE 3000 are:

- Environmental, social and sustainability reports
- Information systems, internal control, and corporate governance processes
- Compliance with grant conditions, contracts and regulations

ISAE 3000 defines an assurance engagement as follows.

Definition

Assurance engagement: An engagement in which a practitioner aims to obtain sufficient appropriate evidence in order to express a conclusion designed to enhance the degree of confidence of the intended users other than the responsible party about the subject matter information (that is, the outcome of the measurement or evaluation of an underlying subject matter against criteria).

(ISAE 3000: para. 12)

1.2 Assurance provided

The level of assurance may be **reasonable** or **limited**. These levels of assurance were discussed in your earlier studies. Remember that absolute assurance can **never** be given on an assurance engagement due to the **inherent limitations** of such engagements.

For revision, the ISAE 3000 definitions are as follows.

Definition

Reasonable assurance engagement: An assurance engagement in which the practitioner reduces engagement risk to an acceptably low level in the circumstances of the engagement as the basis for the practitioner's conclusion. The practitioner's conclusion is expressed in a form that conveys the practitioner's opinion on the outcome of the measurement or evaluation of the underlying subject matter against criteria.

(ISAE 3000: para. 12)

C H A P T E R 14

Definition

Limited assurance engagement: An assurance engagement in which the practitioner reduces engagement risk to a level that is acceptable in the circumstances of the engagement but where that risk is greater than for a reasonable assurance engagement as the basis for expressing a conclusion in a form that conveys whether, based on the procedures performed and evidence obtained, a matter(s) has come to the practitioner's attention to cause the practitioner to believe the subject matter information is materially misstated.

(ISAE 3000: para. 12)

2 Terms of other assurance engagements

Section overview

- It is important to agree terms in the context of a statutory audit

- Think how much more important this is if a firm is appointed to carry out some other type of assignment

- Where there is no detailed regulatory framework there will be a much greater risk of misunderstanding so the negotiation and formal documentation of terms becomes much more important

2.1 Engagement letter for review of financial statements

The objective of a review of financial statements is, according to ISRE 2400 *Engagements to Review Financial Statements*, 'to enable a practitioner to state whether, on the basis of procedures which do not provide all the evidence that would be required in an audit, anything has come to the practitioner's attention that causes the practitioner to believe that the financial statements are not prepared, in all material respects, in accordance with the applicable financial reporting framework.' In other words a review of financial statements results in a limited/moderate level of assurance which is expressed negatively.

The terms of engagement are agreed between the client and the practitioner, unlike an audit engagement where these are determined by law and professional standards.

Interactive question 1: Engagement letter for review of financial statements

To the appropriate representative of management or those charged with governance of ABC Company:

(1) You have requested that we review the general purpose financial statements of ABC Company, which comprise the statement of financial position as at December 31, 20X1, and the statement of comprehensive income, statement of changes in equity and cash flow statement for the year then ended, and a summary of significant accounting policies and other explanatory information. We are pleased to confirm our acceptance and our understanding of this review engagement by means of this letter.

We will perform the following services:

(2) We will review the statement of financial position of ABC Company as of December 31 20X1, and the related statements of income and cash flows for the year then ended, in accordance with the International Standards in Review Engagements (ISRE) 2400 (or refer to relevant national standards or practices applicable to reviews). We will not perform an audit of such financial statements and, accordingly, we will not express an audit opinion on them. Accordingly, we expect to report on the financial statements as follows:

(3) Based on our review, nothing has come to our attention that causes us to believe that the accompanying financial statements do not give a true and fair view (or are not presented fairly, in all material respects) in accordance with International Financial Reporting Standards.

(4) Responsibility for the financial statements, including adequate disclosure, is that of the management of the company. This includes the maintenance of adequate accounting records and internal controls and the selection and application of accounting policies. As part of our review process, we will request written representations from management concerning assertions made in connection with the review.

(5) Our engagement cannot be relied upon to disclose whether fraud or errors, or illegal acts exist. However, we will inform you of any material matters that come to our attention.

(6) Please sign and return the attached copy of this letter to indicate that it is in accordance with your understanding of the arrangements for our review of the financial statements.

XYZ LLP

Acknowledged on behalf of ABC Company by

(Signed)

Name and Title

Date

Requirement

Explain the purpose of each of the numbered paragraphs.

See the **Answer** at the end of this chapter.

2.2 Agreement of terms on engagements to examine prospective financial information

Guidance here is provided by ISRE 3400 *The Examination of Prospective Financial Information*.

If a firm is appointed, for example, to review a cash flow forecast that a client has prepared to support an attempt to raise finance from a bank, there are further issues to consider and to include in the engagement letter:

- The intended use of the information
- Whether the information will be for general or limited distribution
- The nature of the assumptions, that is whether they are best-estimate or hypothetical assumptions
- The elements to be included in the information
- The period covered by the information
- A caveat warning that there could be differences between the forecast and actual performance due to unforeseen circumstances

3 Assurance reports

Section overview

- There is less formal requirement in relation to assurance reports generally than there is for auditor's reports

- Proformas for review reports and other assurance reports are given in international standards

As we saw in Chapter 13, UK auditor's reports are prescribed by International Standards on Auditing (UK) and also by additional guidance in the form of FRC Bulletin (October 2016).

There is less formality surrounding more general assurance reports and these reports will often take the most appropriate form.

3.1 Reviews

International Standard on Review Engagements (ISRE) 2400 (Revised) *Engagements to Review Historical Financial Statements* gives guidance about review reports. Limited assurance is given on review assignments. The ISRE defines limited assurance as 'the level of assurance obtained where engagement risk is reduced to a level that is acceptable in the circumstances of the engagement, but where that risk is greater than for a reasonable assurance engagement, as the basis for expressing a conclusion.'

The practitioner's conclusion 'states that nothing has come to the practitioner's attention that causes the practitioner to believe that the financial statements do not present fairly, in all material respects (or do not give a true and fair view) in accordance with the applicable fair presentation framework.'

The requirements of ISRE 2400 are expressed under the following headings:

- Conduct of a review engagement
- Ethical requirements
- Professional scepticism and professional judgement
- Engagement level quality control
- Acceptance and continuance of client relationships and review engagements
- Communication with management and those charged with governance
- Performing the engagement
- Subsequent events
- Written representations
- Evaluating evidence obtained from the procedures performed
- Forming the practitioner's conclusion on the financial statements
- The practitioner's report
- Documentation

An example of a review report with unmodified conclusions is given in the appendix to the ISRE, and it is reproduced here.

Worked example: Form of Review Report with Unmodified Conclusions

[Appropriate Addressee]

Report on the Financial Statements

We have reviewed the accompanying financial statements of ABC Company, which comprise the statement of financial position as at December 31, 20X1, and the statement of comprehensive income, statement of changes in equity and statement of cash flows for the year then ended, and a summary of significant accounting policies and other explanatory information.

Management's Responsibility for the Financial Statements

Management is responsible for the preparation and fair presentation of these financial statements in accordance with the International Financial Reporting Standard for Small and Medium-sized Entities, and for such internal control as management determines is necessary to enable the preparation of financial statements that are free from material misstatement, whether due to fraud or error.

Practitioner 's Responsibility

Our responsibility is to express a conclusion on the accompanying financial statements. We conducted our review in accordance with International Standard on Review Engagements (ISRE) 2400 (Revised), *Engagements to Review Historical Financial Statements*. ISRE 2400 (Revised) requires us to conclude whether anything has come to our attention that causes us to believe that the financial statements, taken as a whole, are not prepared in all material respects in accordance with the applicable financial reporting framework. This Standard also requires us to comply with relevant ethical requirements.

A review of financial statements in accordance with ISRE 2400 (Revised) is a limited assurance engagement. The practitioner performs procedures, primarily consisting of making inquiries of managementan others within the entity, as appropriate, and applying analytical procedures, and evaluates the evidence obtained.

The procedures performed in a review are substantially less than those performed in an audit conducted in accordance with International Standards on Auditing. Accordingly, we do not express an audit opinion on these financial statements.

Conclusion

Based on our review, nothing has come to our attention that causes us to believe that these financial statements do not present fairly, in all material respects (or *do not give a true and fair view of*) the financial position of ABC Company as at December 31, 20X1, and (*of*) its financial performance and cash flows for the year then ended, in accordance with the International Financial Reporting Standard for Small and Medium-sized Entities.

Report on Other Legal and Regulatory Requirements

[Form and content of this section of the practitioner's report will vary depending on the nature of the practitioner's other reporting responsibilities.]

[Practitioner's signature]

[Date of the practitioner's report]

[Practitioner's address]

Notice the main components of the report:

1   Addressee(s)

    This will depend on the specific terms of the assignment. It may be addressed to the directors, or to a specified third party user such as a bank.

2   Scope and responsibilities

    The scope of the work is defined and the respective responsibilities of management and the practitioner are clarified.

3   Nature of work and level of assurance

    A description of a review and its limitations, and how it differs from an audit.

4 Conclusion

As was explained in Chapter 1, the conclusion is expressed in terms of limited assurance.

If the practitioner determines that the financial statements are materially misstated, the **reasons should be stated** and the conclusion modified depending on the impact of the misstatement.

Impact	Effect on report
Material	Express a qualified conclusion on the limited assurance provided
Pervasive	Give an adverse conclusion that the financial statements do not give a true and fair view

The practitioner may feel there has been a limitation in the scope of the work he intended to carry out for the review. If so, he should **describe the limitation.** The limitation may have the following effects.

Impact	Effect on report
Material to one area	Express a qualified conclusion on the limited assurance provided
Pervasive	Disclaim a conclusion

3.2 Reviews of interim financial information

ISRE 2410 *Review of Interim Financial Information Performed by the Independent Auditor of the Entity* applies the basic principles of conducting reviews and preparing review reports as set out in ISRE 2400 to one specific type of review.

3.3 Reports following examination of prospective information

Chapter 1 explained that the nature of prospective information, such as forecasts and projections, affects the level of assurance that can be given. Reports on these assignments may well contain additional 'warnings' for readers.

The IAASB standard ISAE 3400 *The Examination of Prospective Financial Information* gives the following list of components for this type of report:

(a) Title

(b) Addressee

(c) Identification of the prospective financial information

(d) A reference to the ISAE or relevant national standards

(e) A statement that management is responsible for the prospective financial information including the assumptions on which it is based

(f) When applicable, a reference to the purpose and/or restricted distribution of the prospective financial information

(g) A statement of negative assurance as to whether the assumptions provide a reasonable basis for the prospective financial information

(h) An opinion as to whether the prospective financial information is properly prepared on the basis of the assumptions and is presented in accordance with the relevant financial reporting framework

(i) Appropriate caveats concerning the achievability of the results indicated by the prospective financial information

(j) Date of the report which should be the date procedures have been completed

(k) Reporting accountant's address

(l) Signature

The standard also gives an extract from a report on a review of prospective financial information:

> We have examined the forecast in accordance with the International Standard on Assurance Engagements applicable to the examination of prospective financial information. Management is responsible for the forecast including the assumptions set out in Note X on which it is based.
>
> Based on our examination of the evidence supporting the assumptions, nothing has come to our attention which causes us to believe that these assumptions do not provide a reasonable basis for the forecast. Further, in our opinion the forecast is properly prepared on the basis of the assumptions and is presented in accordance with…
>
> Actual results are likely to be different from the forecast since anticipated events frequently do not occur as expected and the variation may be material.

Notice the extra final paragraph drawing attention to the nature of prospective financial information, illustrating the type of 'caveat' referred to in (i) above.

Interactive question 2: Herbalink Ltd

Herbalink Ltd (Herbalink) is a client of your firm that operates a chain of shops in Cardiff selling ethically produced herbal cosmetics and toiletries. Since opening its first store five years ago the company has expanded and now has 10 outlets in the south Wales area. The directors wish to continue the company's expansion by opening additional stores in major UK cities and by introducing a mail order service.

In order to finance these expansion plans the directors of Herbalink have been discussing an increase in their borrowing with the company's bank. In support of the funding request the directors have prepared profit and cash flow forecasts for the three years ending 31 December 2016, based on assumptions they have made about the future success of the business. Herbalink's bankers require this information to be examined and reported on by independent accountants, and the directors have asked your firm to undertake this assignment.

Two potential properties have been found for the new outlets, both of which are leasehold premises that will require considerable refurbishment to bring them up to the standard of existing stores.

The mail order service, for which postage will be charged, will be run from the main Cardiff branch which incorporates the central delivery warehouse of the company. The packaging for delivered items will be specially designed to protect the products in transit and to reflect the company's logo and ethical trading credentials.

The ingredients for preparing the herbal products are purchased centrally on credit terms. All ingredients are sourced from UK producers and all packaging is made from recycled materials. Employees at Herbalink are paid at rates above the industry average and are also paid bonuses linked to profits made by the company as a whole.

Requirements

(a) From the information provided above, identify the key **receipts** and **payments** that you would expect to be included in the cash flow forecasts prepared by the directors of Herbalink. For each receipt and payment, identify the specific matters you would consider when reviewing the reasonableness of the assumptions in forecasting that receipt or payment.

(b) Explain the role of written representations in the examination of and reporting on forecast information.

(c) Describe the differences between the **conclusion** expressed in an assurance report on forecast information and the **opinion** expressed in an auditor's report on financial statements. Give reasons for these differences.

See **Answer** at the end of this chapter.

Companies may draw up prospective financial information in a format that suits their own management requirements. Since this is internal information it does not have to be presented in accordance with external financial reporting standards. The following proforma examples show a typical layout for a simple profit forecast and for a cash flow forecast. You may come across more complex examples but the principles remain the same.

XYZ Ltd
Profit forecast for the six months to 30 June 20X3

	January £	February £	March £	April £	May £	June £
Revenue	X,XXX	X,XXX	X,XXX	X,XXX	X,XXX	X,XXX
Cost of sales	(X,XXX)	(X,XXX)	(X,XXX)	(X,XXX)	(X,XXX)	(X,XXX)
Gross profit	**X,XXX**	**X,XXX**	**X,XXX**	**X,XXX**	**X,XXX**	**X,XXX**
Expenses/overheads						
Rent and rates	XXX	XXX	XXX	XXX	XXX	XXX
Gas and electricity	XXX	XXX	XXX	XXX	XXX	XXX
Telephone	XXX	XXX	XXX	XXX	XXX	XXX
Insurance	XXX	XXX	XXX	XXX	XXX	XXX
Postage and carriage	XXX	XXX	XXX	XXX	XXX	XXX
Advertising	XXX	XXX	XXX	XXX	XXX	XXX
Bank charges	XXX	XXX	XXX	XXX	XXX	XXX
Stationery	XXX	XXX	XXX	XXX	XXX	XXX
Wages and salaries	XXX	XXX	XXX	XXX	XXX	XXX
Motor expenses	XXX	XXX	XXX	XXX	XXX	XXX
Professional fees	XXX	XXX	XXX	XXX	XXX	XXX
Depreciation	XXX	XXX	XXX	XXX	XXX	XXX
Other expenses	XXX	XXX	XXX	XXX	XXX	XXX
Total expenses	**(X,XXX)**	**(X,XXX)**	**(X,XXX)**	**(X,XXX)**	**(X,XXX)**	**(X,XXX)**
Net profit/(loss)	**XXX**	**XXX**	**XXX**	**XXX**	**XXX**	**XXX**

XYZ Ltd
Cash flow forecast for the six months to 30 June 20X3

	January £	February £	March £	April £	May £	June £
Cash balance at start of month	X,XXX	X,XXX	(X,XXX)	(X,XXX)	X,XXX	X,XXX
Cash in						
Cash sales	X,XXX	X,XXX	X,XXX	X,XXX	X,XXX	X,XXX
Share capital investment	X,XXX	X,XXX	X,XXX	X,XXX	X,XXX	X,XXX
Bank loan	X,XXX	X,XXX	X,XXX	X,XXX	X,XXX	X,XXX
Other external finance	X,XXX	X,XXX	X,XXX	X,XXX	X,XXX	X,XXX
Other cash inflows	XXX	XXX	XXX	XXX	XXX	XXX
Total cash receipts	X,XXX	X,XXX	X,XXX	X,XXX	X,XXX	X,XXX
Cash paid out						
Rent and rates	XXX	XXX	XXX	XXX	XXX	XXX
Gas and electricity	XXX	XXX	XXX	XXX	XXX	XXX
Telephone	XXX	XXX	XXX	XXX	XXX	XXX
Insurance	XXX	XXX	XXX	XXX	XXX	XXX
Postage and carriage	XXX	XXX	XXX	XXX	XXX	XXX
Advertising	XXX	XXX	XXX	XXX	XXX	XXX
Bank charges	XXX	XXX	XXX	XXX	XXX	XXX
Stationery	XXX	XXX	XXX	XXX	XXX	XXX
Wages and salaries	XXX	XXX	XXX	XXX	XXX	XXX
Motor expenses	XXX	XXX	XXX	XXX	XXX	XXX
Professional fees	XXX	XXX	XXX	XXX	XXX	XXX
Other operating expenses	XXX	XXX	XXX	XXX	XXX	XXX
Capital expenditure	X,XXX	X,XXX	X,XXX	X,XXX	X,XXX	XXX
Loan repayments	XXX	XXX	XXX	XXX	XXX	XXX
VAT payment to HMRC	XXX	XXX	XXX	XXX	XXX	XXX
Bank interest paid	XXX	XXX	XXX	XXX	XXX	XXX
Other financing payments	XXX	XXX	XXX	XXX	XXX	XXX
Total cash paid out	X,XXX	X,XXX	X,XXX	X,XXX	X,XXX	X,XXX
Net cash flow for the month	X,XXX	(X,XXX)	(X,XXX)	X,XXX	X,XXX	X,XXX
Cash balance at end of month	X,XXX	(X,XXX)	(X,XXX)	X,XXX	X,XXX	X,XXX

3.4 ISAE 3402 *Assurance Reports on Controls at a Service Organisation*

Entities that use service organisations may require assurance on the internal controls in operation at the service organisation. ISAE 3402 is designed to complement ISA (UK) 402 *Audit Considerations Relating to an Entity Using a Service Organisation*. It applies only when the service organisation is itself responsible for the design and implementation of internal controls.

3.5 ISAE 3410 *Assurance Engagements on Greenhouse Gas Statements*

Entities may prepare greenhouse gas statements (GHG) for a variety of reasons; the statement may be a requirement of a disclosure regime or an emissions trading scheme, or the entity may make voluntary emissions disclosures. From April 2013 all entities listed on the main market of the London Stock Exchange have been required to make mandatory disclosure of greenhouse gas emissions.

ISAE 3410 adopts a risk-based approach to undertaking assurance engagements on greenhouse gas statements, and states that the engagement must also comply with the requirements of ISAE 3000 (Revised) *Assurance Engagements Other than Audits or Reviews of Historical Financial Information*.

The practitioner's report can provide one of two levels of assurance:

(1) Reasonable assurance - an opinion on whether the greenhouse gas statement has been prepared, in all material respects, in accordance with the applicable criteria.

(2) Limited assurance - a conclusion on whether anything has come to the practitioner's attention to make the practitioner believe that the greenhouse gas statements has not been prepared, in all material respects, in accordance with the applicable criteria.

Some of the specific characteristics of a GHG assurance engagement include:

- Multidisciplinary teams, including assurance skills and GHG competencies relating to laws, regulation, quantification and reporting. More complex engagements may also require information systems expertise and scientific and engineering expertise

- Inventory uncertainty relating to incomplete scientific knowledge and the difficulty of estimation and measurement

- Site visits may be required in order to understand the entity and to perform procedures

Summary and Self-test

Summary

Self-test

Answer the following questions.

1 What is limited assurance?

2 When would a practitioner not give any assurance in a review engagement?

Exam-style questions

3 Delta Ltd's sales invoices are produced by its computer system using the relevant price held as standing data on the sales master file. Selling prices are updated by the sales ledger clerk on the verbal authority of the sales director.

Requirement

Draft extracts, suitable for inclusion in the auditor's management letter, which set out the possible consequences, and the recommendations that you would make, in respect of the matters outlined above. **(4 marks)**

4 You are the auditor of Mota Ltd, a distributor of automotive components, and have been provided with the following description of the sales order processing system.

Order entry

Sales orders are taken over the telephone and entered into the computer by a sales order clerk, via a terminal in the sales office, while the customer is on the line. On entry the order details are read back to the customer for confirmation. The computer checks that there are sufficient inventories to meet the order and that the customer's credit limit is not exceeded.

If the goods are unavailable, the customer is asked if he wants the order to be recorded as a 'back order' which will be fulfilled when there is sufficient inventory. Once accepted, the order is automatically given an order number which is relayed to the customer.

Orders which take a customer over his credit limit are referred to the credit controller who decides, in consultation with the chief accountant, whether or not the customer should be allowed to exceed the credit limit or have the credit limit raised. Any adjustments in respect of overrides of, or increases in, credit limits are input, via a terminal in the accounts department, by the credit controller. Printouts of these amendments are not generated and no other review of credit limits is undertaken.

New customers are referred to the credit controller who obtains credit ratings and references and, on the oral authority of the chief accountant, enters the customer account details onto the sales ledger master file via a terminal in the accounts department.

Despatch of goods

Sequentially-numbered packing notes in respect of accepted orders are printed out in the warehouse, and the goods are selected, packed and checked by warehouse staff. Confirmations of packing and any notifications of shortfalls are entered into the computer, via a terminal in the warehouse, by the warehouse supervisor. Two copies of the sequentially-numbered delivery advice are printed in the warehouse and sent with the goods to the customer who is required to sign a copy which is returned by the driver to the accounts department. All despatches are checked at the gatehouse to ensure that they are accompanied by the appropriate documentation. The packing notes are filed in numerical order in the warehouse and the sequence is checked for completeness, on a daily basis, by the warehouse supervisor.

The system does not automatically generate purchase orders with manufacturers when a customer's order cannot be fulfilled.

Computer system

All users of the system are required to log on using identification codes and individual passwords which control their level of access to the system. All passwords are changed every 90 days and when employees leave. Systems support is provided by a supplier where the service agreement provides for availability of a back-up system within 72 hours of a systems failure.

Requirements

(a) Identify the objectives of exercising internal controls over sales order processing. For each objective discuss the extent to which the procedures exercised by Mota Ltd achieve the objective.

Note: You are **not** required to consider sales invoicing or ledger processing. **(8 marks)**

(b) Set out, in a manner suitable for inclusion in a report to management, any deficiencies in the system described above. For each deficiencies you should include the possible consequence of the deficiency and a recommendation to remedy the deficiency.

Note: You are **not** required to write a covering letter. **(10 marks)**

(18 marks)

Now, go back to the Learning outcomes in the Introduction. If you are satisfied that you have achieved these outcomes, please tick them off.

Technical reference

1	Other assurance engagements	ISAE 3000
2	Terms of other assurance engagements	ISRE 2400, ISRE 3400
3	Assurance reports	ISRE 2400

ISRE (UK & Ireland) 2410, ISAE 3000, ISAE 3400, ISAE 3402, ISAE 3410

Answers to Interactive questions

Answer to Interactive question 1

(1) Establishes the purpose of the letter.

(2) Describes the nature of the services to be performed and professional standards that will be followed. The paragraph also emphasises that this is not an audit assignment, and that the nature of the opinion will differ from an audit opinion. This is included to minimise the risk of misunderstandings.

(3) A review gives limited assurance and the opinion will be expressed using a negative form of words. It is important that the directors understand this before the assignment starts, again to eliminate misunderstandings regarding the level of assurance that will be provided.

(4) This paragraph sets out the responsibilities of management in respect of the subject matter of the review.

(5) One of the roles of the engagement letter is to limit the liability being taken on by the practitioner. Here the practitioner is trying to protect himself from being held liable if fraud and errors exist.

(6) It is important that the terms are formally agreed by the two parties so the practitioner requires signed confirmation from the directors that they are in agreement.

Answer to Interactive question 2

(a) Specific matters to consider:

Receipts

Sales receipts: these should include sales from the new outlets and mail order service, which should be staged to reflect the timing of the opening of the new shops and the commencement of the mail order service. In other respects the inflow should reflect the pattern of prior years. Consideration should be given as to whether amounts are prudent given prevailing economic conditions and whether the introduction of the mail order service has an impact on shop takings.

Bank loan: the amount should correspond to what was agreed with the bank, as evidenced by correspondence, and should be sufficient to cover the expansion costs. The timing of the inflow should precede the start of new business activities.

Payments

Refurbishment costs: these should be based on suppliers' quotations and the outflow should precede the start of new business.

Payments for ingredients and packaging: these should reflect the level of forecast revenue and payments should reflect the suppliers' terms of trading.

Mail order operational costs: these should be based on staffing and packaging based on forecast revenue.

Premises costs: to include extra costs, eg, rent and utility costs relating to the new outlets. The rent should reflect the terms of the lease agreements such as up-front costs, rental periods and rent reviews.

Wages and salaries: these should include the costs of additional staff at the new outlets as well as the mail order operation. Rates of pay can be compared with the industry average and bonuses should reflect profits.

Sundry payments: to include advertising, training and recruitment costs relating to the new business. Outflows should precede the commencement of new business. Professional fees will include payments to legal advisors and the reporting accountant.

Loan repayments and finance costs: loan instalments should reflect the repayment terms negotiated with the bank and finance costs should reflect market rates and the level of borrowings. All outflows should be recorded on the anticipated due dates.

Tax payments: PAYE, VAT and corporation tax should be consistent with the relevant figures in the profit forecast and should be paid on the due dates.

Dividend payments: these should be in line with prior years' policies or take into account any anticipated changes in policy which should be confirmed by the directors.

General

Sensitivity analysis should be undertaken on key variables, eg, customer receipts, finance costs and raw ingredients.

(b) Role of written representations:

When conducting an engagement to examine forecast information, written representations are obtained from management regarding:

- The intended use of the forecast information
- The completeness of significant management assumptions
- Management's responsibility for the forecast information

The representations provide evidence that management accepts its responsibilities regarding the assumptions and will reduce the risk of any misunderstandings regarding respective responsibilities (ie, narrow the expectations gap). The representation regarding the intended use of the forecasts may protect the reporting accountant from claims for damages from unforeseen third parties.

(c) Differences between assurance and auditor's reports:

Assurance report

The conclusion of the assurance report on the forecast information will include a statement of negative assurance (ie, limited or moderate assurance) in the form of 'nothing has come to our attention which causes us to believe that the assumptions do not provide a reasonable basis for the forecast'. It will also include an opinion on whether the forecast information is properly prepared on the basis of the assumptions and is presented in accordance with the relevant financial reporting framework.

Auditor's report

The opinion in the auditor's report on financial statements will provide reasonable assurance that the financial statements:

- Give a true and fair view

- Have been properly prepared in accordance with relevant generally accepted accounting practice

- Have been prepared in accordance with the requirements of the Companies Act 2006

Reasons

Financial statements are mainly based on historical information whereas forecast information is based on assumptions about future events. The historical information can be verified to a greater degree than forecasts, which will always be subject to uncertainty.

Answers to Self-test

1 Assurance of a matter in the absence of any evidence to the contrary.

2 When there was a pervasive limitation in the scope of the review or where the practitioner is of the opinion that the report being reviewed is incorrect.

Exam-style questions

3 Consequences

Incorrect prices resulting in undercharging of customers and loss to company or overcharging of customers and loss of customer goodwill.

Recommendations

- All price changes to be recorded on standard documentation which should be signed as authorised by sales director
- Printout of amendments obtained and checked to document authorising amendment
- Printout signed as evidence of checking
- Periodic printout of all selling prices checked on one for one basis to authorised price list held by sales director
- Standing data protected by high level password not known to sales ledger clerk
- Spot checks on invoices prior to despatch

4 (a) Internal controls over sales order processing

Objectives	Extent to which achieved by Mota Ltd's procedures
• To ensure that goods are available for all orders accepted.	• The availability of inventories is checked on the computer system while the customer is on the line. • This will be effective only where the system is continuously updated for new orders and deliveries of inventories.
• To ensure that existing customers are within their credit limits (including the current order being taken).	• The computer system automatically checks that the customer is within his current credit limit. • Adjustments to credit limits are carried out by the credit controller but no review of any amendments is carried out.
• To ensure that new customers are creditworthy before orders are despatched.	• The credit controller carries out credit checks but details are amended on the terminal in the accounts department only after oral authority from the chief accountant, and no subsequent review of new customers is performed.
• To ensure that changes to credit limits are valid.	• As above.

Objectives	Extent to which achieved by Mota Ltd's procedures
• To ensure that the correct goods are despatched to each customer.	• Order details are read back to the customer to confirm their accuracy. • Packing notes are produced in the warehouse giving the details of the order. However, there is no responsibility assigned in respect of dealing with shortfalls of inventories and ensuring that the customer ultimately receives all of the goods ordered.
• To ensure that goods are despatched for all orders accepted.	• Packing notes are sequentially numbered and a completeness check is carried out on a daily basis.
• To ensure that all goods leaving the premises are in respect of valid orders.	• All goods leaving the warehouse are checked at the gatehouse to ensure that they are accompanied by a valid delivery advice.
• To ensure that back orders are fulfilled when inventories become available.	• There are no procedures in place to ensure that, once goods are received by Mota Ltd, back orders are fulfilled.

(b) **Points for inclusion in a report to management**

Deficiency	Consequence	Recommendation
• There is no review of amendments to credit limits once these have been processed on the system.	• Invalid amendments could be made, leading to supply of goods to non-creditworthy customers.	• An exception report should be produced on a weekly basis detailing all changes made to credit limits. This should be reviewed by the chief accountant, and evidenced by his signature, to ensure that all amendments are for valid business reasons.
• Authority to enter new customers onto the system is only given orally with no review of the credit ratings and references obtained.	• Invalid entries of new customers could be made without detection until non-payment of invoices arises.	• The chief accountant should review the credit ratings and references obtained before giving authority to accept the new customer.
• There is no responsibility assigned for dealing with shortfalls in orders when they are being selected in the warehouse.	• Delivery of part-complete orders and non-delivery of parts of orders will lead to loss of customer goodwill and subsequent loss of revenue.	• A daily printout of unprocessed orders should be produced and followed up by the warehouse supervisor.

Deficiency	Consequence	Recommendation
• There are no procedures to ensure that back orders are fulfilled when the goods become available.	• Delay in fulfilling customer orders will again lead to loss of customer goodwill.	• The system should produce a daily list of items that have come into inventory for which there are current back orders. The sales ledger clerk should contact the customer to ensure that the goods are still required and then process the order in the normal manner.
• When back orders are accepted the goods which are unavailable are not immediately reordered.	• There may be significant delays in fulfilling these orders.	• The computer should automatically generate purchase requisitions on a daily basis for items which have been requested but are unavailable. A supervisor should review these purchase requisitions and raise a purchase order where the goods have not already been ordered.

Note: In (b) marks were also awarded for identification of the following:

- Credit control procedures do not take the age of the debt into consideration; this could result in goods being despatched to slow payers.

- In respect of the failure to review credit limits on a regular basis, limits may be unrealistically low for customers with a good payment history, resulting in loss of business.

- Response time in respect of systems support is too slow; this could result in delayed and lost orders.

Glossary of terms

AI	Artificial Intelligence (AI) is the use of computers to do tasks which are thought to require human intelligence. It typically refers to tasks such as learning, knowing, sensing, reasoning, creating things, and generating and understanding language.
Analytical procedures	Evaluations of financial information through analysis of plausible relationships among both financial and non-financial data. Analytical procedures also encompass such investigation as is necessary of identified fluctuations or relationships that are inconsistent with other relevant information or that differ from expected values by a significant amount.
	They include consideration of comparisons of the entity's financial information with other information, and the consideration of relationships among elements of financial information that would be expected to conform to a particular pattern or between financial information and relevant non-financial information.
Anomaly	A misstatement or deviation that is demonstrably not representative of misstatements or deviations in a population.
Application controls	Manual or automated procedures that typically operate at a business process level. Application controls can be preventative or detective in nature and are designed to ensure the integrity of the accounting records. Accordingly, application controls relate to procedures used to initiate, record, process and report transactions or other financial data.
Appropriateness	The measure of the quality or relevance and reliability of the audit evidence
Assurance engagement	An engagement in which a practitioner aims to obtain sufficient appropriate audit evidence in order to express a conclusion designed to enhance the degree of confidence of the intended users other than the responsible party about the subject matter information (that is, the outcome of the measurement or evaluation of an underlying subject matter against criteria).
Assurance team	(a) All members of the engagement team for the assurance engagement.
	(b) All others within a firm who can directly influence the outcome of the assurance engagement.
Audit documentation (working papers)	The record of procedures performed, relevant evidence obtained and conclusions the auditor reached.
Audit evidence	Information used by the auditor in arriving at the conclusions on which the auditor's opinion is based.
Audit plan	An audit plan is more detailed than the strategy and sets out the nature, timing and extent of audit procedures (including risk assessment procedures) to be performed by engagement team members in order to obtain sufficient appropriate audit evidence.
Audit risk	The risk that the auditor expresses an inappropriate audit opinion when the financial statements are materially misstated. Audit risk is a function of the risks of material misstatement and detection risk.

Audit sampling	The application of audit procedures to less than 100% of items within a population of audit relevance such that all sampling units have a chance of selection in order to provide the auditor with a reasonable basis on which to draw conclusions about the entire population.
Audit strategy	The formulation of the general strategy for the audit, which sets the scope, timing and direction of the audit and guides the development of the audit plan.
Audit trail	A stream of evidence that permits the tracing of a transaction forward from its inception to the appropriate ledger accounts or to vouch from the ledger account to the inception of the transaction.
Automation	Automation is the process by which tasks are completed and controlled automatically by machines or computers, with minimal human intervention.
Big data	Datasets whose size is beyond the ability of typical database software to capture, store, manage and analyse.
Business risk	A risk resulting from significant conditions, events, circumstances, actions or inactions that could adversely affect an entity's ability to achieve its objectives and execute its strategies, or from the setting of inappropriate objectives and strategies.
Close family	A parent, child or sibling who is not an immediate family member.
Cloud computing	Cloud computing is a model for enabling ubiquitous, convenient, on-demand network access to a shared pool of configurable computing resources (eg, networks, servers, storage, applications, and services) that can be rapidly provisioned and released with minimal management effort or service provider interaction.
Contingent fee	A fee calculated on a predetermined basis relating to the outcome of a transaction or the result of the services performed by the firm. A fee that is established by a court or other public authority is not a contingent fee.
Control activities	The policies and procedures that help ensure that management directives are carried out.
Control environment	The control environment includes the governance and management functions and the attitudes, awareness and actions of those charged with governance and management concerning the entity's internal control and its importance in the entity. The control environment sets the tone of an organisation, influencing the control consciousness of its people.
Control risk	The risk that a misstatement that could occur in an assertion about a class of transaction, account balance or disclosure and that could be material, either individually or when aggregated with other misstatements, will not be prevented, or detected and corrected, on a timely basis by the entity's internal control.
Cyber risk	Any risk of financial loss, disruption or damage to the reputation of an organisation from some sort of failure of its information technology systems.
Cyber security	The protection of systems, networks and data in cyberspace.

Data analytics	The process of collecting, organising and analysing large sets of data to discover patterns and other useful information which an organisation can use for its future business decisions.
Data protection	When talking about data protection controls in a business:
	Data protection is the use of technology and polices to protect information from theft, corruption or loss.
	However when talking about data protection from the perspective of consumer protection, we could state that:
	Data protection provides the controls over how personal information is used by organisations, businesses or the government.
Detection risk	The risk that the procedures performed by the auditor to reduce audit risk to an acceptably low level will not detect a misstatement that exists and that could be material, either individually or when aggregated with other misstatements.
Digital transformation	Digital transformation is primarily about understanding the existing information and data in your business and then remodelling your business processes and business systems accordingly. Following how data flows through your business (how it is generated, captured, stored, shared and used by which people at which times for what purpose) can ensure that you maximise the use of digital technologies and also help you to challenge existing ways of doing things and restructure accordingly.
Direct financial interest	A financial interest:
	• Owned directly by and under the control of an individual or entity (including those managed on a discretionary basis by others); or
	• Beneficially owned through a collective investment vehicle, estate, trust or other intermediary over which the individual or entity has control, or the ability to influence investment decisions.
Entity's risk assessment process	A component of internal control that is the entity's process for identifying business risks relevant to financial reporting objectives and deciding about actions to address those risks, and the results thereof.
Error	An unintentional misstatement in financial statements, including the omission of an amount or a disclosure.
Fair	Information is free from discrimination and bias in compliance with expected standards and rules. The accounts should reflect the commercial substance of the company's underlying transactions.
Financial interest	An interest in equity or other security, debenture, loan or other debt instrument of an entity, including rights and obligations to acquire such an interest and derivatives directly related to such interest.
Financial statement assertions	Representations by management, explicit or otherwise, that are embodied in the financial statements, as used by the auditor to consider the different types of potential misstatements that may occur.
Fraud	An intentional act by one or more individuals among management, those charged with governance, employees, or third parties, involving the use of deception to obtain an unjust or illegal advantage.

General controls	Policies and procedures that relate to many applications and support the effective function of application controls by helping to ensure the continued proper operation of information systems.
Immediate family	A spouse (or equivalent) or a dependent.
Independence	Freedom from situations and relationships that make it probable that a reasonable and informed third party would conclude that objectivity either is impaired or could be impaired.
Independence in appearance	The avoidance of facts and circumstances that are so significant that a reasonable and informed third party would be likely to conclude, weighing all the specific facts and circumstances, that a firm's, or a member of the assurance team's, integrity, objectivity or professional scepticism has been compromised.
Independence of mind	The state of mind that permits the expression of a conclusion without being affected by influences that compromise professional judgement, allowing an individual to act with integrity, and exercise objectivity and professional scepticism.
Indirect financial interest	A financial interest beneficially owned through a collective investment vehicle, estate, trust or other intermediary over which the individual or entity has no control or ability to influence investment decisions.
Information system relevant to financial reporting	A component of internal control that includes the financial reporting system, and consists of the procedures and records established to initiate, record, process and report entity transactions (as well as events and conditions) and to maintain accountability for the related assets, liabilities and equity.
Informed management	Where the auditors believe that the member of management designated by the audit client to receive the results of a non-audit service provided by the auditor has the capability to make independent management judgements and decisions on the basis of the information provided.
Inherent risk	The susceptibility of an assertion about a class of transaction, account balance or disclosure to a misstatement that could be material, either individually or when aggregated with other misstatements, before consideration of any related controls.
Integrity	This means that an accountant must be straightforward and honest. It implies fair dealing and truthfulness.
Internal audit function	An appraisal activity established or provided as a service to the entity. Its functions include, amongst other things, examining, evaluating and monitoring the adequacy and effectiveness of internal control.
Internal control	The process designed, implemented and maintained by those charged with governance, management, and other personnel to provide reasonable assurance about the achievement of an entity's objectives with regard to reliability of financial reporting, effectiveness and efficiency of operations and compliance with applicable laws and regulations. The term "controls" refers to any aspects of one or more of the components of internal control.
Limited assurance	A meaningful level of assurance, that is more than inconsequential but is less than reasonable assurance, that engagement risk has been reduced to an acceptable level, which then allows a conclusion to be expressed negatively.

Machine learning	Machine learning is a field within AI whereby computers learn to do things rather than follow pre-programmed rules. Through machine learning techniques, computers find patterns in data and use statistical models to classify or make predictions about other pieces of data. There are different types of learning (eg, supervised, unsupervised or reinforced) but all draw on large sets of training data that enable the computer to learn.
Management	The person(s) with executive responsibility for the conduct of the entity's operations. For some entities in some jurisdictions, management includes some or all of those charged with governance, for example, executive members of a governance board, or an owner-manager.
Materiality	An expression of the relative significance or importance of a particular matter in the context of financial statements as a whole. The IFRS *Conceptual Framework for Financial Reporting* states that a matter is material if its omission or misstatement could influence the economic decisions of users taken on the basis of the financial statements.
Misstatement	A difference between the amount, classification, presentation, or disclosure of a reported financial statement item and the amount, classification, presentation, or disclosure that is required for the item to be in accordance with the applicable financial reporting framework. Misstatements can arise from error or fraud.
Non-compliance	Acts of omission or commission intentional or unintentional, committed by the entity, or by those charged with governance, by management or by other individuals working for or under the direction of the entity, which are contrary to the prevailing laws or regulations. Non-compliance does not include personal misconduct unrelated to the business activities of the entity.
Non-sampling risk	The risk that the auditor reaches an erroneous conclusion for any reason not related to sampling risk. For example, the use of inappropriate procedures, or misinterpretation of audit evidence and failure to recognise a misstatement or deviation.
Non-statistical sampling	A sampling approach that does not have the characteristics of statistical sampling (see entry for statistical sampling).
Objectivity	A state of mind that excludes bias, prejudice and compromise and that gives fair and impartial consideration to all matters that are relevant to the task in hand, disregarding those that are not.
Outsourcing	Outsourcing can be defined as "the strategic use of outside resources to perform activities traditionally handled by internal staff and resources." Outsourcing is a strategy by which an organization contracts out major functions to specialized and efficient service providers, who ultimately become valued business partners. And in some cases, outsourcing involves the transfer of employees from the company to the outsourcing company. There are many reasons why a company may choose to outsource certain business functions. Some of the most common reasons include:

- Reducing and controlling operating costs
- Improving company focus
- Gaining access to world-class capabilities

- Freeing internal resources for other purposes
- Streamlining or increasing efficiency for time-consuming functions
- Maximizing use of external resources
- Sharing risks with a partner company

Performance materiality	The amount or amounts set by the auditor at less than materiality for the financial statements as a whole to reduce to an appropriately low level the probability that the aggregate of uncorrected and undetected misstatements exceeds materiality for the financial statements as a whole.
Population	The entire set of data from which a sample is selected and about which an auditor wishes to draw conclusions.
Professional judgement	The application of relevant training, knowledge and experience in making informed decisions about the courses of action that are appropriate in the circumstances of the audit engagement.
Professional scepticism	An attitude that includes a questioning mind, being alert to conditions which may indicate possible misstatement due to error or fraud, and a critical assessment of audit evidence.
Public interest entity	A listed entity; and
	An entity (a) defined by regulation or legislation as a public interest entity or (b) for which the audit is required by regulation or legislation to be conducted in compliance with the same independence requirements that apply to the audit of listed entities. Such regulation may be promulgated by any relevant regulator, including an audit regulator.
Reasonable assurance	A high level of assurance, that is less than absolute assurance, that engagement risk has been reduced to an acceptably low level, which then allows a conclusion to be expressed positively.
Robotic process automation	Robotic process automation (RPA) is the use of software robots to automate standard business processes. The software can be configured to replicate the steps taken by humans and is particularly applicable to processes that are high volume, standard and repeatable.
Sampling risk	The risk that the auditor's conclusion based on a sample may be different from the conclusion if the entire population were subjected to the same audit procedure.
Sampling units	The individual items constituting a population.
Statistical sampling	An approach to sampling that has the following characteristics:
	(i) Random selection of the sample items; and
	(ii) The use of probability theory to evaluate sample results, including measurement of sampling risk.
Substantive procedures	Audit procedures designed to detect material misstatements at the assertion level. Substantive procedures comprise:

- Tests of detail (of classes of transactions, account balances and disclosures).
- Substantive analytical procedures.

Sufficiency	The measure of the quantity of audit evidence.
Tests of controls	Audit procedures designed to evaluate the operating effectiveness of controls in preventing, or detecting and correcting material misstatements at the assertion level.
Tolerable misstatement	A monetary amount set by the auditor in respect of which the auditor seeks to obtain an appropriate level of assurance that the monetary amount set by the auditor is not exceeded by the actual misstatement in the population.
Tolerable rate of deviation	A rate of deviation from prescribed internal control procedures set by the auditor in respect of which the auditor seeks to obtain an appropriate level of assurance that the rate of deviation set by the auditor is not exceeded by the actual rate of deviation in the population.
True	Information is factual and conforms with reality, not false. In addition the information conforms with required standards and law. The accounts have been correctly extracted from the books and records.
Valuation	A combination of the making of assumptions with regard to future developments, the application of appropriate methodologies and techniques, and the combination of both to compute a certain value, or range of values, for an asset, a liability or for a business as a whole.
Vouching	Matching entries in the accounting records to supporting documentation.
Walk-through procedure	A procedure that involves tracing a few transactions through the financial reporting system. Walk-through procedures would normally be performed near the start of the field-work stage of the audit. They involve tracing transactions from the very beginning to the very end, in order to confirm that the auditor has correctly understood how the controls are supposed to operate. Walkthrough procedures aim to test the auditor's understanding, and are not tests of controls.

Index

REVIEW FORM – AUDIT AND ASSURANCE STUDY MANUAL

Your ratings, comments and suggestions would be appreciated on the following areas of this Study Manual.

	Very useful	Useful	Not useful
Chapter Introductions	☐	☐	☐
Examination context	☐	☐	☐
Worked examples	☐	☐	☐
Interactive questions	☐	☐	☐
Quality of explanations	☐	☐	☐
Technical references (where relevant)	☐	☐	☐
Self-test questions	☐	☐	☐
Self-test answers	☐	☐	☐
Index	☐	☐	☐

	Excellent	Good	Adequate	Poor
Overall opinion of this Study Manual	☐	☐	☐	☐

Please add further comments below:

Please return completed form to:

The Learning Team
Learning and Professional Department
ICAEW
Metropolitan House
321 Avebury Boulevard
Milton Keynes
MK9 2FZ
E learning@icaew.com